ECUMENICAL FAITH
IN EVANGELICAL PERSPECTIVE

ECUMENICAL FAITH
IN
EVANGELICAL PERSPECTIVE

Gabriel Fackre

WILLIAM B. EERDMANS PUBLISHING COMPANY
GRAND RAPIDS, MICHIGAN

Copyright © 1993 by Wm. B. Eerdmans Publishing Co.
255 Jefferson Ave. S.E., Grand Rapids, Mich. 49503

Printed in the United States of America

Library of Congress Cataloging-in-Publication Data

Fackre, Gabriel J.
Ecumenical faith in evangelical perspective / Gabriel J. Fackre.
p.   cm.
Includes bibliographical references.
ISBN 0-8028-0668-6 (pbk.)
1. Evangelicalism. 2. Theology — 20th century. I. Title.
BR1640.F33   1993
270.8′2 — dc20   93-1218
CIP

CONTENTS

v

To the ecumenical evangelicals —
partners in conversation and mission

INTRODUCTION

I AM an "ecumenical" who has enjoyed increasing contact with self-identified "evangelicals" since the evangelism ferment of the early 1970s. Mainline churches, including my own United Church of Christ, struggled at that time to put together "the deed" of the preceding activist decade with a raised awareness about sharing "the Word," the mandate to "tell the Story."[1] In this developing alliance I found that evangelical mentors — C. S. Lewis, for example — were the same figures that also powerfully shaped our own family piety. Kinships with this evangelism era deepened in the following years, especially with those then called "young evangelicals" or "neo-evangelicals." We found ourselves together in social action ventures, evangelism sorties, conferences, and book collections.[2]

Further consciousness-raising for me about current evangelical belief took place with work on the Carl Henry chapter in a 1984 revision of the *Handbook of Christian Theologians*

---

1. As chronicled in my *Do and Tell: Engagement Evangelism in the '70s* (Grand Rapids: Eerdmans, 1973) and *Word and Deed: Theological Themes in Evangelism* (Grand Rapids: Eerdmans, 1975).

2. For examples of the last, see Robert K. Johnston, ed., *The Use of the Bible in Theology: Evangelical Options* (Atlanta: John Knox, 1985); and Mark A. Noll and David Wells, eds., *Christian Faith and Practice in the Modern World: Theology from an Evangelical Point of View* (Grand Rapids: Eerdmans, 1988).

(Henry was the first evangelical to be recognized in this important resource).[3] The prolonged exposure to Henry's thought and to his person in the American Theological Society, and my increased collaboration with some evangelical historians (Mark Noll, George Marsden, Timothy Smith, Nathan Hatch, Joel Carpenter) and theological colleagues (Donald Bloesch, Orlando Costas, David Wells, Clark Pinnock, Robert Johnston, Samuel Solivan, Roger Nicole, Eleonore Stump, Richard Lints, Mary Stewart Van Leeuwen, Arthur Holmes, Robert Pazmiño), made me aware of the intellectual rigor of evangelical thought. Why were these figures and points of view not known and encountered in mainline churches and theological academia? Why were the works of evangelicals not as visible on the reading lists of ecumenical institutions as ecumenical scholarship was in evangelical institutions? The answers have to do with stereotypes of evangelicalism that still abound.[4] To their shame, many in religious studies circles and in mainline seminaries remain ignorant of evangelical theology.

This book, therefore, has a missionary purpose. It aims to demonstrate to ecumenicals what they are missing in evangelicals, and to show evangelicals that ecumenicals have not completely overlooked or failed to engage evangelicals.

One might say that I stand on a boundary between these two territories with news to convey to each. But this Tillichian figure ("the boundary") is not quite right; it suggests the absence of citizenship, one "without a country." No, I live somewhere — in the church catholic and ecumenical. I explain "evangelical catholicity" in chapter 2. But there, and in other formulations, "evangelical" is the adjective and the larger Christian community the noun. I am an "evangelical ecumenical."

---

3. "Carl Henry," in *A Handbook of Christian Theologians*, ed. Martin E. Marty and Dean G. Peerman, rev. and enl. ed. (Nashville: Abingdon, 1984), pp. 583-607.

4. I discovered some answers in research done on the teaching of systematics in evangelical and ecumenical seminaries. See my "The State of Systematics: Research and Commentary," *Dialog* 31, no. 1 (1992): 54-61.

An *evangelical* ecumenical is one who shares with the Reformation the centrality of justification by faith and Holy Scripture (its "material" and "formal" principles, as they are sometimes called). Also with evangelicals today, an evangelical ecumenical affirms the experiential appropriation of justification and Scripture with its overflow in evangelization. The gospel is a word that warms the heart and opens the mouth. An evangelical *ecumenical* is one who joins these commitments to a classical trinitarian faith, as transmitted in credal, liturgical, and sacramental traditions, and who vigorously participates in an ecumenical movement that both seeks ecclesial unity and is deeply immersed in today's struggles for justice, peace, and the integrity of creation. In this sense, the topic treated herein is ecumenical faith in evangelical perspective.

Evangelical ecumenicals regularly find themselves in alliances and overlaps with "ecumenical evangelicals." The latter are associated first and foremost with self-consciously evangelical constituencies and their networks, and trace their personal Christian beginnings to the experience of new birth, often (though not always) maintaining that this experience is the key to authentic faith. The adjective *ecumenical,* however, means an openness to connect and to associate with those in the formally designated ecumenical movement, including Roman Catholic and Eastern Orthodox believers as well as Reformation heirs. With these believers they share a doctrinal orthodoxy, especially as it is found in credal, catechetical, and confessional traditions, and worry about its erosion today in both popular culture and academia. Ecumenical evangelicals also often share the mission agendas — both evangelization and social action — of this larger ecumenical community. In addition, they are conversant with the literature and formative ideas of a wider circle of theological inquiry, although often critical of its tendencies. Ecumenical evangelicalism is both a subcommunity within, and a tendency to be found throughout, contemporary evangelicalism.

This series of essays takes up topics and persons from the vantage point of evangelical-ecumenical convergence. The substance of each chapter has appeared in either evangelical or ecumenical publications or fora. I hope that the view from this edge will give a fresh perspective on matters vital to both constituencies. I am grateful for the colleagues and comrades who have made this location habitable.

MAPPING THE TERRITORY

WHAT EVANGELICALS
BELIEVE ABOUT THE BIBLE:
COMMONALITY AND DIVERSITY

CAN anything good come from evangelical hermeneutics? In the standard world of academic theology, the answer is no. Typical is a recent work by David Tracy.[1] While making a thoughtful case for "interpretation-as-conversation," he engages no evangelical viewpoint, and no evangelical appears in the index of three hundred names. How open is the conversation?

Some assumptions about evangelicalism account for its exile: its precritical worldview; a fundamentalist fanaticism incompatible with learned inquiry; an absolutism resistant to modern pluralism; a traditionalism irrelevant in secular society.

Serious encounter with evangelical interpreters quickly exposes all these caricatures. Much evangelical hermeneutics is postcritical; many evangelicals repudiate fundamentalism; evangelical inquiry tends to be encyclopedic; evangelical hermeneutics is fiercely pluralist; evangelicalism is not marginal to modern society but is increasingly formative both culturally and ecclesially. It is time to end academic parochialism and invite evangelicals into the conversation.

---

1. David Tracy, *Plurality and Ambiguity: Hermeneutics, Religion, Hope* (San Francisco: Harper & Row, 1987). An exception to the general rule of inattention is James Barr. But his polemic in *Fundamentalism* (Philadelphia: Westminster, 1978) and *Beyond Fundamentalism* (Philadelphia: Westminster, 1984) regularly obscures the distinctions and dynamisms examined in this essay.

THE EVANGELICAL PHENOMENON

What is an evangelical? Definitions abound both within and without this company. Here I shall root the word *evangelical* in sixteenth-century soil but follow its tendrils beyond.[2] The word was (and still is) associated with the Reformation evangel: justification by faith according to the authority of Scripture. (Justification by faith is sometimes called the material principle, and Scripture the formal principle, of Protestantism.) The encounter of each priestly believer with the biblical text and the personal appropriation of grace by the trusting heart were taken further by the subsequent movements of Pietism, Puritanism, the Awakenings, and revivalism. Scriptural loyalties and the experience of faith were thus radicalized and interiorized, their intensification evidenced by a rigorous personal morality and a passion for sharing the gospel. Thus the popular description of an evangelical as a "born-again" Christian is not off the mark: for an evangelical, justification is a conversion experience and Scripture is engaged with a commensurate devotion, manifesting itself in evangelical piety and evangelistic zeal.

EVANGELICAL INTERPRETATION: A SPECTRUM

Following general evangelical usage in terminology, one may define hermeneutics as the science and art of biblical interpretation.[3] Evangelical hermeneutics can be initially located on the

---

2. The definitions used here are elaborated in my entry, "Evangelical, Evangelicalism," in *Westminster Dictionary of Christian Theology,* ed. Alan Richardson and John Bowden (Philadelphia: Westminster, 1983), pp. 191-92.

3. For example, Bernard Ramm, *Protestant Biblical Interpretation: A Textbook of Hermeneutics,* 3d ed. (Grand Rapids: Baker, 1970); and Walter M. Dunnett, *The Interpretation of Scripture* (Nashville: Nelson, 1984). While covering other topics, Carl Henry's six-volume work, *God, Revelation and Authority* (Waco: Word, 1976–83), is the most developed statement of evangelical hermeneutics in this generation.

larger landscape of authority options in the Christian tradition. One can identify major alternatives according to the priority of Bible, church, or world.[4] So understood, the choice is clear for evangelicals. Whatever subsidiary sources they may recognize — the role of the church and its traditions or the place of the world of human experience — Scripture is primary. How it is primary is the question of hermeneutics. The answers given constitute the diversity within evangelicalism.[5]

The variety of perspectives makes a dramatic appearance in the current "battle for the Bible."[6] At the center of the controversy is inerrancy. Partisans of the term contend that it expresses the logic of evangelicalism. Strongly disagreeing are those who espouse infallibility.[7] Yet each includes subtypes that may be as significant as the differences between the two positions. Others contest both: to the right, oracularity; and to the left, catholicity. Under these four headings one can explore the vitalities and complexities of evangelical hermeneutics today.[8]

---

4. As in Karl Barth, *Church Dogmatics,* IV/3/1, trans. G. W. Bromiley, ed. Bromiley and T. F. Torrance (Edinburgh: T. & T. Clark, 1961), pp. 87-165 and passim. I employ these types in *The Christian Story,* vol. 2: *Authority: Scripture in the Church for the World* (Grand Rapids: Eerdmans, 1987).

5. See especially the work of Robert K. Johnston, *Evangelicals at an Impasse* (Atlanta: John Knox, 1980); and *The Use of the Bible in Theology: Evangelical Options,* ed. Robert K. Johnston (Atlanta: John Knox, 1985).

6. So Harold Lindsell, *The Battle for the Bible* (Grand Rapids: Zondervan, 1976); and Harold O. J. Brown, "The Arian Connection: Presuppositions of Errancy," in *Challenges to Inerrancy: A Theological Response,* ed. Gordon Lewis and Bruce Demarest (Chicago: Moody, 1984), pp. 383-401.

7. The debate is reflected in revisions of institutional statements of faith. Fuller Seminary's hermeneutical journey is a case in point, described in the illuminating study by George Marsden, *Reforming Fundamentalism: Fuller Seminary and the New Evangelicalism* (Grand Rapids: Eerdmans, 1987).

8. Other typologies can be found in Robert Gnuse, *The Authority of the Bible: Theories of Inspiration, Revelation and the Canon of Scripture* (New York: Paulist, 1985); Johnston, *Evangelicals at an Impasse;* and Clark Pinnock, *Biblical Revelation* (Chicago: Moody, 1971).

ORACULARITY

"But the Bible says . . . !" With the Book held high, the tele-vangelist assures the multitudes that its truth comes from the mouth of God through the pen of the writer to the eye and ear of the believer. The Scriptures are the oracles of God.

Oracularity is a potent view in some circles of popular fundamentalism. It holds that God communicated the very words of the Bible to designated amanuenses. In its earthiest expression, oracular reliability includes transmission as well as transcription, although more formal argument limits it to the original writings.

Evangelical scholarship describes this position as the dictation theory, or the mantic or mechanical dictation view, and consistently repudiates it. Although the language of dictation occurs in early Protestant scholasticism, even there it is qualified.[9] Most conservative evangelicals, including fundamentalists, take great pains to distinguish their conception of biblical authority from oracularity.[10] Nevertheless, critics regularly attribute oracularity to them, thereby confirming suspicions that the evangelical phenomenon is not well understood.[11]

Intellectual defenders of dictation or oracularity are hard to find. One must look to Islamic traditions that refuse to translate an oracular Koran or to Mormon teaching about its mantic text for the apologetics of oracularity.

---

9. Citations appear in Heinrich Heppe, *Reformed Dogmatics,* rev. and ed. Ernst Bizer, trans. G. T. Thomson (Grand Rapids: Baker, repr. 1978), pp. 17-20. Explicit rejection by inerrantists of verbal dictation began over a century ago with A. A. Hodge and Benjamin Warfield.

10. Henry, *God, Revelation and Authority,* 4:140-61.

11. Even dictionary editor and writer Alan Richardson makes this mistake in "Fundamentalism," *Chamber's Encyclopedia,* new ed. (London: George Newnes, 1959), 6:114.

INERRANCY

Inerrantists put distance between themselves and oracularists by acknowledging the human factor in the writing process. Dictation is precluded by the varied vocabulary pools and literary styles within the books of the Bible and the influence on authors of historical circumstance. The Holy Spirit superintends the author's words but otherwise allows for human particularity. Such oversight assures the deliverance of revealed propositional truth in the autographs. These original writings are "God-breathed," as declared in the locus classicus of inerrancy, 2 Timothy 3:16. That view entails not only the inbreathing of the Spirit into the mind and heart of the inspired prophet and apostle but also the breathing out of the words themselves. This plenary verbal inspiration, as noted, is not dictation but rather the protection of the author's words from error.

As plenarily inspired, the autographs are without error in all about which they speak, matters historical and scientific as well as doctrinal and moral.[12] Inerrantists stress this point in their sharp controversy with the infallibilists.

Inerrancy would seem to be a tight hermeneutic, excluding much-criticized pick-and-choose alternatives. But at least three views of inerrancy exist: conservative, moderate, and liberal.

Transmissive Inerrancy

The most conservative reading of inerrancy reduces the human role in the revelatory process to a minimum. Although acknowledging the human literary processes, these conservatives suspect the effort to understand them through standard methods of scholarship. They consider critical inquiry so fraught with the dangers of secular humanism that they give little attention, for

---

12. See Article 4 of the "Chicago Statement on Biblical Inerrancy." For commentary on this article, see James Montgomery Boice, *Does Inerrancy Matter?* (Wheaton, Ill.: Tyndale House, 1980).

example, to how the genre employed in ancient writing affects its meaning. Transmissive inerrantists take the text as it is, reading it in grammatical-historical fashion.

Accounts of a past Edenic paradise with specific geography and occupancy, and of a future millennial kingdom preceded by a timetable of turbulence in the Middle East, the rapture of believers, seven years of tribulation, and so forth,[13] are indicators of a transmissive reading. Campaigns for creationism, on the one hand, and apocalyptic forecasts of things to come, on the other, are often associated with conservative inerrancy.

Reliable transmission takes place as well between the time of the autographs and their present-day reception. Superintendence means the protection of the inerrant Word of God along the very route of editing and translating.[14] An indication of this trust in (approved) present texts is the preoccupation with harmonization. These inerrantists zealously defend the absolute trustworthiness of historical reportage, the scientific veracity of accounts of miraculous phenomena, the reliability of self-referential literary sources, and the reconcilability of apparently conflicting chronicles. Fundamentalists, who specialize in these things, are therefore consistently conservative inerrantists, although not all conservative inerrantists are fundamentalists.

Trajectory Inerrancy

The human underside of the revelatory process comes to higher prominence in moderate or trajectory inerrancy. These inerrantists give more attention to historical and literary factors, and thus allow a role to critical scholarship, albeit a modest one, because they still judge much biblical scholarship to be ruled by

---

13. For a revealing conversation among advocates of different millennial views, see "Our Future Hope: Eschatology and Its Role in the Church," *Christianity Today* 31, no. 2 (Feb. 6, 1987): 11-141.

14. Lindsell holds that copies and acceptable versions, as well as autographs, may be considered the inerrant Word of God (*Battle*, p. 37). Henry disagrees (*God, Revelation and Authority*, 4:230-31).

secular premises.[15] Further, they believe that one cannot give the interpretation of Scripture over to a scholarly magisterium. The divine Word is accessible through grammatical-historical study, commonsense exegesis based on the Protestant principle of perspicuity.

The Word so heard is not neoorthodoxy's event/Event with its elusive subjectivity. Rather, the epistemic Word congeals in the propositional truths of Scripture. Although deposited in culture-relative language, the words of the autographs are protected from error — historical and scientific as well as doctrinal and moral. Sound interpretation requires, however, that literary genre be honored. To treat Genesis and Revelation as straightforward reporting of the world's beginnings and endings is to succumb to secularism by reading into ancient texts the assumptions of modern historiography. Indeed, Genesis provides cosmological information about origins (e.g., the significance of the order of the days), but casts it in literary forms with a basic theological intent.[16] Thus moderate inerrantists do not defend a creationist young-earth scenario, although they do stress the hypothetical nature of evolutionary theory.

Moderate inerrantists do not engage in extensive harmonization. Acknowledging the human side of the text allows for oriental hyperbole and inexactitude in numbering and in the specifics of ancient chronicles.[17] An epistemic Providence does watch over transmission but secures the center, not the circumference, of Scripture. Acceptable Greek and Hebrew texts are infallible — trustworthy in doctrine and morals and in

---

15. "The Uses and Abuses of Historical Criticism" (Henry, *God, Revelation and Authority,* 4:385-404) is a frequently cited statement of moderate inerrancy.

16. So Henry in ibid., 6:133-55.

17. On acceptable variations, as well as general principles of interpretation, see Roger Nicole, "The Nature of Inerrancy," in *Inerrancy and Common Sense,* ed. Roger R. Nicole and J. Ramsey Michaels (Grand Rapids: Baker, 1980), pp. 71-95.

general not error-prone.[18] Yet mistakes may appear on marginal matters of science and history. The quest for autographical purity becomes very important, hence the emphasis on textual criticism. Confidence in the inerrancy of the autographs, but the freedom from tight divine control after the launch from the inspired autographs, prompts the label "trajectory."

Along with conservative inerrantists, moderates hold to other standard features of traditional Protestant hermeneutics:

1. *Sola Scriptura,* understood in its most restricted sense: Scripture as the sole and sufficient authority, not the sole occupant of the seat of ultimate authority. (Reason does play a surprisingly prominent role in a stream of apologetic inerrancy.)[19]

2. Perspicuity: the clarity and accessibility of Scripture to the common sense *(sensus literalis)* of the whole people of God, and thus without dependence on a teaching office, ecclesial or academic, or deferral to the claims of mystical cognoscenti.

3. Analogy of faith: the reading of unclear texts in the light of clear ones and thus the canon as the literary context for interpreting the text. Hence the venerable hermeneutical principle: Scripture is its own interpreter.

Intentional Inerrancy

This subtype comprises those who are reluctant to use the word *inerrancy,* or who want to distinguish themselves from strict inerrantists.[20] This subtype makes yet greater room for the

---

18. Henry, "The Infallibility of the Copies," *God, Revelation and Authority,* 4:220-55.

19. For various approaches in evangelical apologetics, see Gordon Lewis, *Testing Christianity's Truth Claims* (Chicago: Moody, 1976).

20. On the latter, see Clark Pinnock, *The Scripture Principle* (San Francisco: Harper & Row, 1984), pp. 57-60, 78-79, 126-29, 222-26. On the former, see J. Ramsey Michaels's preference for verbal inspiration (with its space for critical genre study) in "Inerrancy or Verbal Inspiration? An Evangelical Dilemma," in *Inerrancy and Common Sense,* pp. 49-70.

humanity of the text. The distinguishing feature is its accent on authorial intention.

Modern interpreters must not allow their concerns and premises to override the writer's purposed meaning. Discerning that intention requires careful scrutiny of the historical circumstances and literary form of the text, and thus the employment of critical apparatus. Recognizing this human substratum and giving critical scholarship a significant role in probing it make for a liberal inerrancy — inerrancy, because the rightly perceived intended meaning is without flaw and because of a general inerrantist suspicion of the antisupernaturalist bias in the methods and findings of critical scholarship; liberal, because these inerrantists assign historical and literary criticism a larger resource role in the understanding of Scripture than other inerrantists.

Assessment of Scripture's accounts of beginnings and endings again is indicative of placement on the evangelical spectrum. These inerrantists read Genesis on creation as a theological statement with no sacrosanct information intended on the when, where, and how of the world's origins.[21] These inerrantists are often amillennialists, treating Revelation as metaphorical disclosure of the ultimate whats and whys.

Intentional inerrantists are often under fire from conservative and moderate inerrantists. Their critics believe that these liberals have put their feet on a slippery slope, so humanizing Scripture that they imperil its sacred nature. By inordinate attention to critical approaches, and by denying the informational status of key stretches of historical record, they have succumbed to secularity.

---

21. J. I. Packer, *Beyond the Battle for the Bible* (Westchester, Ill.: Cornerstone, 1980).

INFALLIBILITY

The next major category is evangelicals with strict views on the authority of Scripture but without the presumption of inerrant autographs. Although some may still argue that the originals are without error (defining error as the intention to deceive), most infallibilists believe that the autographs could contain mistakes. Yet these errors do not affect the fundamental purpose of the Word of God, which is (*pace* 2 Tim. 3:16 inerrantists) "for teaching, for reproof, for correction, and for training in righteousness." Scripture is for soteric knowledge, revealed truth offered to make one "wise unto salvation" (2 Tim. 3:15, AV). Infallibilists cite the Westminster Confession's statement that "the whole counsel of God concerning all things necessary for his own glory, man's salvation, faith and life, is either expressly set down in Scripture, or by good and necessary consequence may be deduced from Scripture." Thus the Bible is "given by inspiration of God to be the rule of faith and life."[22]

Given its soteric purpose, Scripture is not required to be definitive in matters scientific and historical. For such information one turns to the appropriate human disciplines. One must not confuse the gospel with the Bible's ancient cosmologies and chronologies. The Chalcedonian paradox applies to the epistemic Word as well as the incarnate Word, giving in both cases treasure in earthen vessels. Within this category are differing positions, identifiable as conservative, moderate, and liberal.

---

22. A major dispute within evangelicalism focused on the volume by Jack Rogers and Donald K. McKim, *The Authority and Interpretation of the Bible: An Historical Approach* (New York: Harper & Row, 1979), which argues that the Reformers, together with the church fathers, held to a soteric view of Scripture. For a rejoinder, see John D. Woodbridge, *Biblical Authority: A Critique of the Rogers and McKim Proposal* (Grand Rapids: Zondervan, 1982).

Prominent works on infallibilism include G. C. Berkouwer, *Holy Scripture*, trans. Jack Rogers (Grand Rapids: Eerdmans, 1970); Ramm, *Protestant Biblical Interpretation;* and Dewey Beegle, *Scripture, Tradition, and Infallibility* (Grand Rapids: Eerdmans, 1973).

Unitive Infallibility

Conservative infallibilists are often embattled inerrantists, weary from the warfare and convinced that the defense of evangelical faith does not take place at the Maginot Line of errorless autographs. For example, having argued for an inerrancy that makes room for inaccuracies in the transmission process, or having stressed the theological rather than the literal interpretation of cosmological passages, it is a short step to saying simply, "The Bible is the Word of God for faith and life." All the intricate justifications now seem to be circumlocutions. The Bible is not a textbook of science and history but the good news of salvation for sinners. Indeed, infallibilism is no stranger to the experientialism of evangelical faith. A religion of the heart can easily conclude that inerrancy is left-brain logic chopping, imperial reason run amok.

The conservative position of unitive infallibility assumes the oneness of the message of salvation found throughout Scripture. The progressive revelation in the Bible does not call into question the harmony of all biblical teaching on faith and morals.

For some who come out of inerrancy, conservative infallibility proves to be an unstable position. To those who have left behind the inerrancy ethos and now employ more actively the methods of biblical criticism, the question comes: How can one reconcile the seeming differences in theological viewpoints within Scripture? Doesn't the Bible contain some doubtful moral judgments and some dubious ideas about the ways of God? What *is* the infallible Word spoken through the varied human words?

Essentialist Infallibility

The authoritative Word God speaks in Scripture comes as "the essentials of evangelical theology."[23] The Bible gives the funda-

---

23. The category is suggested by the title of Donald Bloesch's two-

mentals of faith. One cannot read it as a flat surface of uniform teaching, nor as an evenly developing progressive revelation. Scripture has peaks and valleys, in both Testaments. One needs a guide to find a way out of the valleys and up to the peaks. The Bible itself provides this guide: Scripture is its own interpreter. While the inner testimony of the Holy Spirit convicts the heart of its truth, the inspired text conveys to the mind the gospel's content. Running like a red thread through Scripture is its saving knowledge. This evangelical disclosure includes teaching about the deity and humanity of Christ, Christ's virginal conception and bodily resurrection, the doctrine of substitutionary atonement, justification by grace through faith, the triune nature of God, the bodily return of Christ, and so forth. Scripture also gives standards for the moral life and the ways of personal piety. Thus moderate infallibilists look to the Bible for the substance of Christian faith and life. The essentials constitute the lens through which they read the text, providing principles of selection and interpretation.

As with all forms of infallibilism, essentialist infallibilists make no claims for the consistent veracity of scientific or historical detail. But regarding those theological distinctives that entail statements bordering on science and history (i.e., the virginal conception and bodily resurrection), infallibilists challenge the closed system of antisupernaturalism.

As one moves along the evangelical spectrum, one should note the role of tradition in hermeneutical judgments. The formulation of evangelical basics bears the obvious marks of historical debate. Essentialists often acknowledge the stamp of ecclesiality, as in the citation of Reformation confessions, but they tend to see tradition more as a passive recipient for the revealed Word than as an active partner in the hermeneutical

---

volume systematics, *The Essentials of Evangelical Theology* (San Francisco: Harper & Row, 1978–79). He develops his view also in "A Christological Hermeneutic: Crisis and Conflict in Hermeneutics," in *Use of the Bible*, pp. 78-102.

task. So too they do not usually assign reason or experience a formative role in interpreting Scripture, although these resources function in that way for those who legitimate critical scholarship.[24] The self-conscious activation of those resources occurs in the catholic evangelical hermeneutics described later. In moderate infallibilism the knowledge of God's saving truth is the heart of God's holy Word.

Christocentric Infallibility

Old differences between Reformed and Lutheran hermeneutics have their echoes in the evangelical debate about the Bible. Calvinists understood Christ, the Word, to be coextensive with Scripture, hence their esteem for the Old Testament. Classical Lutheranism also interpreted the Bible christologically but tended to read it according to the norm of Christ/gospel/justification. Similarly, inerrantists and the first two forms of infallibilism see Christ as coterminous with the autographs, or manifest through the faith and moral instruction within it, a Calvinist turn. Like Lutheran hermeneutics, christocentric views today (evangelical and otherwise) use the norm of Jesus Christ to interpret the text, making a distinction within Scripture comparable to law and gospel. Nonevangelical options may develop a christological reading of the text as such, and that in its various forms.[25] By contrast, liberal infallibilism continues the essentialist commitment to a propositional core but makes active use of the standard of Jesus Christ in both interpreting and selecting its constitutive elements.

This view invites collision with inherited readings of Scripture, as in the contemporary dispute about the status and role of women. Can an evangelical disagree with Paul? Yes. His cultural limitations have to pass muster before the norm of Jesus

---

24. Ramm, *Protestant Biblical Interpretation,* passim.
25. For the variety in christological hermeneutics, see my *Christian Story,* 2:78-91.

Christ. Indeed, the Paul of Galatians 3:28 must judge inadequate the Paul who demands silence from women and assigns them a role of subservience, especially as that christological criterion takes account of Jesus' relationship with, and teaching about, women. In the same way, one must scrutinize all evangelical doctrine by the standard of Jesus Christ. One must honestly question scriptural content short of this norm and venture fresh interpretations of the substance of Scripture.[26]

CATHOLICITY

Catholicity is a word and concept beginning to make its appearance in contemporary evangelicalism.[27] This fourth type includes the sacramental movement already noted, but it comprises a more encompassing constituency, one whose roots reach back to the evangelical catholicity of another time.[28] Hermeneutical catholicity incorporates all historic authority claimants — Bible, church, world — according to the priorities and functions assigned to them by an evangelical doctrine of revelation.

In this view, Scripture is the *source* of authority, based on its unique prophetic-apostolic inspiration. The church (as the whole people of God) and its classical tradition constitute the authoritative *resource* for interpreting the Bible, warranted by the Spirit's gift to the church of illumination, but always standing under Scripture. The world of general human experience — rational, moral, affective — constitutes the *setting* in which one

---

26. On this position, see Paul K. Jewett, *Man as Male and Female* (Grand Rapids: Eerdmans, 1975).

27. Bloesch describes catholic evangelicalism in *The Future of Evangelical Christianity* (Garden City, N.Y.: Doubleday, 1983). Robert Webber discusses "An Evangelical and Catholic Methodology" in *Use of the Bible,* pp. 137-58.

28. In particular, to the evangelical catholicity of the Mercersburg theology. See *The Mercersburg Theology,* ed. James Hastings Nichols (New York: Oxford University Press, 1966).

16

reads Scripture and tradition, so legitimated by a common grace at work in general revelation.

With its inclusive bent, evangelical catholic hermeneutics appropriates learnings from inerrantists and infallibilists. From inerrancy it learns loyalty to the whole canon, holding that the plenarily inspired Bible is capable of surprises and future disclosures, an openness that talk of a canon within the canon would preclude. From inerrantists and infallibilists it adopts the traditional principle of the analogy of faith, thereby establishing the canon as the literary context for interpreting the text. It is in debt to the infallibilists for stressing the canonical substance of essential belief and its christological center.

The relative emphasis placed on the two junior partners to Scripture varies. Thus context (world) may bulk large in a view influenced by liberation accents,[29] or focused on cross-cultural studies,[30] or engaging the issues of philosophical hermeneutics.[31] Ecclesial tradition (church) may figure prominently in the hermeneutical equation, as in sacramental evangelicalism. Yet in both cases, world and church are ministerial, while Scripture is always magisterial.

Also variable is the kind of experience (world) that is hermeneutically formative. Where apologetic interests are high, stress upon "the light of nature," dimmed but not destroyed by the fall, brings reason into partnership with faith. In affective

---

29. As in Orlando Costas, *Christ Outside the Gate* (Maryknoll, N.Y.: Orbis, 1982); and René Padilla, *Mission Between the Times* (Grand Rapids: Eerdmans, 1985). Evangelical feminism's contextuality ranges from Virginia Ramey Mollenkott's *The Divine Feminine* (New York: Crossroad, 1983) to Faith Martin's *Call Me Blessed* (Grand Rapids: Eerdmans, 1988). See also the journal *Daughters of Sarah*.

30. See Charles Kraft, *Christianity in Culture* (Maryknoll, N.Y.: Orbis, 1984).

31. Anthony C. Thiselton's major work, *The Two Horizons: New Testament Hermeneutics and Philosophical Description* (Grand Rapids: Eerdmans, 1980), and his proposal of an action model in hermeneutics (Roger Lundin, Anthony Thiselton, and Clarence Walhout, *The Responsibility of Hermeneutics* [Grand Rapids: Eerdmans, 1985], pp. 110-11), represent significant responses to deconstructionist and reader-response theory.

17

traditions, feeling replaces reason in the correlative role. Where justice and peace or personal ethics are to the fore, moral sensibilities are active in the junior partnership. One could make the case that these three emphases constitute the equivalent of conservative, moderate, and liberal divisions in the category of catholicity. But the crosscurrents within, and the complexity of, this combinationist hermeneutic make such internal distinctions difficult.[32]

Every evangelical hermeneutic, functionally if not formally, finds some place in its authority structure for church and world. Even in the extremes of oracularity, one cannot deny the role of the church in the canonization process, in spite of its assignment to a place of passivity. Also, although conservative evangelicals often do not acknowledge it, strong dogmatic traditions shape the way one reads a *sola Scriptura* text. Oracularists, inerrantists, or infallibilists who deny a place for the world in their hermeneutics often reveal its subtle effects when taking political and social stands that purport to be directly from Scripture. These hidden operations argue for a more self-conscious, and therefore more critical, appreciation of ecclesial and secular factors in hermeneutical theory and practice, as evangelical catholicity attempts.

CONCLUSION

Some self-identified evangelicals will not find themselves in the foregoing categories. Among that number may be those who have discovered Karl Barth and thus are ambivalent, at best, about talk of Scripture's propositional truths and are critical of the rationalist tenor of some evangelical debates.[33] From a very

---

32. See my *Christian Story,* 2:91-124.

33. For Bernard Ramm's pilgrimage toward Barth, see Ramm, *After Fundamentalism* (San Francisco: Harper & Row, 1983). See also Gregory G. Bolich, *Karl Barth and Evangelicalism* (Downers Grove, Ill.: InterVarsity, 1980).

different perspective, others would consider dispensationalism integral to inerrancy. Yet others might declare for inerrancy or infallibility but disavow the evangelical label on the grounds of Roman Catholic or Eastern Orthodox commitment. Exceptions acknowledged, the typology presented here seeks to describe the overall evangelical movement today and its dominant hermeneutical constituencies.

I have established the boundary of evangelical hermeneutics on the left at catholicity. Beyond that are those who do not identify themselves as evangelicals but do hold to the primacy of Scripture, either loosening the cords of propositionality or reducing or reconceiving its normative content. Thus a conceptual hermeneutic locates defining ideas or motifs within Scripture, an historical view fixes upon the saving deeds of God, various christological positions make Christ or Jesus the content or norm of Scripture, and other forms of catholicity assign a larger or different role to other kinds of tradition or context. Beyond these are the other two major authority types in which the church and its tradition or the world of human experience replace Scripture as primary. Thus, for all its diversity, evangelicalism represents a distinct and important perspective on the controverted questions of authority and interpretation. Its voice needs to be heard in the ongoing hermeneutical conversation.

POLITICAL FUNDAMENTALISM:
DISTINCTIONS AND DIRECTIONS

THE influence of the Religious Right on the 1980 elections, its success in subsequent single-issue campaigns, the high visibility of television evangelists, and the media attention to all these things pointed to a new phenomenon in contemporary culture. But was it not, finally, one more transient American fancy? The Bakker and Swaggart scandals, the "invisible army" of Robertson that never materialized, Falwell's announcement that he was "backing off of politics" — are these not indicators of the end of a short-lived era?

To write the obituary of political fundamentalism now is a measure of the naiveté of any popular commentary. The invisible army that managed to propel a candidate into the presidential arena is still there, far more dispersed than the sages of "Nightline" and "Frontline" thought to be the case. It lives still in the political arena. It dwells as well in the church and as part of a wider evangelical constituency. Indeed, one cannot understand its political presence and future unless one grasps its ecclesial meaning. To that end I engage here in some necessary theological analysis. Such inquiry requires attention to basic definitions with special reference to key distinctions within and beyond the movement in question. With those in hand one can discern potential directions.

EVANGELICALISM

The first set of confusions that one must address has to do with the words *evangelical* and *evangelicalism* and their relation to fundamentalism. As noted in chapter 1, the description of a theological point of view as "evangelical" came into usage in the sixteenth century to identify Protestants who believed that "the evangel," the good news, centered in justification by grace through faith as attested by the authority of Scripture.

Today evangelicalism refers to these same two accents as they have been radicalized and interiorized by the historic movements of Pietism, Wesleyanism, Puritanism, the Great Awakenings, and modern revivalism. Evangelicals have an intense personal experience of justification (and thus are "born-again" Christians) and make rigorous use of Scripture, a piety that issues in evangelistic zeal and strong moral codes.

Although these characteristics locate modern evangelicals within the current theological spectrum, one must go further: contemporary evangelicalism is no undivided empire. One can discern at least six varieties:

1. Fundamentalists. Here the discursive side of the movement takes precedence, the Word written. Ultra-inerrancy is the criterion of faithfulness. With it goes the polemical and separatist mentality that characterizes every religious and secular fundamentalism, but Christian fundamentalism is no monolith. It can be apocalyptic or nonapocalyptic, political or apolitical (or combinations thereof, as in the neo-fundamentalist phenomenon of the Religious Right).

2. Old Evangelicals. The affective side is in ascendancy, personal experience of regeneration being decisive, together with its expression in mass evangelism. Billy Graham and those who stress personal conversion and mass evangelism are in this category.

3. New Evangelicals. The term *neo-evangelical* came into use in the 1950s to describe those who stressed the social import of faith and its apologetic persuasiveness and criticized funda-

22

mentalist sectarianism.[1] It is associated in this country with the periodical *Christianity Today*.

4. Justice and Peace Evangelicals. Influenced by the anti-establishment social movements of the 1960s and since, related often to communitarian experiments, these activist evangelicals advocate a political agenda drastically at variance with the Religious Right. Its representative journal is *Sojourners,* espousing a radical political agenda in the Anabaptist tradition.

5. Charismatic Evangelicals. New birth leads to second blessings — glossolalia, healing, celebrative worship, intense group experience.

6. Ecumenical Evangelicals. More a tendency than a constituency, ecumenical evangelicals edge the movement toward relationships with the larger Christian community. This tendency evidences itself in a variety of ways, from sacramental rediscoveries[2] to alliances with mainline Christians on common social concerns.

FUNDAMENTALISM

"Political fundamentalism" is a subset of the first type.[3] It is both a version of evangelical faith and an expression of a more universal human phenomenon. In the latter respect, it shares with other religious and political movements a mind-set, as in Islamic fundamentalism, Roman Catholic fundamentalism, Jewish fundamentalism, Marxist fundamentalism, and so on. (The literature of the organization Fundamentalists Anonymous — made up largely of Protestant ex-fundamentalists —

---

1. Carl Henry gives a firsthand account of formative events and persons in his autobiography, *Confessions of a Theologian* (Waco: Word, 1987).

2. See Robert E. Webber, *Evangelicals on the Canterbury Trail* (Waco: Word, 1985).

3. These categories appear in my entry, "Evangelical, Evangelicalism," in *Westminster Dictionary of Christian Theology,* ed. Alan Richardson and John Bowden (Philadelphia: Westminster, 1983), pp. 191-92.

is a storehouse of information on the mind-set.)[4] Associated therewith are the familiar words *absolutist, dogmatic,* and *polemical,* which reflect attitudes grounded in a deeper set of the mind, a worldview. In this worldview, reality is at war with itself. History, indeed the cosmos, is sharply divided between the legions of light and the armies of night (coming to metaphysical expression in the dualism of specific religious traditions such as Manichaeism and Zoroastrianism). Thus proponents of this view draw a decisive line between "us" and "them," and the true believer guards it with the weaponry of inner conformity and outer assault. By rigid discipline one must keep the righteous empire unsullied, and by means appropriate to dealing with satanic forces one must subject the evil empire to unremitting attack. Hence the campaigns mounted to purge its institutions (as in the efforts of fundamentalists in the Southern Baptist Convention during the 1980s), or to separate itself from the infidel parent organizations (the "independent Baptist" movement associated with Falwellian fundamentalism). Combining this mind-set with an apocalyptic reading of current history — an imminent end of the world — intensifies all these features.

Apocalypticism points toward an important theological aspect of fundamentalism. But before attending to these key eschatological themes, one must understand fundamentalist hermeneutics, the interpretation of the Bible that warrants the end-time scenario of much political fundamentalism.

Fundamentalist Hermeneutics

As mentioned in chapter 1, fundamentalist biblical interpretation is based on the principle of inerrancy. The errorlessness of Scripture was one of five planks in the early twentieth-century

---

4. See *The FA Networker,* especially vol. 3, no. 1 (Spring 1987), published by Fundamentalists Anonymous, P.O. Box 20324, Greeley Square Station, New York, N.Y. 10001.

fundamentalist movement as it attacked modernism. Fundamentalism today, however, fixes upon scriptural interpretation as the key issue, with ultra-inerrancy as the test of orthodoxy.

Yet even inerrantists disagree among themselves, a fact to keep in mind when attempting to understand major denominational disputes as well as the political landscape (e.g., the moderate inerrantists who teach in Southern Baptist seminaries and the fundamentalist inerrantists who want to remove them). Fundamentalists are ultra-inerrantists or transmissive inerrantists.[5] The transmission from God to authors takes place with minimal human contribution, and from authors to modern readers with no human distortion, by virtue of a "grace of preservation." The intellectual expression of this view appears in the zeal to harmonize apparently conflicting historical narratives and to treat biblical cosmology and nature marvels as scientific reportage.

Fundamentalism is a version of transmissive inerrancy that uses this doctrine as the criterion of orthodoxy, with special attention to the accounts of beginnings (Genesis) and endings (Revelation) — hence the creationists' efforts to rewrite public school textbooks, on the one hand, and the high profile of apocalyptic eschatology among many (not all) fundamentalists, on the other.

Apocalyptic Fundamentalism

Distinctive as it is from other kinds of evangelicalism, fundamentalism itself is not an undivided empire. Intense struggles go on within its own ranks, indeed, exacerbated by the "us and them" mentality that tends to make even small deviance cause for major splits. In regard to the immediate issues of politics and apocalyptic, for example, one can discern four camps: politi-

---

5. I discuss the transmissive view and other forms of inerrancy (and infallibility) teaching in *The Christian Story,* vol. 2: *Authority: Scripture in the Church for the World* (Grand Rapids: Eerdmans, 1987), pp. 62-75.

cal, apolitical, apocalyptic, and nonapocalyptic fundamentalism. The phenomenon I am examining is largely a case of political apocalyptic fundamentalism.

Apocalyptic fundamentalism refers to ultra-inerrantists who anticipate the imminent closure of human and cosmic history, discernible by secret knowledge of cataclysmic events either presently taking place or immediately forthcoming.[6] The form apocalypticism often takes in political fundamentalism is that of pretribulational premillennialism, with its roots in the dispensationalist thought of John Darby and the Scofield Bible.[7] As *pre*millennialists, they believe that Christ will come from heaven with his church to establish a thousand-year reign of peace and plenty on the earth, a view contrasting with that of erring *post*millennialists who hold that Christ will come *after* a thousand-year period of peace, missionary success, and plenty. As *pre*tribulationists, they hold that a rapture will take place in which Christ will come for his church (Christ descending halfway to earth to gather the living saints and the resurrected dead saints into the heavenly regions), thereby protecting believers from seven horrifying years of tribulation that will then be unleashed upon the earth before Christ comes to establish the millennium.

This comforting thought of "pretrib premils" (as the cognoscenti identify them) contrasts with the discomforting thought of "posttrib premils" and "midtrib premils," who anticipate that the saints will have to endure all or some of the tribulation. Pretrib, posttrib, and midtrib premils watch carefully the signs of the times through the lens of the apocalyptic passages of Scripture (found especially in Daniel, Revelation, 2 Thessaloni-

---

6. Graphically portrayed in color, for example, by Charles R. Taylor, "The Destiny Chart" (Cypress, Calif.: Today in Bible Prophecy, 1978).

7. Described in such works as George Ladd, *The Blessed Hope* (Grand Rapids: Eerdmans, 1956); Ernest Sandeen, *The Roots of Fundamentalism* (Chicago: University of Chicago Press, 1970); Robert Gundry, *The Church and the Tribulation* (Grand Rapids: Zondervan, 1973); and Dave MacPherson, *The Great Rapture Hoax* (Fletcher, N.C.: New Puritan Library, 1983).

ans, Matthew 24, and Mark 13), often interpreting the establishment of the state of Israel in 1948, the formation of ten nations into the European Common Market, and events in the Middle East as portentous of things to come. Posttribs and midtribs can identify tribulation figures of the Antichrist, the "abomination of desolation," and so on in the present, a practice denied to pretribs, for whom these events can take place only after the rapture.

All premillennialists continue and conclude their apocalypse with a final uprising of Satan and his legions after the millennium, put down then by Christ, who dispatches the enemy to a lake of fire and passes final judgment on the reprobate, sending them to eternal damnation and establishing a new heaven and a new earth where the saints dwell in glory.

Political Apocalyptic Fundamentalism

Apocalyptic premillennialism has in earlier eras tended to be apolitical: the end is coming, "rescue the perishing," gather the church apart from a world on the way to destruction. The groups under examination are therefore neo-fundamentalists in that they combine intense this-worldly political commitments with their apocalypticism. Neo-fundamentalists draw a straight line from the apocalyptic preview of coming attractions to specific programs, parties, and candidates. The believers prepare the way for the coming of the Lord by service to causes that are commensurate with the standards of the arriving kingdom. Loyalty to them pits the legions of the coming King against the satanic forces that now, as in the future, contest Christ's rule. The political cum evangelistic zeal and attendant organizational energy that arises from this kind of theology of hope is something to behold, as in the Robertson crusade and the vigor of neo-fundamentalist single-issue campaigns.

One should note in passing that the neo-fundamentalists who constitute much of the current Religious Right differ from the religious expressions of the radical right in this country. In earlier decades of this century, and still today, some fundamentalists have pronounced political agendas of a hypernationalist and sometimes of an avowedly racist sort. Thus Carl McIntire is a soft radical of superpatriotic bent. Hard radicals include groups that range from the Ku Klux Klan and neo-Nazis to the newer survivalist movements who link Christian symbols and fundamentalist hermeneutics to nativist and racist programs with violent overtones.[8] Neo-fundamentalists are distinguished from the radical Christian right not only in their rejection of avowedly superpatriotic and racist views but also in their mainstreaming political intentions. They do not attack the establishment from outside in ad hoc raids and political hyperbole, as is the case with radical rightists, but seek to change what they also believe to be a Satan-captive terrain from within by accepted processes of political and social action. Using many of the tactics employed by other movements of social protest — electioneering, petitioning for redress of grievances, letter writing, rallying, demonstrating, boycotting, and in some cases civil disobedience — they seek to change laws, lawmakers, and the social, economic, and educational institutions of society.

By mapping the territory within a section of today's evangelical empire, I have tried to identify the features of one aggressive religiopolitical movement that will have significant impact on the future of this country, including its quest for peace. Understanding its politics requires this kind of theological investigation with all its distinctions, indeed tedious and fine distinctions. In sum, this movement is a neo-fundamentalism within evangelicalism, largely wedded to a pretribulational premillennialism with imminent apocalyptic expectations, drawing political conclusions and tapping political energies. With this understanding one can anticipate more clearly the directions this movement may take.

Before turning to that topic, however, I must make passing

---

8. I investigate these distinctions in *The Religious Right and Christian Faith* (Grand Rapids: Eerdmans, 1982), pp. 1-5.

reference to one version of political fundamentalism that is postmillennialist rather than premillennialist, one that has a growing following in the United States. This is the reconstructionist movement mentored by R. J. Rushdoony and given visibility in a recent Bill Moyers documentary. Reconstructionism is an intellectually complex ideology in the Reformed tradition that seeks to order society on the basis of strict Old Testament legal as well as moral codes in the expectation that the biblicizing of society is promised as a millennial hope before the return of Christ.[9]

DIRECTIONS

Political fundamentalism is a volatile movement, active in a volatile society going through volatile times. All this volatility makes prognostication about directions hazardous. For example, while writing in 1982 about the Religious Right, I commented on its susceptibility to the seductions of power because of naiveté about its presumed righteousness. But I was myself naive about the vulnerability of its leaders to more prurient temptations. Although risky, projections are nevertheless possible, especially when grounded in an understanding of the theological assumptions of the movement.

The apocalyptic premillennialism of neo-fundamentalism will fuel its own political fires for the foreseeable future. The invisible army will continue to march because ardent hope mobilizes for action (as Jürgen Moltmann has argued and history has demonstrated). Nontheological factors will certainly play their part in its momentum, including the cultural and economic disenfranchisement felt by many of its participants. Indeed, the tumults and historical peril of these times are social facts that feed apocalypticism, because theological visions are inextricable

---

9. See Rousas J. Rushdoony, *The Institutes of Biblical Law* (Phillipsburg, N.J.: Presbyterian and Reformed, 1973).

from their socioeconomic habitat. Many analysts point out this earthy underside, but they regularly fall prey in their analyses to a reductionism that fails to assess the influence of belief systems in social change. The latter sociologism, in combination with uncritical assumptions about an omnipresent and irreversible secularization process, makes it difficult for most popular and much academic commentary on political fundamentalism to grasp its factuality and durability. Neo-fundamentalism is here in force and is here to stay.

I have already outlined the diversity within a wider evangelicalism and in fundamentalism itself. That diversity should give some indication about the ways evangelicalism will influence the political process. Even secular commentators can see by now that evangelicalism is no bloc vote. Jesse Jackson's following among African-American evangelicals, who make up a large part of African-American church life, should put to rest all early media stereotypes about the monolithic nature of the evangelical vote. The poor showing of Robertson forces, the fundamentalist leaders prominent in the Bush and Kemp campaigns, and so forth should underscore the diversity in fundamentalist party politics. Nevertheless, one can see signs of fundamentalist political unity on single issues, both those connecting directly with its hermeneutics (e.g., public school textbooks and prayer in public schools) and those in which its agenda converges with the secular New Right (on issues that run from personal morality to foreign policy).

Two factors, one obvious and the other less so, could weaken or slow down the continuing presence and influence of political fundamentalism. The first is public exposure of the moral flaws of some of its leaders. Fundamentalists are supposed to practice what they preach, especially when they so sharply draw the lines between the forces of good and the cadres of evil. This sense of betrayal has already taken its toll on the income and thus the institutions of prominent media figures, including those not exposed for hypocrisy (the cutback on the television programming of Falwell and the unsuccessful effort of Robertson to distance himself from the scandals). Further, neo-fundamentalists are children of their times — whether they admit it or not — and thus bad publicity embarrasses them, a fact that could account for such things as the final decision of the Assemblies of God not to exempt Swaggart from its rules for rehabilitation after a period of equivocation, and also the apparent slowing in 1988 of the campaign of Southern Baptist fundamentalists to take over Southern Baptist educational institutions.

The second factor that could significantly retard neo-fundamentalist political momentum has to do with a twofold theological contradiction. First, in spite of its professed loyalty to biblical authority, including its rigorously literalist hermeneutic, neo-fundamentalism does not espouse the radical understanding of the fall found in Scripture. Sin does not stubbornly persist in the life of the redeemed but has been evacuated to the exclusive region of Satan outside the precincts of the saints, creating the "us and them" mentality already discussed. Because the saints are so preserved in their saintliness and thus enjoined to carry on holy wars against the sinners, they have no place for a piety of self-criticism and no system of checks and balances or sober procedures of monitoring within their institutions that might anticipate the corruptibility to which all persons and institutions in a fallen world are susceptible. In the absence of both these elements (e.g., no regular corporate confession of sin within its liturgies, and no modes of self-examination in personal piety and institutional self-scrutiny, as in financial accountability to its constituency or to the wider public), persons at the top of pyramidal organizations have fallen prey to the predictably attendant temptations. Indeed, money, sex, and power, three seductions to which neo-fundamentalists have succumbed, are directly related to this naiveté about the invulnerability of saints, aggravated further by the "us and them" apocalyptic of neo-fundamentalism. An older tradition that demanded of its saints (the monks) the taking of vows of poverty, chastity, and obedience knew about the corruptibility of the pious, even though

31

its ascetic alternative is inadequate. In view of the universality of sin manifest in the temptations that grow with the accumulation of power, including spiritual power, both a sober piety and institutional self-monitoring are necessary. Their absence in political fundamentalism could prove its undoing. Time will tell.

The second contradiction emerges when one asks: Can apocalyptic theology sustain over time its political rationale? If the end is coming soon, one in which believers will be raptured and a time of devastating tribulation is expected, then why should they want to change political institutions? Apocalypse forecasts their imminent dissolution with the attendant removal to heaven of believers. Why should a neo-fundamentalist want to build a university that will compete with Notre Dame (Falwell) or a Christian Broadcasting Network (Robertson) or Christian theme parks (Bakker) or publishing houses (Swaggart) or hospitals (Roberts), or want to run for president (Robertson)? Both the political and institutional programs launched seem to assume more hope and a longer future for human history than premillennialist horizons would allow. The sociologist Jeffrey Hadden has noticed this seeming theological incoherence, and he wonders if a postmillennialist turn is in the offing for the televangelists.[10] Indeed, the growth of the postmillennialist reconstructionist movement may be a straw in the wind. Then one must ask if the abandonment of apocalyptic that goes with such a move would, in turn, affect the degree of political energy generated by it. This second theological caveat may argue for a potential change in the political trajectory of the phenomenon.

Although one cannot know the ultimate direction of political fundamentalism any more than one can penetrate the eschatological future God has in store for humanity (seen as it is "in a mirror, dimly," and not through the transparencies of

---

10. Jeffrey Hadden, "Religious Broadcasting and the Mobilization of the New Christian Right," *Journal for the Scientific Study of Religion* 26, no. 1 (March 1987): 23-24.

apocalyptic), one can make an educated guess about its penultimate future. Barring the pitfalls identified, this army will continue to be about its holy wars, and evangelical ecumenicals and ecumenical evangelicals will have to ask about the clarity of their own eschatological vision and their political will to pursue it.

EXPLORING THE BOUNDARIES

THE USE OF SCRIPTURE
IN THEOLOGY

The answer to the question — Well, how do you do it? — will be given by stopping the action in mid-course and examining its features. That means looking at a current inquiry on the soteriological singularity of Christian faith.[1]

JESUS CHRIST, THE LIFE OF THE WORLD

INCREASING religious pluralism in modern societies poses sharp questions for Christians about their claim that Christ is *the* way, truth, and life. This contemporary "plural shock" (companion to "culture shock" and "future shock") has caused more than a few cases of christological heart failure. I have sought to identify that kind of response and other reactions in a typology that runs from views which eliminate or significantly alter Christian assertions of finality (parallel pluralism, synthetic pluralism, degree pluralism) through the qualified particularist themes of Rahner and Barth

---

1. I have formulated these theses in "The Scandals of Particularity and Universality," *Mid-Stream* 22, no. 1 (January 1983): 32-52. For my more extensive development of the material found there and in this chapter see *The Christian Story*, vol. 2: *Authority: Scripture in the Church for the World* (Grand Rapids: Eerdmans, 1987).

(centripetal singularity and centrifugal singularity) to positions of radical exclusiveness (imperial singularity). Do these current types exhaust the possible alternatives? A quest for an answer takes me to the biblical texts.

My starting point is the locus classicus for the scandal of particularity, John 14:6. Making use of both traditional and contemporary methods of interpretation,[2] as well as theological exegesis,[3] the inquirer seeks to discern the meaning of this awesome affirmation of the Johannine Christ: "I am the way, and the truth, and the life; no one comes to the Father except through me." Three major motifs emerge as constitutive of assertions about the decisiveness of Jesus Christ. (1) God's saving *way* into the world was by the singular route of the birth, life, death, and resurrection of Jesus Christ. (2) The definitive *truth* of revelation is manifested in these events. (3) The decisive

---

2. I follow Raymond Brown here in the interpretation of "the way" as primary predicate and one read against the background of its Hebrew Bible usage (as in the parallelism of Ps. 86:11) with modifications by Qumran tradition, rather than as shaped by Mandaean and Hermetic sources. Nevertheless, de la Potterie's arguments for the linkages of the Johannine "way" with God's making of a way through the desert underscore the feature of action that is assumed in Brown but is somewhat muted by his noetic preoccupation. With Schnackenburg I read "truth" and "life" as the expression and clarification of "way," rather than as the rationale for it. (One can construe the epexegetical "truth" and "life" in either sense.) Indeed, Christ as revealer is a dominant note in John and is seen as the giver of life to those who know the truth. But the subjective soteriological assertion is the issue of the unity of Father and Son, one rendered possible by the way that the Son made into the world. One may have life because it comes from the Source through the Stream as it breaks forth in our midst. As one reads Johannine texts like this in the context of the canon (according to the hermeneutical procedure described subsequently), the kind of incarnational singularity stressed in the Johannine "way" is complementary to other New Testament perspectives on the decisive action of Christ: its portrayal in the Pauline corpus in terms of his vicarious work or in the Synoptic delineations of the eschatological prophet and the resurrection.

3. On the validity of theological exegesis see T. F. Torrance, *Reality and Evangelical Theology* (Philadelphia: Westminster, 1982), pp. 42, 48-51, 68-71. My own use of this method relates a text to Scripture in its entirety as interpreted by evangelical substance and christological norm, on the one hand, and to tradition on the other. More about this matter subsequently.

life of redemption is made available to human beings through these events. Thus in Jesus Christ God does a *deed,* makes a *disclosure,* and effects a *deliverance.* Any response to pluralism that is faithful to biblical warrants must cohere with these awesome claims to particularity.

Has the way the tradition of imperial singularity has read this text and its auxiliaries done justice to the depth of their meanings? In the field of systematics some twentieth-century theologies have sought to be faithful to the scandalous particularity but have claimed to discover aspects of universality neglected by imperial views. Thus both Barth and Rahner, each in his own very different way, assert a deed and disclosure of finality in Jesus Christ, yet they go on to declare for a universality in the soteriological effects and relationships of the singular action to all humanity. But the conception of "anonymous Christianity" in Rahner and mission as "vocation" in Barth compromises the singularity of deliverance in Christ — that in him alone the believer can find life and salvation by grace through faith.[4] The issue of Christian response to pluralism seems to be joined most critically here around the meaning of life and salvation or, more technically, around the application of the benefits of Christ's saving work (redemption applied).[5]

A survey of texts that deal with the New Testament assumptions about the appropriation of the benefits of Christ's work makes an overwhelming case for the inextricable unity of the faith response to the good news of saving grace, however one conceives of any of these terms, whoever the writer, whatever the community, wherever the layer of tradition. In each case one hears the refrain as a key Johannine "life" text formulates it: "God so loved the world that he gave his only

---

4. Waldron Scott has astutely identified this point in Barth's soteriology. See his *Karl Barth's Theology of Mission* (Downers Grove, Ill.: InterVarsity, 1978).

5. John Murray, *Redemption: Accomplished and Applied* (Grand Rapids: Eerdmans, 1955, repr. 1978).

Son, so that everyone who believes in him may not perish but may have eternal life" (John 3:16). A systematics rooted in Scripture and responding to pluralism must think within the framework of the claim to singularity found in the following passages:

Matthew 8:10-13; 9:1-8, 19-22, 28-38; 10:32-33, 37-40; 11:27-30; 12:36-37; 17:19-20

Mark 2:5-12, 34; 8:34-38; 9:23-25; 10:52; 11:22-26

Luke 5:20-25; 7:9-10, 50; 8:48-50; 10:25-28; 15:7; 18:29-30

John 1:12-13, 16-18; 3:3-8, 16-18, 28, 36; 4:10-14, 22, 42; 5:24; 6:29, 33-40, 47-51, 53-58, 68-69; 10:10; 11:25-26; 12:25-26, 50; 14:1-7, 23-24; 15:1-11; 17:1-5, 25-26; 20:30-31

Acts 2:36-39, 47; 3:17-19; 4:11-12; 8:21-22; 10:43; 11:13-18; 13:38-39, 48; 15:6-11; 16:30-34; 20:21, 32; 26:16-18

Romans 1:16-17; 3:21-22, 25-31; 4:3-17; 5:1-2, 8-11; 6:23; 8:28-30; 10:9-13; 11:1-6, 11, 13-14, 21-22

1 Corinthians 1:9, 18-29, 21-24; 3:15; 5:5; 6:9-11; 15:1

2 Corinthians 2:14-16; 4:4, 14; 5:18-21; 6:2; 7:9-10; 8:7-9; 10:7; 13:4-5

Galatians 1:4; 2:15-16, 19-21; 3:6-14, 22-29; 4:4-7; 5:4-6; 6:8-9, 15

Ephesians 1:4-7; 2:3-5, 8-9, 13, 16, 18-19; 3:10-12, 17-19; 4:30-32; 5:8

Philippians 2:12-13, 15-16; 3:8-11

Colossians 1:12-14, 20-23, 26-28; 2:2, 6, 12-13; 3:1-4, 12-13

1 Thessalonians 1:9-10; 2:11-12, 16; 4:12, 14, 16; 5:5, 23-24

2 Thessalonians 1:3-10; 2:10, 12; 3:1-2

1 Timothy 1:16, 19; 2:3-6; 4:1, 16; 5:8; 6:12

2 Timothy 1:5-10, 18; 2:11-13, 15

Titus 1:1-3; 3:5-8

Hebrews 4:2-3; 5:9-10, 12; 6:5-6; 7:24-25; 9:14-15; 10:32-36, 39; 13:20-21

James 1:17-18, 21; 2:5, 20-26; 5:20

1 Peter 1:5-9, 19-23; 2:23; 4:17-19; 5:10

2 Peter 1:3-4, 10-11
1 John 1:1-7; 2:1-3; 3:1-4, 23-24; 4:9-10, 13-15; 5:4-5, 11-33
2 John 1:9
Jude 1:20-23
Revelation 14:12.

The overwhelming New Testament evidence for the union of confession of faith with salvation converges with the testimony of the traditions of Christian piety that stress decision and personal engagement. Thus the two major features of evangelicalism — commitment to the authority of the Bible and centrality of the act of faith — are integral to any evangelical option in soteriology.[6]

The foregoing consideration precludes one significant attempt to respond to questions posed by pluralism. A mention of it here helps to clarify the methodological issues with which this essay struggles. A minority opinion in the Reformed tradition, expressed by such men as Charles Hodge and Benjamin Warfield, holds that all humans who die in infancy are redeemed by the transfer to them of the benefits of Christ's saving work.[7] The development and influence of this charitable *theologoumenon* correspond to the heightening awareness in Western theology of both global reality with its teeming populations, unreached and unreachable, and the magnitude of disease, desolation, and infant mortality, an expanded horizon akin to what I have called plural shock. The meeting between this cultural sensibility and a Reformed theology that blends the mercy work of Christ with the *Grundmotif* of divine sovereignty helped to shape this view, which adjudges the role of decision or faith, underscored in the foregoing plethora of

---

6. For elaboration see my article, "Evangelical, Evangelicalism," in *Westminster Dictionary of Christian Theology,* ed. Alan Richardson and John Bowden (Philadelphia: Westminster, 1983), pp. 191-92; see also chap. 1 above.

7. Charles Hodge, *Systematic Theology* (New York: Scribner, Armstrong, and Co., 1871), 1:26-27; and Benjamin B. Warfield, *Two Studies in the History of Doctrine* (New York: Christian Literature Co., 1897), p. 230.

passages, as applying only to adults. The same nineteenth-century Christian problematic had other responses that stayed closer to both the textual warrants and evangelical experience, which I discuss shortly (see pp. 45-46). Here points one should note from the Hodge-Warfield experiment are, on the one hand, the readiness within a rigorously biblical tradition to develop doctrine beyond older formulations, and that readiness in apparent response to an era's perceptions and questions, and, on the other hand, the too easy accommodation to culture when speculatively shaped doctrinal presuppositions bypass the biblical evidence.

Pluralism does not exhaust the meaning in which the issue of soteriological singularity is currently cast. Modernity brings with it the focus on the *humanum*. In the 1980s two aspects of human reality claimed special force. On the one hand, peoples long marginalized began to demand access to the essentials of human life — from food, clothing, and shelter to the right to participate in the decisions that affect their destiny — in other words, to justice and freedom for all. On the other hand, peril to the whole human enterprise mounted because of the ever-present, planet-threatening nuclear weaponry. The latter quantum leap in destructive capability in combination with the revolution of rising expectations constituted a new angle of vision for viewing the biblical testimony to redemption. The first responses to it were nervous, both in secular theologies that reduce the meaning of salvation to social or personal change in the horizontal dimension and in apocalyptic theologies that reduce it to a catastrophic verticality. These predictable, first encounters of the Christian community with new cultural fact (similar to the accommodationist and imperialist first encounters with pluralism) put this question: Can a commitment to Christ as the life of the world find a place for the *rudiments* of life as health of the body and historical relationships, as well as for the *fundaments* of life as health of the soul and its transhistorical relationships?

A scriptural search for an answer gives an overwhelming yes. In *Cry Justice!* Ronald Sider has done a significant piece of this investigative work.[8] He traces the red thread of a two-testament witness in which God wills life, hope, and wholeness for human beings in their physical and historical being. A sampling of these passages includes the following:

Exodus 3:7-10; 6:2-9; 20:1-3, 13, 15, 17; 22:25-27; 23:6-8, 10
Leviticus 5:7-11; 12:6-8; 14:1-22; 19:9-10, 11-18, 32-34, 35-36; 23:22; 25:8-17, 35-55
Deuteronomy 1:16-17; 8:1-20; 10:17-19; 15:1-11; 16:18-20; 23:19-20; 24:10-11, 17-22; 25:13-16; 26:1-11; 27:19; 32:4
1 Samuel 2:8
2 Samuel 11:1-4, 6, 14-15; 12:1-7
1 Kings 21:1-19
Nehemiah 10:31
Job 5:11-16; 22:5-9; 24:1-12, 19-22; 29:1-17
Psalms 9:7-12, 18; 10:2-4, 15-18; 12:5; 15:1-5; 35:19; 37:22-26; 41:1-2; 68:5-6; 69:30-33; 72:1-4, 12-14; 82:1-5; 89:14; 94:1-15, 20-23; 96:10-13; 103:6-7; 109:30-31; 113:5-9; 140:12; 146:1-10
Proverbs 14:21, 31; 15:25; 16:11-12; 17:5; 19:17; 21:13; 22:9, 16, 22-23; 23:10-11; 28:3, 8, 27; 29:4-7, 14, 26; 31:8-9
Ecclesiastes 4:1
Isaiah 1:10-17, 21-26; 3:13-25; 5:8-13, 15-16, 22-24; 9:6-7; 10:13-19; 11:1-4; 25:6-8; 26:5-6; 29:17-21; 32:1-3, 6-8, 15-17; 33:14-16; 42:1-7; 58:1-10; 61:1
Jeremiah 7:1-15; 12:1-2, 5, 7; 22:1-5, 11-12
Lamentations 3:34-46
Ezekiel 18:5-9; 22:1-3, 6-12, 15-16, 23-31; 45:9-10
Amos 2:6-8; 4:1-3; 5:6-15, 21-24; 6:4-7; 7:10-17; 8:4-8
Micah 2:1-10; 3:1-4, 9-12; 4:1-4; 6:6-8, 9-15
Habakkuk 2:5-12
Zephaniah 3:1
Zechariah 7:8-10; 8:14-17

---

8. Ronald Sider, *Cry Justice!: The Bible on Hunger and Poverty* (New York: Paulist, 1980).

Malachi 3:5
Matthew 5:17-20; 6:1-4, 11, 24-33; 7:12; 10:42; 12:1-8, 15-21; 19:16-30; 23:23; 25:31-46
Mark 8:1-9; 10:41-45
Luke 1:46-55; 3:7-11; 4:16-21; 6:20-25; 7:18-23; 11:42; 12:32-34; 14:12-14, 15-23; 16:19-31; 19:1-10; 20:45-47
John 2:13-16; 13:1-17, 34-35
Acts 2:41-47; 4:32-37; 6:1-7; 9:36-41; 11:27-30; 20:32-35
Ephesians 4:28
1 Timothy 4:4-7
James 2:1-9, 14-17; 5:1-6
1 John 3:11-18; 4:7-12
Revelation 7:13-17; 21:4-5, 22-27.

Decisive for the interpretation of these texts is the christological lens. How can Christians speak of redemption in any less terms than Christ spoke and acted? In the texts cited and in the pattern of his activity and preaching, as detected by either a historical-critical or a grammatical-historical reading of the New Testament, one can have no doubt that he was a healer of and carer for body as well as soul. He brought good news to the economically poor as well as to the poor in spirit. He brings peace to a broken world as well as to a broken heart. Further, all the rudimentary healings that have to do with the life of bodies in societies happen by a christic grace that works in those who do not know its source, as such, as well as in those who do (Matt. 25:31-46; John 1:3-5, 9-10). By the presence of the Word, Jesus Christ, light and hope — truth and healing — happen where the name is not named in the common venture of life.

The texts and their christological guide press one to honor a soteriological work done by the Savior wherever life is rendered livable in its most elemental sense. Using the distinction made in Cruden's *Concordance* between two biblical usages of the concept and word *salvation*, one can ascertain deliverance from evil as well as deliverance from sin and guilt throughout the Scriptures — salvation from war, oppression, sickness, destruction, enemies, poverty, hunger. To believe that Jesus Christ is Savior is to understand the release from this bondage as his saving work. For the eye of faith, Christ is present incognito wherever human life is made and kept human in its rudimentary sense, including the work of that grace in those aspects of the teaching and practice of other religions or people of no religion. An imperial singularity, which does not acknowledge this universal activity of salvation (by grace through love) from the powers of evil, obscures a basic biblical refrain.

The fullness of salvation cannot be encompassed by the grace aforementioned, the one that assures bread and breath. One does not live by them alone. Humans are destined for a dimension of life *coram Deo,* eternal life, another kind of hunger and hope. This life with God is liberation from sin and guilt, hence reconciliation with the One with whom humans finally have to do. To one community the good news of this salvation in Jesus Christ is given. Herein lies the evangelical mandate to tell the Story, through the hearing of which saving faith is born.

If these fundaments of salvation, salvation in its verticality, are promised to those who hear and accept the good news, is one then driven ineluctably to the position of imperial singularity? I have already differed from this view in discerning in Scripture the two dimensions of salvation; now I want to add another distinction. In the same century in which Hodge had propounded the theory of infant universalism, others wrestled with the questions posed by pluralism, especially as it rose from the missionary situation. As ones for whom the evangelical decision was crucial, yet whose knowledge of the unreached and unreachable millions weighed upon them, a different dynamic was put in motion.[9] A

---

9. Egbert C. Smyth, "Probation After Death," *Homiletical Review* 11, no. 4 (April 1886): 281-91; and Thomas Field, "The 'Andover Theory' of Future Probation," *Andover Review* 7, no. 41 (May 1887): 461-75. As in Paul's struggle with the place of Israel in God's saving purposes (Rom. 9–11), so here too those who are heirs to Abraham, the father of faith, have a unique soteriological and eschatological relationship (one more complex than can be treated in these pages).

thread of texts came into focus: 1 Peter 3:19-20; 4:6; Ephesians 4:8-9; John 5:25-29; Matthew 8:11; 12:40; Luke 13:28-30; Hebrews 9:15; Romans 10:7; Revelation 21:25. In one way or another these passages indicate the postmortem possibilities of grace. The Petrine centerpiece, which had to deal with a question raised by the lengthening eschatological horizon (the question here), formulates its response with christological firmness. These texts describe the overall New Testament picture of the implacable love of a just Savior as reaching the unreached dead in eschatological proclamation. Thus the glorified Christ as well as his Body on earth is the organ of the good news, the hound of heaven whose pursuit cannot be confined to human calendars and timetables. A patristic tradition that put to the fore "the descent into hades" (the place of the dead) in the developing rule of faith was an early strand of doctrinal exposition of the texts in question along just these lines. Thus tradition, ancient and modern, constitutes a resource for understanding the biblical source.

Working out of these various textual strands, in dialogue with primary and secondary traditions, and guided by a christological vision, I try to confront a fundamental question posed by culture. The response is grounded in a firm commitment to the claims of christological and soteriological particularity and in the consequent rejection of various accommodationist views. At the same time, the fresh cultural context opens up aspects of biblical universality heretofore obscured by earlier formulations. Thus the trajectory of received interpretation is followed, its direction revised (not reversed) to do justice to both the scandal of particularity and that of universality. I now turn to the assumptions about the use of Scripture that lie underneath this inquiry in systematics.

THE ROLE OF THE CHRISTIAN COMMUNITY
IN THE INTERPRETATION OF SCRIPTURE

I had not brought to full awareness the extent to which the Christian community functions in my use of Scripture until this exercise in methodological self-examination. The following companions have left tracks in the snow.

1. Although there is no identifiable doctrine as such, a composite of traditional assertions about the person and work of Christ and about the nature of revelation and salvation constitutes the claim to particularity that I have characterized as reconciliation, revelation, and redemption. This inherited pattern of thought functions in the theological exegesis of John 14:6 and its counterparts. Here, then, is doctrinal sedimentation, discoverable in wide ranges of the life, thought, worship, and witness of the Christian community (its catholicity), and thus tradition (in the sense in which that word is often used).

2. The community appears in another way, as does its doctrinal distillation, in the more focused assumptions of the Reformation tradition.[10] Thus the personal response of faith plays a critical role in the dynamics of redemption. The texts assembled are read in the light of *(a)* the importance of hearing and responding, *(b)* the cruciality of justification by grace through faith, *(c)* the explicit belief element in faith (necessary albeit not sufficient), and *(d)* the inseparability of applied redemption from faith (a premise overturned by Hodge's emphasis on divine sovereignty).[11]

---

10. This tradition is a gift to the church universal, an offering assimilable by a genuinely catholic understanding of Christian belief. The same is true about the special gifts to the wholeness of faith by Roman Catholic and Eastern Orthodox traditions in other areas of faith. On this complementarity see Peter Toon, *The Development of Doctrine in the Church* (Grand Rapids: Eerdmans, 1979), pp. 105-26.

11. In an excellent study of Paul Althaus's theology, with particular reference to the question of Christian faith and world religions, Paul Knitter has discovered the import of the Reformation theme. His rejection of this theme and his pursuit of another course along the lines of Rahner's anonymous Christianity dissolve the classic claims to both epistemological and soteriological singularity, a fact that alerted me to the importance of the faith act in each of these dimensions. See Paul Knitter, "Jesus — Buddha — Krishna: Still Present?" *Journal of Ecumenical Studies* 16, no. 4 (Fall 1979): 650-71; "Christianity as Religion: True and Absolute? A Roman Catholic Perspective," *Concilium* 136 (1980): 12-21; and *No Other Name?* (Maryknoll, N.Y.: Orbis, 1985).

3. The Reformation perspective is underscored at the points of personal appropriation and depth of decision by the evangelical tradition as contributory to the interpretation of the redemption texts. Evangelical experience cannot require all believers to replicate the cataclysmic nature of choice, but neither can it conceive of salvation as being without an explicit yes to Jesus Christ. "Tradition" here refers not only to doctrinal deposits but also to the more encompassing environment of life, worship, and mission.[12]

4. Although few recognize it, the phenomenon of "critical scholarship" is in fact a community of critical scholars, one that develops from time to time its consensus points or relative consensus points.[13] In the more restricted sense of the use of the historical-critical method, critical scholarship is invited into the textual discussion at various points. In a wider sense, one that would include a range from the new literary criticism and canon criticism to grammatical-historical and word studies, this subcommunity of biblical reflection plays its role in the work here on soteriology. But more about the specifics of textual inquiry in the next section.

The acknowledgment of the role of tradition in these various senses is captured in an observation from a Faith and Order Study of the World Council of Churches. After twenty-five years of research and colloquy on the authority of the Bible in the churches, a participant noted, "The biblical texts can never be interpreted *ab ovo;* interpretation is always conditioned by the tradition in which the interpreter stands."[14] The explora-

---

12. For some illuminating observations on this wider view of tradition see Avery Dulles, "Tradition and Theology: A Roman Catholic Response to Clark Pinnock," *TSF Bulletin* 6, no. 3 (January-February 1983): 6-8.

13. Kierkegaard makes this point forcefully in his struggle to turn the abstractions "the press" and "the public" into their human constituents. See *The Present Age,* trans. Alexander Dru (New York: Harper & Row, 1962); and *Attack Upon Christendom,* trans. Walter Lowrie (Princeton, N.J.: Princeton University Press, 1968).

14. Ellen Flesseman-van Leer (ed.), "Introduction," Faith and Order Paper no. 99, in *The Bible: Its Authority and Interpretation in the Ecumenical Movement* (Geneva: World Council of Churches, 1980), p. 2.

tion of the use of the Bible in Christian theology could take an important step forward if this kind of recognition was more widespread.[15]

How tradition functions vis-à-vis Scripture is another matter. Two convictions are at work in soteriological investigations. *(a)* The discernment of the riches of the text relates directly to the depth and width of ecclesial vision. Narrow perceptions of biblical meaning come predictably from slit-eyed exegesis. This is a powerful argument for ecumenical tradition. *(b)* The function of tradition in relation to Scripture is heuristic. Tradition is ministerial and Scripture is magisterial.[16]

The church and its postbiblical tradition(s) constitute the *resource* for understanding the scriptural *source*. But the source is just that, the ultimate authority in systematic theology. Hence the distinction between Scripture as the rule that rules *(norma normans)* and tradition as the rule that is ruled *(norma normata)* functions in my systematic proposals.[17] These observations prepare the way to examine the role of the text itself.

---

15. The evidence of its use even by the most rigorous inerrantist is: *(a)* the consistently selective use of texts and their derivative doctrinal formulations; and *(b)* the tacit assumption that acceptable received versions of the Bible, while guarded by a grace of preservation, have come to us over the centuries through the instrumental cause of the Christian community, a convergence of divine and human similar to that of the process of canonization. Not to affirm this conjunction of grace and church would be to fall into an ecclesiastical docetism or monophysitism.

16. See Clark Pinnock's exposition of this aspect in his American Theological Society paper, "How I Use Tradition in Doing Theology," *TSF Bulletin* 6, no. 1 (September-October 1982): 2-5.

17. The reworking of terminology, as in the WCC Faith and Order rendering of tradition as the encompassing category in the sense of "the gospel," and the Bible and postbiblical lore as deposits thereof, are intriguing, related as they are both to New Testament scholarship on the development of traditions and to ecumenical dialogue. I retain the older usage here to assure criteriological clarity: postbiblical tradition as always ministerial to the prophetic-apostolic testimony of canonical Scripture.

CANON, COMMON SENSE, AND CONTINUITY

Final recourse to the text for the systematic theology done in this soteriological inquiry means answers to three kinds of questions: Wherefore? What? Why?

Wherefore text, when one has said the text cannot be detached from ecclesial context?[18] The answer is twofold. (1) To acknowledge the influence of ecclesial perspective does not require an historical-relativist ideology, ecclesial or cultural, one that would deny the possibility of cross-cultural and transtemporal communication, one that is less rather than more (and strives to be less rather than more) controlled by perspectival commitments and thus able to discern the intended meaning of Scripture. The belief that human beings, rather than treat the common life as a battlefield where raw power decides policy, can emerge sufficiently from their commitments and conditionings to enter into conversation on matters of importance is the basis for civil discourse and rational decision making in the human community. Also, contextual orthodoxies are being challenged today by proposals addressed to both the time and the space gap, as in the "merging of horizons,"[19] and by theories about the relative rates of change in ephemeral, conjunctural, and structural history.[20] Accessibility of the text's meaning is assumed in the use made of Scripture in this soteriological inquiry, given the meeting of the hermeneutical conditions here developed. One is not so locked into ecclesial or cultural positions that its truth cannot make itself known — the Word

---

18. A secular historical relativism would put the same kind of question, holding that cultural contextualization denies access to the text.

19. Hans-Georg Gadamer, *Truth and Method,* trans. and ed. Garrett Barden and John Cumming (New York: Seabury, 1975). For a penetrating exposition of Gadamer's thought and its relationship to other perspectives in New Testament hermeneutic and philosophical inquiry, see Anthony C. Thiselton, *The Two Horizons: New Testament Hermeneutics and Philosophical Description* (Grand Rapids: Eerdmans, 1980).

20. As developed by cultural historians F. Braudel and P. Chaunu.

addresses the hearer — even to the extent that a contemporary perspective from which one views a text can be challenged, modified, and overturned by the text. (2) Cultural and ecclesial relativisms deny in fact what they assert in theory. The orthodoxy that one can allow no historical truth claim is itself exempt from the rule of relativity. What's sauce for the goose is sauce for the gander.[21]

What does the text as last court of appeal entail? Here a configuration of themes comes into play: perspicuity, intentionality, honesty, analogy, unity, continuity, propositionality.

Perspicuity refers to the accessibility of Scripture. The plain meaning of the text is its controlling significance. As such, its understanding is not confined to a privileged few (i.e., ecclesiastical or academic cognoscenti). I have noted that both the ecclesial and critical communities do make their contributions, but they do not hold the keys that unlock the mysteries. The Bible is an open book. Here the priesthood of all believers (and thus the availability of the Scriptures to all with the will, mind, and heart to encounter them) is a crucial hermeneutical presupposition.

Intentionality has to do with the purposed meaning of the text. What the author intends, in the context and way that purpose is executed, is normative for exegesis. Indeed, a text may have both implications and applications far beyond the authorial purpose (the former has to do with the *sensus plenior,* about which I shall speak subsequently, and the latter is the homiletical challenge every Sunday morning), but original textual intention must adjudicate these proposals.[22]

---

21. Carl F. H. Henry underscores this point regularly in his 6 volumes on *God, Revelation and Authority* (Waco: Word, 1976–83).

22. Current talk of the polyvalence of texts by exegetes using the new literary criticism and Jungian categories fails to take adequate account of the controls of intentionality. That one can honor the richness of textual meaning within the bounds set by the author's purpose is illustrated by David Steinmetz in a provocative essay on the continuing relevance of medieval exegesis (fourfold meaning: literal, allegorical, tropological, anagogical). See David C. Steinmetz, "The Superiority of Pre-critical Exegesis," *Theology Today* 37, no. 1 (April 1980): 27-38.

For clarification of intention the best tools of scholarship are welcome. The honest study of genre, grammar, word usage, historical context, and textual form and development are resources in this process. A responsible encounter with the text is marked by integrity of inquiry, using the tested instruments of historical and literary analysis.

Given the singular nature of the Scriptures, the warrants for which I discuss in the next section, the aforementioned disciplines cannot have the final word on textual intention. Influenced as these inquiries in their present state are by value frameworks of their own and in consideration of the divergent opinions in the present state of the art, the decisive interpretive framework for a text is the whole canonical context. Thus Scripture is its own best interpreter. Key to this point is the principle of analogy in which one reads the more elusive texts in the light of clearer ones.[23]

Assumed in the canonical environment for a given text is the unity of Scripture. That is, the Bible has an overall coherence and directionality that constitutes the horizon against which the reader views the biblical drama and declarations. This unity is established by the divine action itself as it moves through events in the great narrative of salvation — the deeds, centering in Christ's liberating and reconciling work, as they are presented and interpreted in prophetic-apostolic testimony. In speaking about this big picture in which the textual microcosm is situated, I have of necessity anticipated some of the "why" questions and will return to them.

Texts make truth claims. That is the point of those who declare for the propositional status of Scripture, which bears particularly on systematic theology. One may define propositions as expressions in language or signs of something that one can believe, doubt, or deny, or that are either true or false; thus propositions do occur in the Bible and are derivable from biblical

---

23. See R. C. Sproul, "Biblical Interpretation and the Analogy of Faith," in *Inerrancy and Common Sense,* ed. Roger R. Nicole and J. Ramsey Michaels (Grand Rapids: Baker, 1980), pp. 119-36.

materials in the form of doctrinal assertions. In the next section I argue that one can better describe the evocative and expressive nature of biblical truth claims as "affirmations," but here the point is simply that this systematic theology cannot do without statements having the referents of human and divine reality to which the terms *yes* and *no* are appropriate, without expression in language or signs of something that is either true or false.

One can see the presence of each of these foregoing themes in the use of Scripture in this soteriological inquiry. The plain meaning of the texts is at work in the passages dealing with salvation in both microcosmic and macrocosmic dimensions, as is the canonical resonance. Central features of the drama of continuity were presupposed in the unpacking of the paradigmatic text. The canonical range of authority functions in the uncovering of surprises in the Scriptures as in the eschatological soteriology texts obscured by inherited patterns of exegesis and doctrine. The whole investigation assumes the propositional status of textual evidence.

Why must one be responsible to the intended meaning of texts with theological import? The answer lies in the doctrine of revelation presupposed in one's view of biblical theology. The former is the underside of the latter.[24] A brief exploration of revelatory assumptions is therefore appropriate.

Revelation happens along the time line of the biblical narrative. What God *does* in that drama to reconcile the parties alienated from the divine purpose is inextricably bound up with what God *discloses;* the deeds of God are foundational to the knowledge of God. Although one cannot reduce revelation to the acts of reconciliation, as some versions of *Heilsgeschichte* conceptuality, biblical theology, and so forth tended to do, neither can one sever it from them.[25]

---

24. I give both exposition and visualization in *The Christian Story*, vol. 1: *A Narrative Interpretation of Basic Christian Doctrine* (Grand Rapids: Eerdmans, 1984), pp. 40-55; and in my *Christian Story*, 2:49-59, 341-50.

25. Some think that Langdon Gilkey's 1961 essay on the incoherence of the concept "acts of God" ("Cosmology, Ontology, and the Travail of

In the history of Christian theology — both its catecheti-
cal/confessional and its systematic/speculative expressions —
doctrinal affirmation follows the time line of the biblical drama.
From the first rules of faith and the early economic Trinity,
through the credal formulations and their interpreters (viz.,
Athanasius), to later confessional symbols and traditional dogmatics, the great saga constitutes the outline of statements of
Christian faith: the missions of the triune God in creation, fall,
and covenant; in Christ's life, death, and resurrection; in the
church, salvation, and consummation. Here I draw on the resource of tradition to make the point. But while tradition in-
structs, Scripture must confirm (the Scots Confession, chap. 20).
It does so in setting forth the movement from creation to consummation. In all this one learns that the power that patterns
revelation is constituted by the deeds of reconciliation.

Revelation is grounded in, but not exhausted by, the history
of the reconciling acts of God. The events of this narrative are
witnessed to, and interpreted by, seers whose eyes are opened
to their inner meaning. Thus a doctrine of inspiration is a
necessary part of a doctrine of revelation, a point that proponents of "revelation as event" regularly ignore in their eagerness to avoid fundamentalist views of the Bible.[26] The process
of revelation includes, therefore, a reliable account of the definitive events in the biblical narrative, including the trustworthy

---

Biblical Language," *Journal of Religion* 41 [1961]: 194-205) gave the coup
de grace to this theme. On closer inspection, Gilkey's argument shows itself
to be a variation on the Ebionite refrain that has appeared in every doctrinal
debate since the early christological controversies. The paradox of divine-
human coterminality is found not only in the person of Christ but also in the
doctrines of salvation, the church, the sacraments, etc., and is always challenged by reductionists of either a humanizing or divinizing stamp.

26. Some have attempted to change this situation, e.g., Paul Achtemeier,
The Inspiration of Scripture: Problems and Proposals (Philadelphia: Westminster, 1980). From the evangelical side, see the effort of William Abraham to
reconceptualize inspiration by blending an acts theology with divine speech
themes, in *The Divine Inspiration of Holy Scripture* (New York: Oxford
University Press, 1981).

interpretation of those events. The Holy Spirit, whose power brings the events to be, also grants the biblical envisioner insight into them and is present in that mysterious pilgrimage in which insight, affect, idea, and word make their journey together toward one. Thus the inspired prophetic-apostolic testimony is part and parcel of the revelatory process.

Because of the inseparability of the partners in this pilgrimage, the words and imagery in their canonical appearance are under the custodianship of the Spirit. In this sense one has to do here with verbal inspiration. The Spirit working in the community grants this charter with its special fusion of deed, interpretation, and word. One returns always to this language of Canaan as the font of systematic theology. The inspiration is plenary in that no one's decision, doctrinal or methodological, can restrict the range of words and insights to selected preserves within the full canon and thereby restrict the full range of the Spirit's work and the surprises of the Spirit that may await one in what appear to be the most unpromising — uninspiring by human reckoning — stretches of Scripture.

The verbal nature of inspiration is associated with the kind of writing the Bible is and that, in turn, with the character of revelation itself. A faith whose substance is what God does and discloses in an historical drama, one with a view to engaging the reader personally in the action, will be cast in the genre of story with its plot developing in characters and events moving over time and space through conflict toward resolution. As such, its language is critical to its purpose, featuring tensive symbols that, on the one hand, express the tone of the action and, on the other hand, evoke the response of the whole person, addressing the affective as well as the cognitive self. Austin Farrer has described inspiration in similar terms, viewing it as the gift of insight in images.[27] Long before him John Bunyan wrote:

---

27. Austin Farrer, *The Glass of Vision* (Westminster, Md.: Dacre, 1948), pp. 38-56. On the unity of biblical language and thought, see also Bernhard W. Anderson, *The Living World of the Bible* (Philadelphia: Westminster, 1979).

Solidity indeed becomes the Pen
Of him that writeth things Divine to men;
But must I needs want solidness, because
By Metaphors I speak? Were not God's Laws,
His Gospel-Laws, in olden time held forth
By Types, Shadows, and Metaphors? Yet loth
Will any sober man be to find fault
With them, lest he be found for to assault
The highest Wisdom. No, he rather stoops,
And seeks to find out what by Pins and Loops,
By Calves, and Sheep, by Heifers, and by Rams,
By Birds, and Herbs, and by the blood of Lambs,
God speaketh to him. And happy is he
That finds the light and grace that in them be.
. . . .

Dark Figures, Allegories? Yet there springs
From that same Book that lustre, and those rays
Of light, that turns our darkest nights to days.[28]

The function of story and symbol in biblical interpretation
has been brought to the fore by the use of tools from the new
literary criticism.[29] This perspective has given to the role of

---

28. John Bunyan, *The Pilgrim's Progress,* Harvard Classics, vol. 15, ed.
Charles W. Eliot (New York: P. F. Collier & Son, 1909), pp. 7-8.

29. The considerable interest in narrative theology is related both to the
recovery of imagination and the recognition that discursive thought has limits
in matters of ultimate commitment and to the narrative structure of biblical
faith itself as a plot with characters moving over time and space through
conflict toward resolution. Storytelling theology comes in various forms that
often overlap.

(1) A literary-aesthetic view of narrative influenced by critics like Erich
Auerbach and Northrop Frye and shaped significantly by the work of Amos
Wilder and Stephen Crites. Biblical texts, especially the parables, are the focal
point of inquiry, with classic and contemporary literature providing reference
points. Contributing significantly to the current discussion are Sallie McFague,
Dominic Crossan, Dan Via, Robert Funk, Robert Roth, and Robert Detweiler.

(2) An interpretation of story in terms of personal formation and ex-

imagination in Scripture the attention that it deserves but that it has not always received in biblical studies and rarely receives in the world of systematic theology. Nonetheless, enthusiasm for this dimension has obscured and even denied, in some quarters, the cognitive weight and transcendent referents of biblical narrative and symbol. The biblical story is true to life (human and divine) objectively as well as true for me subjectively. It makes assertions about the way things are, identifiable by affirmation, and brings one into relationship to the way things are by the power of symbol. Wilbur Urban's defense of the complementarity of "the truth of the symbol" (the reliability of its objective reference) and "symbolic truth" (the power of its subjective impact) in religious language is a helpful way of honoring the dual dimensions of biblical imagery and saga.[30] By insisting upon the former, the concern of the propositionalist

---

pression influenced in some cases by learning from psychology, frequently that of Carl Jung, in others by pedagogical issues, in others by social-ethical concerns, and in still others by some aspects of Karl Barth's theology. The story in psychological context finds expression in the work of such figures as James Hillman and Sam Keen, and in Catholic idiom in Thomas Cooper, John Navonne, and John Dunne. Johannes Metz, James McClendon, Robert McAfee Brown, and Michael Goldberg explore its social-ethical dimensions. Thomas Groome has developed its catechetical possibilities and Richard Jensen its homiletical implications. George Stroup examines its meaning at the point of collision between personal and community stories. David Stuart has investigated its role in personal testimonies.

(3) A theological employment of narrative in which the macrostory of redemption is the focal point. Drawing on a tradition with roots in the biblical saga itself, expressed in the primitive kerygma and more systematically in the economic Trinity and the classical creeds, nineteenth- and twentieth-century salvation history perspectives lifted up the drama that stretched from creation to consummation with its critical-historical trajectory running from the exodus to Easter. Oscar Cullmann, G. Ernest Wright, and Bernhard Anderson are among its better-known interpreters, and Karl Barth is its profoundest twentieth-century expositor. Current narrative theologians who work with these categories in one way or another are Hans Frei, Ulrich Simon, Robert Roth, and Amos Wilder. For an exploration of these varying uses of story and a case made for an encompassing reformulation of the third view, see my "Narrative Theology: An Overview," *Interpretation* 37, no. 4 (Fall 1983): 340-52.

30. Wilbur Urban, *Language and Reality* (New York: Macmillan, 1939).

is honored. Yet the way truth claims are made in the biblical setting is by an *affirmation* from the world of life and death, drama and commitment, not by a proposition from the spectator world of formal logic.[31]

---

31. One should distinguish between weighing biblical assertions as propositions in the second sense and propositionalism, a theory that goes beyond the biblical usage of them. As I construe it here, propositionalism does not take the following into account adequately:

(1) The analogical character of all biblical statements and doctrinal assertions as they touch upon transcendent reality. In reaction to subjectivism, legitimate as that reaction is, propositionalists insist upon the univocity of theological language. But this univocity flies in the face of Scripture's own testimony to the nature of its seers' perceptions as "seen through a glass darkly." A venerable tradition of analogy that asserts uncompromisingly the truth of theological declarations acknowledges the finitude of human language: theological language is necessary but not sufficient access to the divine glory.

(2) The exfoliation possibilities inherent in biblical language. Thus propositionalism does not sufficiently recognize the potential of Christian doctrine to develop. The assumption that one can find specific doctrinal assertions lying on the surface of Scripture and that one can appropriate them in unchangeable form in the work of theology does not take into account the catholic nature of revelation. If the truth claims of Christian faith are to be true for all times and places, then the inspired original language and ideas of the Bible must be subject to unfolding over these times and places, dealing with the issues and in the idiom of them. That process, to which I shall give attention in a subsequent section, does not overturn doctrinal perceptions grounded firmly in Scripture, but it does enlarge their scope in meaning. Doctrine develops. My soteriological exposition enriches rather than overturns the received tradition.

(3) That the word *proposition* does not adequately convey the character of biblical truth claims. Its association with formal logic (in which it is a theorem or problem that one can demonstrate or perform) conveys the meaning of discursive reasoning. But biblical assertions call for decisions and entail life-and-death commitments. Truth claims in Christian teaching therefore are best denominated *affirmations,* not propositions. One cannot make the claims without associating them with acts of engagement and the import of ultimacy. To say that Christ is the way, the truth, and the life is to make such an affirmation, an assertion eminently more than the setting forth of a proposition. An unambiguous truth claim is operative in my use of Scripture, one attested by the accent of proposition in current discussion of biblical authority but better expressed in affirmational and analogical fashion.

SUBSTANCE: THE BIBLICAL NARRATIVE

What is really at stake in the determination to hold the affirmational (propositional) status of scriptural language are the truth claims of the biblical metastory, the great drama that moves from creation to consummation. It is no accident that modern partisans of inerrancy are also passionate defenders of "the fundamentals."[32] For others who support inerrancy, but for whom the term *fundamentalist* would be inappropriate (e.g., Carl Henry), the heart of the biblical witness is clearly the narrative of God's purposes and deeds of deliverance from beginning to end.[33] What these events were, are, and will be and their valid interpretation constitute the refrains of classical Christian belief.

Functionally, the inerrantist stress on the fundamentals (the nonnegotiables of Christian conviction, historic faith) converges with the emphasis of the infallibilists on the Bible as authoritative in soteric knowledge, although the former believe that the doctrinal assertions and assumptions of the Bible can be protected only by the inerrancy of the text in its entirety.[34] As already noted, inerrantists do make a contribution to the use of Scripture in systematic theology in the various emphases; so too do the infallibilists, especially at the

---

32. See the treatment of these fundamentals in essays by Kenneth Kantzer and John Gerstner in *The Evangelicals,* ed. David F. Wells and John D. Woodbridge (Nashville: Abingdon, 1975). Also consult George Marsden, *Fundamentalism and American Culture* (New York: Oxford University Press, 1980); and essays by Ed Dobson and Ed Hinson in *The Fundamentalist Phenomenon,* ed. Jerry Falwell (Garden City: Doubleday, 1981).

33. Henry, *God, Revelation and Authority,* 4:465.

34. Because we do not have the autographs and thus the total errorlessness that they guarantee, but only derivative copies for which one cannot make comparable claims, the inerrantist argument against the infallibilist view proves to be logically flawed: the reliability of the biblical teaching of the inerrantist is also associated with a theoretically errant received text. If God can use a theoretically errant received text in the hands of the believing Christian to convey sound doctrine to the inerrantist, one has no warrant for denying the same claim made by the defenders of a soteric view of biblical authority.

point where the purpose of Scripture for faith and life is brought to the fore.[35]

Indeed, the soteric use of Scripture is a natural correlate of evangelical piety. Evangelicalism at the Reformation — with justification by faith as its material principle and scriptural authority as its formal principle — employed Scripture as a source of saving knowledge rather than a textbook for scholastic speculation. As "evangelical" came to be understood more and more in terms of intensification of justification in personal experience and the rigor of obedience, the Bible continued to be instrumental to that end. When advance in the natural and social sciences and the importance of scholarly apparatus in the study of Scripture raised questions about the reliability of biblical cosmology and chronology, that tradition, based as it was on the evangelical use of Scripture for saving knowledge, did not deem its source of authority imperiled, and today it finds its earlier focus on the evangelical core confirmed. This evangel — the good news of God's saving deeds done over the time line of the Christian narrative — constitutes the substance of the scriptural source. As such the gospel story is the principle of interpretation of the Bible's rich and variegated materials. The canon in its entirety is viewed through the lens of the divine saga with Jesus Christ as its center.

To return to the discussion of symbol, the macrostory is the horizon against which one should view all microstories and their expositions. Thus this systematic work uses Scripture as classical theology has regularly used it over the centuries, not as an encyclopedia of varied information but as "the sacred writings that are able to instruct you for salvation through faith in Christ Jesus . . . useful for teaching, for reproof, for correction, and for training in righteousness, so that everyone who belongs to God may be proficient, equipped for every good

---

35. That is the way the Bible functions in most Christian theology, including, as noted, those who insist that scriptural authority extends to matters in the areas of the natural and social sciences.

work" (2 Tim. 3:15-17). To that end, "all scripture is inspired by God" (2 Tim. 3:16a).

Discussion of the soteric use of Scripture is not complete without reference to the "internal testimony of the Holy Spirit." Because this Book has an Author who works in, with, and under the authors of these books, neither source nor substance comes home until the truth of the affirmations met here convicts and converts. Illumination in its deepest sense includes hearing the Word within the words and thus being transformed by this confrontation with God. One can encounter God only in a way that is commensurate with who God is and how God comes to humans — in suffering struggle and personal commitment.[36] Thus readiness to learn from this Book means a posture befitting the gift, a meeting with the text in hope and fear, whetted expectation and trembling. Thus a double subjectivity is bound up with the soteric use of Scripture: God the subject by the power of the Holy Spirit present in the believer's subjectivity of encounter. When this encounter happens, the doctrine of sin becomes the confession of it, and the doctrine of grace becomes a cry of exultation.

THE SETTING FOR SOURCE AND SUBSTANCE

Another element involved in the use made of Scripture in the above exercise has been variously described and justified in terms of reason, context, contemporary experience, historical method, and cultural or sociological analysis. The warrants for its use have

---

36. "The speculative philosopher . . . proposes to contemplate Christianity from the philosophical standpoint. It is a matter of indifference to him whether anyone accepts it or not; such anxieties are left to theologues and laymen — and also surely to those who really are Christians, and who are by no means indifferent as to whether they are Christians or not. . . . Only the like is understood by the like . . . *quidquid cognoscitur, per modum cognoscentis cognoscitur*" (Søren Kierkegaard, *Concluding Unscientific Postscript*, trans. David F. Swenson and Walter Lowrie [Princeton: Princeton University Press, 1941], p. 51).

been associated traditionally with concepts like general revelation, common grace, the hidden Christ, and the image or likeness of God in humans. Here I choose to speak of the first concept as the "what" — as human experience in its richness and variety with special reference to its rational, moral, and affective dimensions.[37] Its legitimacy or the "why" is grounded in the presence of a universal grace, one to which the previous soteriological inquiry already pointed. Christ's healing work in creation includes a grace that renders one's general experience reliable enough at critical junctures to allow the great saga to move forward. Human experience is indeed so corrupted by a will in bondage that human thoughts, moral perceptions, and intuitions, as such, can neither discern the divine purpose nor power one toward it. But the Son of God has not left this world so bereft that intimations of an individual's destiny are denied. This universal grace enables one to go ahead, literally, with the day-to-day business of making and keeping life livable "toward the future."

The role of human experience so conceived is apparent at these points in scriptural interpretation: (1) Reliance upon the canons of logic. Ordinary discourse and argument presuppose elemental rules such as the law of noncontradiction, and these are assumed here also.[38] (2) The use of biblical scholarship in all its traditions — precritical, critical, and postcritical. The influence of culture and doctrine on these arts, and their offering as subcommunities of tradition in the conversation about a text (see previous comments on tradition) means that they are resources, not *the* source of authority. They are tools for a "faith seeking understanding." (3) Help from the moral perceptions of a time, place,

---

37. With rough correspondence to the distinctions of thinking, doing, and feeling in Schleiermacher's *The Christian Faith,* ed. H. R. Mackintosh and J. S. Stewart, 2 vols. (New York: Harper & Row, 1963), and to the classical categories of truth, goodness, and beauty.

38. On the law of noncontradiction see Henry, *God, Revelation and Authority,* 4:49, 59, 114, 227; and E. L. Mascall in his defense of the "Intellectual Principle," in *Whatever Happened to the Human Mind?* (London: SPCK, 1980), pp. 1-27.

or constituency. God raises up from stones children of Abraham (Matt. 3:9; Luke 3:8) and uses Assyria as the rod of divine anger (Isa. 10:5). Movements that seek justice, freedom, and peace in times of forgetfulness, including the amnesia of the Christian community, bring to awareness visions and commitments within one's own biblical charter. Texts are read with a sensitivity to the meaning intended in them by their Author when eyes are opened to them by forces outside the communities of biblical faith. Perceptions of both a cognitive and a spiritual sort, as well as moral perceptions, may enrich the capacity to see what Scripture has to say to a time and place. (4) Finally, an era poses questions. At the level of affect, but not excluding discursive elements, human experience at a given time and place sensitizes one to issues of high moment, often best expressed in the art and literature of a period. In such a *kairos,* Scripture speaks a special Word.[39] In sum, human experience conceived in this way constitutes the *setting* in which the scriptural *source* and gospel *substance* is read.

What effect does this understanding of human experience have on systematic theology? The consequence is twofold: first, the translation of biblical substance into language that connects with the settings, perceptions, and questions and is coherent according to the laws of logic; second, the development of doctrine along the trajectory established by earlier resource tradition and in conformity with the biblical source. In the first case, systematic theology perceives *applications* to this time and place in the idiom of this time and place in modes different from other times and places. In the second case, systematic theology draws out *implications* of the substance of the Bible not seen in earlier formulations of doctrine. In this sense key texts used in systematic inquiry can have a *sensus plenior.* Thus the intention of the text as a faithful expression of the divine purpose holds a meaning that

---

39. Tillich's "method of correlation" expresses this idea formally, but other agendas take over his execution of the method. The formulations of "the question" of the modern era are influenced to such a degree by his philosophical presuppositions that significant features of the classical Christian answer disappear from view.

earlier exegetes did not grasp in its fuller implications because the necessary setting of human experience was not present, and the exegete was not therefore positioned at the angle of vision to see that signification. Human experience in the sense of ever-new contexts of question and perception performs a catalytic function in the use of Scripture. This function is at work in the historical and eschatological aspects of soteriology developed in the inquiry here.

JESUS CHRIST

One of the ironies of the modern hermeneutical discussion is the way the name of Jesus Christ has come into dispute and even into disrepute. Whereas classical Christianity maintained that he is the eternal Word to which all of Scripture testifies, and Reformation Christianity used christological language to interpret the meaning and force of the Bible *(was Christum treibt)*, today the use of similar categories evokes suspicion.[40] Indeed, there are reasons for some of this suspicion. In the struggle against fundamentalism and a speculative biblicism, both neoorthodox and liberal protagonists have sought to validate Scripture by an appeal either to themes within it believed to be out of range of critical scholarship or to a way of encountering the Bible that is faithful to its invitation to personal engagement. Thus "Christ" as the Word heard "within" the biblical words or Scripture as "witness to the Word" has become a familiar counterinterpretation of the Bible's authority.

Within many of these proposals other dynamics were often at work. One was the denial of the cognitive weight of biblical assertions, a judgment influenced by existentialist fears that claims to objective knowledge would deflect the believer from

---

40. As in Affirmation 1 of the 1982 Declaration of the International Council on Biblical Inerrancy. See Tom Minnery, "What the Bible Means," *Christianity Today* 26, no. 20 (Dec. 17, 1982): 45-47.

subjective encounter.[41] Revelatory significance was then transferred either to the encounter with Christ itself or to the figure of
Jesus. From here it was a short step to interpreting "Christ" as the
historical Jesus recovered by the scholarship of the new quest. The
work of Edward Schillebeeckx and Hans Küng and also the
increasing use of a critical reconstruction of the Jesus of history
by various liberation and process theologies are examples of the
strong influence of this historical Jesus view.[42]

Appeal to the Jesus of history as recovered in modest form
by new-quest scholarship moves the post-Easter apostolic testimony to Jesus' significance from its classical place as authoritative canonical teaching to that of first contextual interpretation, with the respect indeed due to its proximity to origins but
similar in kind to subsequent efforts at appropriating Jesus for
other times and places.[43] Thus fundamental teaching about the
person and work of Christ disappears from the "Christ" distilled
from the Scripture. Further, in many cases the content poured
into the word *Christ* — where critical scholarship sketches its
picture of Jesus, and where it does not — is supplied by a philosophical conceptuality, sociopolitical program, psychological
construct, or cultural agenda. Thus one has good reasons for
scrutinizing carefully any proposal to incorporate a christological norm into the interpretation of Scripture.

With these risks in mind, I seek to show how Jesus Christ

---

41. A commitment traceable to Kierkegaard's defense of "subjectivity"
in his critique of Hegelian speculation on the one hand and "the Christian
crowd" on the other. See *Concluding Unscientific Postscript,* pp. 115-224.

42. See Edward Schillebeeckx, *Jesus: An Experiment in Christology,*
trans. Hubert Hoskins (New York: Seabury, 1979); and *Christ: The Experience
of Jesus as Lord,* trans. John Bowden (New York: Seabury, 1980); Hans Küng,
On Being a Christian, trans. Edward Quinn (Garden City, N.Y.: Doubleday,
1976).

43. For a monumental effort to make this category change and attempt
to argue its consonance with traditional understandings of apostolic authority,
see Schillebeeckx's *Jesus,* passim, and my critique of it in "Bones Strong and
Weak in the Skeletal Structure of Schillebeeckx's Christology," *Journal of
Ecumenical Studies* 21, no. 2 (Spring 1984): 248-77.

can be understood as the final standard in the use of the Bible in systematic theology. The following constitute the christological norm: (1) Theology begins in prayer and ends in praise (Aquinas, et al.). The Christian theologian lives and works out of prayer in the name of Jesus and looks to the eternal Word for illumination. Christ is the Alpha and Omega of all that is thought and said. A prayer that is always close to me in study and writing is: "Speak to us the Word that we need, and let that Word abide in us until it has wrought in us your holy will." (2) With the authority of canonical Scripture here affirmed in conjunction with the narrative framework for interpreting it, one is driven to ask how Scripture is construed at the very center of that saga. How does Jesus Christ himself use Scripture? The answer is found in the following passages:

Matthew 4:4, 6, 7, 10; 5:21, 27, 31, 33, 38, 43; 7:12; 8:17; 9:13; 11:10, 13, 17, 22-24; 12:3-7, 18-21, 39-42; 13:14-15, 35; 15:4-9; 16:4; 19:5, 7, 18-19; 21:13, 16, 42; 22:29-30, 31-32, 35-40, 44; 24:15, 24, 31; 27:46
Mark 2:25-26; 4:12; 7:6-7, 9-10; 9:12; 10:3-6; 11:17; 12:10-11, 24-27, 29-31, 35-37; 14:21, 27, 49; 15:34
Luke 4:4, 8, 10-12, 17-19, 25-28; 6:3-4; 7:22-23, 27, 32; 10:13-15, 26-28; 11:29-32, 49; 13:4, 28-29, 34; 16:16, 29-31; 17:26-30; 18:20; 19:46; 20:17-18, 28, 37-38, 41-44; 22:37; 23:46; 24:25-27, 44-47
John 5:39-40; 9:2-3; 13:18; 14:6; 15:25.

The clear message of these texts is that Jesus used the Scriptures to witness to his person and work. The passages that the Christ of the New Testament cited from the Hebrew Bible were read by him in the light of a christological norm. The apostles followed their teacher in that same usage of texts from the Hebrew Bible. As Scripture's own record of its Lord's practices, the christological norm becomes decisive for me as a systematic theologian. Thus Scripture in its entirety is the source of Christian teaching, but Jesus Christ in his particularity is the norm.

I must now unpack the meaning of this statement with a view to the perils of modernizing mentioned previously.

Christ is the Word who speaks through the Bible in two senses that one must clearly distinguish. (1) As the light of the divine life, Jesus Christ does the work of convincing the believer of biblical truth. The truth of the text comes home, it persuades, because Christ speaks through the words by the power of the Holy Spirit. The Spirit of God the Son attests by internal movement *(testimonium Spiritus Sancti internum)* that what is said is so. As such, truth for *all* becomes truth for *me* — a general declaration becomes a personal conviction. Here is the presence and power of Christ in the subject, hence the "subjectivity" of the christological norm. (2) Subjectivity is not subjectivism; the complementary work of Jesus Christ is the act of *testing* objectively as well as *attesting* subjectively.[44] Statements in theology, which are claimed as biblical warrants for positions held, must pass muster before the norm of Jesus Christ.

This examination works in two ways in my systematic theology. I ask the questions: Do traditional claims stand up under the scrutiny of what the Bible declares about Jesus Christ? Are there new dimensions to inherited Christian doctrine not perceived in earlier formulations? As noted before, the setting of a given time and place resituates the theologian and provides a fresh vantage point for viewing the great narrative of faith. In this new historical location, one may expose delimited understandings of faith and discern enriched understandings. The figures of reduction and enrichment are purposely used here because they suggest the ongoing character of Christian teaching — a journey in faith. That is, Christian doctrine is revisable but not reversible; it develops along the line of the trajectory that comes from its origins. That is why ever-new truth and light do really break forth from God's Word. Underneath this conviction is the trust that the Holy Spirit is present in the church in the

---

44. As suggested by Robert Clyde Johnson's discussion of the same in *Authority in Protestant Theology* (Philadelphia: Westminster, 1959), pp. 15ff.

ministerial work of the tradition, in this sense of rightness of direction. Thus the noetic work of the Spirit in *illumination* undergirds the central tradition of the Christian community as resource, just as the noetic work of the Spirit in *inspiration* makes possible Scripture as source.

The soteriological question made important use of the norm of Jesus Christ. Proposals for enriching traditional understandings of salvation by recovering the biblical duality of redemption from sin and guilt, on the one hand, and of redemption from evil, on the other, were catalyzed by the questions and perceptions of life on an imperiled planet and movements to sustain life in the face of its varied threats. Then the proposals were finally tested by the words and works of Jesus Christ, who struggled against the forces of evil and sin and who overcame death in its most rudimentary and fullest meaning. Also, questions posed by the heightened awareness of religious pluralism uncovered veins of biblical ore waiting to be mined further, namely, those on the theme of eschatological confrontation. Here again, christological discernment was decisive. Both the implacable love of Christ in his historical career searching for the lost and the last (a commitment also present in the infant salvation scenarios of Hodge and Warfield) and the specific textual warrants for speaking about the love of Christ that pursues the unreached into eternity lead me to seek to hold together particularity and universality in a different and, I hope, more biblically developed fashion.

CONCLUSION

The way Scripture is used in this exercise in self-understanding reflects a fundamental premise of my work: the richness of faith requires a full-orbed approach to it. In the foregoing analysis a variety of perspectives are at work: the contributions of inerrantists as well as infallibilists, the insights of both event-oriented and propositionalist hermeneutics, the use of historical-critical as well as grammatical-historical methods, attention to the "truth of the symbol" as well as "symbolic truth," the role of tradition as well as of Scripture, the cultural setting as well as the christological norm. Efforts at inclusive thinking in this as in other theological matters can be, finally, an irenic but muddleheaded eclecticism. What preserves the quest for a full-orbed faith from this kind of ersatz holism is the clear understanding of the role each partner plays, and the warrants thereof, as set forth throughout this essay. I conclude with a visual presentation of the components and their interrelationships.

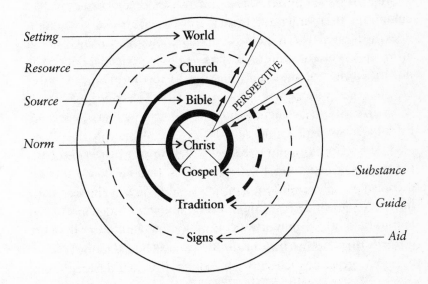

The *world* leaves its imprint on all systematics; a self-critical theology seeks to deal with the formative questions and perceptions of a given time and place. A *perspective* shaped by the special peril and promise of modern life and by the fact of religious pluralism sets the stage for one's encounter with the soteriological affirmations of Scripture. The way into the biblical center is traversed with the assistance of the *church's* two thousand years of struggle with these themes, especially as it has crystallized its lore in the inner ecclesial orb of *tradition*, a thickened line yet one open to development, as indicated by its brokenness, but always along the arc formed by its original direction. This reach in toward the truth is met by the *biblical source,* the texts that address the question in the context of the canon, as both participate in the *substance* of the *gospel* story. Theological affirmations that rise from this encounter are put to the final test by the *christological norm,* even as their truth comes home to one personally by the internal attestation of the Spirit of the Son. (Turning these circles to profile position would indicate the revelatory work of the Spirit that underlies and shapes the cone of authority.) Doctrinal assertions emerging from this pilgrimage return by the same route to address the *setting* of theological discourse, there both to challenge culture and to communicate with it. This hermeneutical circulation does not entail the adjudication of christologically warranted affirmations by the cultural setting — the experiential context is *not* the arbiter of the biblical text — as in too much uncritical usage of the circle metaphor in hermeneutics. Here one may think of an arrowlike movement to a destination, yet a journey with its dynamic movement in and out.

This effort to honor the contribution of a variety of constituencies is a special kind of evangelical option. Its Corinthian modality is an expression of ecumenical evangelicalism. Standing in a long tradition of commitment to the universality of faith and to the faith community, yet grounded unambiguously in the gospel distinctives, it is a decision for evangelical catholicity.[45]

---

45. The commitment to catholicity in the use of Scripture is kindred in spirit to Avery Dulles's effort to honor the truth in various conceptions of revelation in his important work, *Models of Revelation* (Garden City, N.Y.: Doubleday, 1983), although different in focus (Scripture in one, revelation in the other), in the status accorded the Roman Catholic magisterium, and in questions I would raise about using the symbolic model as the organizing principle for restatement. Again, while I do not employ here David Kelsey's specific distinctions of how Scripture is used in contemporary theology and am unpersuaded by his functionalist proposals, many of the positions he examines appear in the foregoing discussion. The normative work here goes beyond Kelsey's project by drawing on elements from one or another usage, identifying the respective roles they play, and seeking to integrate them. See David H. Kelsey, *The Uses of Scripture in Recent Theology* (Philadelphia: Fortress, 1975).

EVANGELICAL CATHOLICITY

"EVANGELICAL catholicity" are fighting words in some parts of the church. Hear this from Gerhard Forde protesting its advocacy among today's Lutherans:

> One comes away reading . . . one dominant message: If we want to be saved from going under with mainline American Protestantism we had better become something called "evangelical catholics." . . . What is going on here? . . . Why is it that the lines seem to be drawn in terms of certain loaded adjectives one can bandy about indiscriminately? What means this attempt to fix up or damn historical movements by adjective-mongering? "Catholic" is suddenly gussied up enough to meet with general approval by adding the adjective "evangelical"?[1]

Jeffrey Gros, Roman Catholic theologian who served as director of the Faith and Order Commission of the National Council of Churches, is also interested in evangelical catholicity. Here is what he has to say in a review of George Shriver's book on Philip Schaff:

---

1. Gerhard Forde, "Lutheran for the Time Being," *Dialog* 27, no. 3 (Summer 1988): 164-65.

The discussion of "evangelical catholicism" rose to prominence around the founding of the Evangelical Lutheran Church in America (1988) and its selection of its name. For many this discussion was new. This volume chronicles the life of a man who gave currency to the term a century and a half ago, Philip Schaff. . . . Indeed, his dream of an ecumenically united Christianity has begun to take shape in the United Church of Christ in the US, a Church which is heir to his German Reformed, Pennsylvania denomination among others.[2]

Ironies abound here. Lutherans who want to distance themselves from mainline churches discover a new fighting word, "evangelical catholicity." Yet the words and concept come from a tradition and history these critics of the mainline are eager to repudiate. Indeed, the United Church of Christ, shaped by the evangelical catholic heritage, is viewed as a prime example of acculturated Protestantism. To top it off, an important Roman Catholic theologian reminds the Lutherans of the roots of evangelical catholicity in the Reformed ancestors of the United Church of Christ!

The Evangelical Lutheran Church in America "catholic" caucus may be wiser in its intuitions than in its formulations. The Mercersburg understanding of evangelical catholicity has a more radical — root — critique than some of its new recruits realize. It has to do with an ecumenical legacy more encompassing than the Lutheran–Roman Catholic dialogue focal to their particular interests. It goes beyond the challenge to denominationalism, as important as that is. I am referring to fundamental theological method and content.

To give attention to this aspect of the Mercersburg theology I draw heavily on Philip Schaff's inaugural address, *The Principle of Protestantism*, which is the manifesto of evangelical

---

2. Brother Jeffrey Gros, FSC, review of George Shriver, *Philip Schaff: Christian Scholar and Ecumenical Prophet* (Mimeographed, 1988).

catholicity.[3] Interestingly, a second inaugural address, that of John Payne on the occasion of his installation in the new Lancaster Seminary chair of Mercersburg and Ecumenical Theology, takes up the key theme of catholic unity articulated by his predecessor.[4] My remarks are an interpretation of theses found in each, as they touch on the state of theology in the churches today. I also try to connect with issues identified in Linden De Bie's essay, "Saving Evangelical Catholicism Today."[5]

Some of the persons who bore faithful witness to evangelical catholicity have been on my mind as these thoughts took form, sainted dead of recent memory: George Geisler, Theodore Trost, Sr., Bard Thompson, George Bricker. Over the past years, I have worked with one or another of these faithful pastors and teachers of the gospel. They now know in the communion of saints the catholicity to which those on earth can only point in hope. I dedicate this paper to them.

THE SECT AND THE TRIBE

The spread of the "sect principle," the "sect system," yes, the "sect plague," was the occasion for the Mercersburg theologians' exposition of evangelical catholicity. Is there an equivalent environment today? Yes. Yesterday's sectarianism is today's tribalism.

By definition, a tribe is an aggregation of people of common stock, united by a community of customs and traditions. Tribalism is a state of affairs in which fundamental identity is established by participation in one or another separate commu-

---

3. Philip Schaff, *The Principle of Protestantism*, trans. John W. Nevin, ed. Bard Thompson and George Bricker, Lancaster Series on the Mercersburg Theology, vol. 1 (Philadelphia: United Church Press, 1964).

4. John B. Payne, "Mercersburg and Ecumenical Theology: What's the Connection?" *New Mercersburg Review* no. 7 (Spring 1990): 3-13.

5. Linden J. De Bie, "Saving Evangelical Catholicism Today," *New Mercersburg Review* no. 6 (Autumn 1989): 11-21.

nity of common stock. Theological tribalism happens in the Christian community when fundamental Christian identity is associated with loyalty to the *subcommunity* of common stock with its attendant customs and traditions. Evangelical catholicity today struggles against the tribal system, as evangelical catholicity yesterday stood against the sectarian system.

Tribal sectarianism today comes in two varieties, although it also has hybrid forms. Each is related to powerful cultural currents, secularization and pluralization, with their related modern and postmodern orthodoxies. I label the first variety imperial tribalism and the second confessional tribalism.

Imperial Tribalism

Imperial tribalism reflects both the premise and the focus of a secular modernity. Truth comes by right knowledge of the world of time and space, and exists to make that world livable. Today's historically conscious secularity is well aware that knowledge is inseparable from historical circumstance and vested interest. Thus understanding of what is the case, and what makes life livable, is not so easily accessible as precritical confidences assumed. But there is a way. The door to the truth is unlocked by engagement. Kierkegaard and Marx long ago turned Hegel upside down and shook the key from his pocket. To be in touch with the dynamisms of the Really Real is to be there in the midst of the movement, not alienated from it by thought or power. Thus history is on the side of the actor (not the thinker) and the oppressed (not the oppressor). The same is true of knowledge, hence "the epistemological privilege" of the actor against oppression. Truth can be known, injustice can be overcome, the one world in which humans dwell can be made livable. How it happens depends on the mobilization of the powerless and our solidarity with their cause.

Where these familiar themes of modernity connect with the issue of tribalism is at the point of individual engagement, the "who" point. Who is the actor? As the measure of real injustice has been taken in recent decades — in this country, from the civil rights struggles of the 1960s on — the number of engaged individuals has multiplied. Callous is the Christian who has not done serious soul-searching as each marginalized constituency has made its case.

Significant epistemological claims are made in association with the demands of justice. Modern advocacy groups are in this respect the children of Kierkegaard and Marx: what is to be known can only be known in a commensurate mode. More simply put, the doer is the knower. Thus oppression, experienced and acted against, is the revelatory locus. To know God, to encounter Christ, and to discern Scripture's meaning require participation in this communal place of epistemological privilege. Truth is tribal.

The tribalism so far discussed is one active in both theological academia and the mainline churches. But a variation of it is also found in countries far distant from the shores of the American Academy of Religion and the National Council of Churches. This evangelical empire makes a strikingly similar claim of epistemological privilege. But the *experience* is worlds away from the political and social barricades of the change agent. This time the oppressor is the devil, and deliverance is from the thralldom of sin and guilt. Here the tribal rite is the born-again experience, and the armies of conversion march with imperial design.

Because truth is accessible in all tribalism only to those of common stock, relationships with outsiders can only be polemical or calls to conversion. No conversation is conceivable; it would undercut the assumption of privileged loci. Where imperial tribalism reigns, the theological forum, or the church, begins to look like an armed camp. The city of Beirut replaces the City of God.

Confessional Tribalism

Postmodern protagonists smile at the warfare of epistemological empires. Truth found here or there? But there *is* no there, there — only illusory claims and interest-laden agendas ripe for deconstruction. Humans cannot know states of affairs, human or divine. One can never find "the truth"; one must be content with what one has, not things truthful but things meaningful. Or, one could say, the meaningful *is* the truthful, that which works, maximally for "us," or minimally for "them."

Confessional tribalism comes down on the "for us." Influenced, consciously or otherwise, by developments in cultural anthropology and linguistics, and grounded in a Kantian agnosticism about knowledge of ultimate reality, the confessionalist fixes upon the features and boundaries of tribal self-definition. This land, these graves, these heroes, this lore, this language, these totems are who we are. We cannot step out of our skin, and we choose not to do so. Let us learn *our* language, love *our* lore, and live by *our* codes.

There is no tribal warfare here, only border patrol. "Don't tread on me": Don't claim you are in when you are out. You have your turf, and we have ours. This capacious country has plenty of room for all. The horizons are limitless. Our tribe will not claim sovereignty. We live and let live. We confess who we are, and you can do the same. No imperialism here, but neither is there warrant for conversation and cross-pollination. Pluralism baptizes the status quo.

An important version of confessional tribalism appears to move toward the imperial view by its more strident self-definition: those of common stock who are not faithful to the boundaries risk contamination by alien tribes. There is no desire to take "the others" by storm, in the fashion of imperial modes, but rather to assure the loyalty of one's own to one's own. Something of a fortress mentality obtains, the "sect-type" in Troeltsch's famous schematization. The self-identified tradition, denomination, or confession becomes the principle of inclusion and exclusion.

Like the imperial view, the confessional view makes telling points. Christians *are* creatures of their history, community, and heritage; the fact of pluralization forces one to acknowledge and live with the reality of many and varied worldviews; the recovery of forgotten lore is fundamental to faith today. But the question is: What is the definitive history, community, and heritage for Christian believers? What are the alternatives? And what lore gives Christians their fundamental identity?

Clues to the answer to tribalism today are found in the Mercersburg theologians' struggle with sectarianism yesterday.

CORINTHIAN CATHOLICITY

According to Schaff, sect pollution had been unleashed upon the land: "Poisonous weeds shoot up thus wild and luxuriant in our Protestant garden."[6] What is this disease?

> Anyone who has, or fancies he has, some inward experience and a ready tongue may persuade himself that he is called to be a reformer; and so proceeds in spiritual vanity and pride in a revolutionary rupture with the historical life of the church, to which he holds himself immeasurably superior . . . the deceived multitude, having no power to discern spirits, is converted not to Christ and his truth, but to the arbitrary fancies and baseless opinions of an individual who is only of yesterday . . . a variegated sampler of all conceivable chimeras and dreams.[7]

The response to all this must be "Protestant Catholicism," or later "evangelical catholicism" and "evangelical catholicity." To define this alternative Schaff drew from the storehouse of current European philosophy, romanticist and idealist — the

6. Schaff, *Principle*, p. 150.
7. Ibid., pp. 149-50.

Schlegels, Novalis, Schelling, Hegel, and their theological appropriators, Schleiermacher, Neander, Dorner, Hengstenberg. Even in the title of the key chapter 5, these cultural debts are clear: "The True Standpoint: Protestant Catholicism or Historical Progress."[8] So all the catchwords of the age found their way into the Mercersburg theology: organism, growth, progress, history, diversity.

Mercersburg can be explored against the background of its culture, but it cannot be explained in reductionist fashion by the social or philosophical currents of its time. It borrowed, somewhat eclectically, categories from the intellectual atmosphere of the day to defend and interpret the faith as it understood it. (John Payne gives evidence of this eclecticism when he notes that in *The Principle of Protestantism* Schaff uses two theories of development "which he holds together in uneasy tension: the romantic, organic and the idealist, dialectical,"[9] one stressing continuities and the other oppositions.) If the foes were the individualism, rationalism, and subjectivism of the hour, then one hefted into position any weapon at hand that one could use responsibly. But one must not mistake the weapon for the vision and the passion.

One does not have to look far to find the latter in the text. To the one who

> has any right idea of the church, as the communion of saints, this state of things must be the source of deep distress. The loss of all earthly possessions, the death of his dearest friend, however severely felt, would be as nothing to him, compared to the grief he felt for such division and distraction of the church of God, the Body of Jesus Christ. Not for the price of the whole world with all its treasures, could he be induced to appear as the founder of a new sect. . . . Not a solitary passage of the Bible is on their side. . . . The Lord is come to make of twain one; to gather the dispersed children of God

8. Ibid., p. 165.
9. Payne, "Mercersburg," p. 4.

throughout the whole world into one fold, under one Shepherd. His last commission to his disciples was that they should love one another, and serve one another. . . . His last prayer before his bitter passion was that his followers might be made perfect in one, as he was in the Father and the Father in him. . . . Paul exhorts the Corinthians in the name of Jesus Christ that they should all speak the same thing and that there should be no division among them, but that they should be perfectly joined together in the same mind and in the same judgment. They must not call themselves after Paul, or Apollos, or Cephas, or Christ in the way of party or sect. For Christ is not divided.[10]

Schaff pursues Paul's Corinthian image in some interesting ways, indeed using a Hegelian walking stick on the path. As in Corinth, so on the Pennsylvania frontier, to name the party spirit was not to deny the partisans' gift.

The divine significance of sects, then, their value in the history of the church, consists in this, that they are a disciplinary scourge, a voice of awakening and admonition by which the church is urged to new life and a more conscientious discharge of her duties. The system has a favorable operation further, as it tends to spread religious interest and stimulate Christian zeal. In this country, perhaps, if there were no sects, we should have half as many congregations and houses of worship as we have now, and many blessings of the Gospel altogether.[11]

Schaff's irenicism includes, specifically, a good word for the so-called Puritans:

The deep moral earnestness, the stern self-discipline, the unbending force of character must fill the unprejudiced historian

10. Schaff, *Principle,* pp. 151-52.
11. Ibid., pp. 171-72.

with admiration. There are reasons for its war against false forms. . . . We may never ungratefully forget that it was this generation of godly Pilgrims which once and for all stamped upon our country that charter of deep moral earnestness . . . that peculiar zeal for the Sabbath and the Bible that have raised it so high a place in the history of the Christian Church, and enabled it to compare so favorably with the countries of the Old World. For our German emigration in particular it must be counted a high privilege that it is here brought into contact with the practical piety of the English community, and by degrees also imbued more or less with its power; though with the loss, to be regretted on the other side, of many German peculiarities. Thousands of souls that might have died in vanity and unbelief in their native land, have thus been rescued, we may trust, from eternal perdition.[12]

With all these good things, why rage against the "sect plague"? The answer is its violation of Corinthian catholicity. The sect takes the good gift given to it by the Holy Spirit and makes it the be-all and end-all of Christ's church. To the sectarian must come the Word: "The eye cannot say to the hand, 'I have no need of you.' . . . If the whole body were an eye, where would the hearing be?" (1 Cor. 12:21, 17).

Said in the incarnational and ecclesial language of Mercersburg: the divine-human person of Christ lives now as the Body of Christ on earth, giving it unity, apostolicity, sanctity, and catholicity. To draw apart from the living Body, to set oneself up in arrogance outside it, and more, to claim one's little sect to be the true church, is to be cut off from the life of the Body. Sects can only be born to die in their insularity.

The alternative? One could honor the continuities, refusing to overleap the centuries in a vain attempt to repristinate beginnings. Specifically, one could recognize the gifts brought to the

---

12. Ibid., p. 147. On the roots of Schaff's irenicism see Shriver, review, pp. 8-10.

church by patristic and medieval Christianity and celebrate the Reformation advances. But one should not abort a growth that looks beyond these to yet greater things to come. From Neander (cum Hegel) one can learn about the dialectic: the church of Peter (thesis), the church of Paul (antithesis), the church of John (synthesis).

EVANGELICAL NORMS

For Mercersburg, authentic catholicity is evangelical. Schaff spends sixty-one pages expounding the "advance" in historical development represented by the Reformation. At its heart are the affirmation of justification by grace through faith alone and the final authority of Scripture, the "material" and "formal" principles that are "two different sides . . . of one and the same principle" — the *Protestant principle*.[13]

Sola Fide

Schaff calls justification — the material principle — the "article of life," the article by which the church stands or falls. He describes it in this manner:

> This all-sufficient satisfaction of Christ takes hold upon the individual subjectively in justification. This is a judicial, declarative act on the part of God, by which he first pronounces the sin-crushed, contrite sinner free from guilt as it regards the past, for the sake of the only-begotten Son, and then . . . makes over to him in boundless mercy the full righteousness of the same, to be counted and to be in fact his own. It is in this way (1) negatively, *remissio peccatorum* . . . and (2) positively, *imputatio justitiae* and *adoptio in filios Dei*. . . . Man by justification steps into the place of Christ, as Christ had

---

13. Schaff, *Principle*, p. 99.

previously stepped into the place of man. In this way, all Pelagian and semi-Pelagian self-righteousness is torn up by the roots. . . . While the merit of Christ is thus viewed as the only ground, the only means of appropriation . . . is presented to us in faith. This is . . . the free gift of God, which is offered and imparted to [us] through the word of sacraments.[14]

In an otherwise standard-brand statement of Reformation soteriology, Schaff's phrases "to be in fact his own" and "imparted to [us]" reflect his second-Adam Christology and his attempt to respond to Roman Catholic charges that the Reformers endorsed an abstract view of the work of Christ and a loveless faith. Further, this Christology presupposes a sweeping Reformed vision of God's covenantal history:

God, before whom the dimensions of time all give way in the same vast eternity, looks upon men in their inmost nature as rooted in Christ, with whom they are brought into living union by faith. For the relation of Christ to humanity is not outward but inward and essential. He is the second Adam, the spiritual head of the race. . . . The justifying act becomes itself the occasion, by which the principle is actualized in its subject, having creative force, quickening the dead . . . and thus lodges in his person a life germ altogether new, in which is comprehended from the start the entire growth of holiness.[15]

Schaff makes several moves here. First, in typical Reformed fashion, he stretches back into the eternal covenant between the first and second persons of the Trinity, and thence to the plan that unfolds from Adam through the fall to incarnation and atonement. His second move is forward through the church's word and sacraments to the "application of the benefits" of Christ's person

---

14. Ibid., pp. 87-88.
15. Ibid., pp. 94-95.

and work. The article by which the church stands or falls is the evangelical word to the sinner: *sola fide*. But it cannot be torn from a sentence that includes *sola gratia* in its full covenantal range and *solus Christus* in its historical particularity. Justification is God's gracious work from beginning to end, as well as in its personal application to the contrite sinner. For Mercersburg, catholicity applies to the Protestant principle itself: its very definition resists reductionism. Thus the full sweep of the Story is taken into the meaning of the *evangel* in "evangelical" — the good news of God, from covenant to creation to Christ to consummation.

Sola Scriptura

Scripture alone is the final authority for evangelical faith. "To the material or life principle of the Reformation accordingly is joined as its necessary complement the formal or knowledge principle, which consists in this, that the word of God, as it has been handed down to us in the canonical books of the Old and New Testaments, is the pure and proper source as well as the only certain measure of all saving truth."[16]

What is the "word of God"? "If there is any unerring fountain of truth . . . it can be found only in the word of God, who is himself the truth; and this becomes consequently the highest norm and rule by which we measure all human truth, all ecclesiastical tradition and all synodical decrees. . . . Infallibility belongs to Christ and his word alone."[17]

As *sola fide* is inseparable from its companions in Mercersburg's catholicity, so too is *sola Scriptura*. Scripture is read through the lens of Christ. Because Christ is the eternal Word of God, one is taken once again to the gracious Word that was in the beginning, the Word that brought creation to be, the Word that is enfleshed in Christ, who will come again in triumph. *Solus Christus* and *sola gratia* join *sola Scriptura*.

---

16. Ibid., p. 98.
17. Ibid., p. 106.

Catholicity leaves its mark again on the relation of Scripture to tradition. Evangelical faith recognizes the historical necessity of tradition, the Spirit's gift of illumination given to the church in ritual, historical, and dogmatic forms. But it rejects any claim to parity with Scripture, or worse, regency over it. Tradition is always measured by the biblical source and norm.

The highest form of tradition is its dogmatic form as found in the ecumenical creeds and the Reformation confessions. "Tradition in this sense is absolutely indispensable. By its means we come first to the contents of the Bible. . . . This tradition therefore is not a part of the divine word separately from that which is written, but the contents of Scripture itself as apprehended and settled by the church against heresies past and always new appearing."[18]

Thus the "church of Paul" makes its witness to the church catholic. Without the evangelical principle in both of its expressions there is no faithful and scriptural Christianity. Catholicity means, as well, that the two need each other: "The material element without the objective basis of the formal becomes swarming inwardism, and in the end sheer subjectivity. The formal element without the material, however, conducts to stiff, lifeless and soulless externalism, the idolatry of the letter."[19] Hence evangelical catholicity entails a catholic evangel at its Reformation center, determinedly Pauline, but set within a Johannine circumference.

EVANGELICAL CATHOLICITY TODAY

A Corinthian word should be spoken to the times of tribalism. It needs to be heard in two ways.

The first has to do with the mode of discourse necessary in the Christian community. The Corinthian church was the

---

18. Ibid., p. 116.
19. Ibid., p. 123.

body of those baptized in Christ. Paul soon enough discovered that this included all manner of folk who conceived of membership exclusively in terms meaningful to their particular charisms — prophecy, tongues, helping, healing, administration, and so forth. First Corinthians 12 affirms the legitimacy of the diversity but excoriates the drive to hegemony. Chapter 13 takes it a step further, pressing beyond mutual recognition to mutual coinherence, the *agape* that God is in the inner-trinitarian life together reflected in the *agape* and *koinonia* of Corinthian life together.

Schaff traced this "church of love," as he called it, to the perichoretic unity of the Father and the Son (John 17:6). It meant a sharp no to loveless fissiparousness in any form, the "sect plague." That unity required an upsetting openness of the Reformation churches to each other, to their predecessors, and to development toward a larger unity beyond each and all. For believers today it means a sharp no to tribalism, a no to imperial claims that this or that modern charism is the sum and substance of the gospel, the place of epistemological privilege to which all must come to know Christ and be the Body. It also means a no to confessional tribalism satisfied with its location and lore, needing no other charism, content and complete in what it is and has. If ecclesial sin comes twinned, then the former is arrogance and the latter apathy, or in the language of the tradition, *superbia* and *accedia*.

The beginning of openness is the readiness to engage in colloquy. Luther spoke of the "mutual conversation and consolation" of the sisters and brothers in the congregation as a veritable means of grace. Catholicity of this sort means the rebirth of theological conversation in the church. It means a household of common talk. All retreat into comfortable rooms is over, for the bell calls all to the common table. It is time for table talk in the family of God.[20]

---

20. "Colloquy" and "table talk" have been important features of my involvement with Mercersburg's contemporary witness: Craigville Colloquies I-X, 1984–93, which have sought to bring together the diversity of perspec-

Catholicity entails more than mutual conversation. It also means mutual correction. In the midst of colloquy the Spirit can work a change of heart and mind. When the Mercersburg theologians came out of their solitary confinement to the Protestant room and walked the hallways with medieval and patristic housemates, they had to leave behind ultra-Protestant ideology. Just so, one can recognize the diseases of confinement: individualism, uncritical private judgment, subjectivism, biblicism.

Can catholicity today make for comparable vulnerability and self-criticism? To be open to correction and complementarity means that the charisms of the most strident advocacy groups are welcomed by others. The hermeneutics of suspicion and the hermeneutics of partisanship do have a word from the places of suffering and oppression: to know and serve the Christ of the hungry and hopeless is to keep company with them there, to learn to look at the gospel in new ways as good news for the poor and the captive. But the road to Corinth is a two-way street. The gospel is good news for the sinner as well as the sufferer, and an evangel that proclaims triumph over death as well as oppression. The fullness of the gospel proclaimed in the church will be in direct proportion to the mutual correction and completion of the church's tribal monologues. Let the imperialist who raids and the confessionalist who patrols dismantle their juggernauts and take down their barricades. Open borders and welcomed strangers bring strength and growth.

The mutual correction that comes from open conversation brings with it, therefore, a far richer grasp of the content of faith. Tribalism produces doctrinal fragmentation — heresy; a catholic life together nurtures a full-orbed faith.

Standing alone, catholicity could be a worse alternative than the tribalism it purports to challenge — a new normless

tives in the United Church of Christ in the quest for a larger unity; "Theological Tabletalk" at Lancaster Theological Seminary, 1962–70, and at Andover Newton Theological School, 1971 to the present, weekly gatherings of clergy, theological students, and teachers to discuss current theological works.

tribe with no self-critical principle, a process ideology that asserts interaction for its own sake. Mercersburg faced the same option in the romanticism and idealism of its own day and chose the better part: the "Protestant principle," *evangelical* catholicity. Entry into the Johannine "church of love" was by the Pauline corridor: the justifying work of God in Christ according to the testimony of Scripture. For believers today the same standard must obtain. Both the mode and the content of catholicity live under the evangelical norm. The claims of each tribe, what they give to and receive from other charisms, must pass muster before Scripture as read in the light of the full gospel and according to its center, Jesus Christ. I have noted that the material principle of gospel justification brings complementarity of content to those captive to today's interiorities and pietisms, on the one hand, and social reductionisms and utopianisms on the other. The church should attend to the impact of the evangelical Scripture principle at this point.

In both imperial and confessional tribalism, human experience is normative: in the former, the epistemological privilege of the engaged — the actor in the drama of liberation; in the latter, the nonepistemological act of loyalty to the warp and woof of group experience. Truth *is* or truth *as* the company of the committed. Scripture is the creature of the community, the Word *of* the tribe.

The Word of God, Jesus Christ, as Scripture attests to him, is captive to no one and no thing. Human experience, whether it be the experience of the oppressed, of the Christian community, or of the evangelical being born again, is not the final word one has "to trust and obey." That sovereign Word can be spoken *against* all these experiences, and it always must be understood as spoken *to* them, not *from* them. This is the evangelical Scripture principle to which all tribalisms are accountable.

Faithfulness to a *catholic* evangelical principle means that one cannot scorn the gifts brought by experiential charisms to the Body of Christ. The Word is sovereign enough not to be bound by its freedom *from* believers. It can be free *for* one and *in* one, even free enough to use one's experience, social or personal, in or outside the church. Indeed, the promise of the covenant with Noah is that one has a right to look for signs in one's human experience of truth, and thus in the experience of the most imperial of tribes. But because this common grace is that of the eternal Word, Jesus Christ, the instrument of discernment is always the Christ known in and disclosed by Scripture. Further, a solemn promise was made at Pentecost that the Holy Spirit would never desert the Body of Christ. So the most restrictive of confessional tribes may have gifts to bring. The self-authenticating Word spoken to humans in Scripture is, again, the principle of discernment and interpretation of all tribal claims.

CONCLUSION

Evangelical catholicity has telling significance for these tribal times. Those who believe this statement should share the gift given to them in the church struggles of today, but not as one more sect claiming to have the definitive word. That would be the ultimate irony. Rather, one should let this charism do a catalytic work wherever it finds itself. In the communities of faith in which one lives, one should bear witness to the Corinthian vision as illumined by the evangelical Word.

A NARRATIVE THEOLOGY
OF REVELATION

THE gospel speaks forthrightly of One who reveals what is hidden. The words of disclosure are about deeds of deliverance. The good news is not that mysteries formerly veiled from the ignorant are now uncovered, but that the ultimate bondage and alienation are overcome. Whatever else evangelical faith has to say to its contemporaries within and beyond the church, it is this: The fundamental question, given sin, is how can an estranged world be reconciled to God? Whatever humans know about who God is and what God has disclosed finally comes down to that.

Modernity does not ask this question, as Karl Menninger argues persuasively in *Whatever Became of Sin?*[1] Of the perennial human quandaries, ignorance, death, suffering, and sin, it is suffering — as misery and hopelessness — that comes center stage today.[2] The starvation of multitudes, the oppression of the poor and powerless, tyranny that denies human freedom, injustice to class, race, sex, age, and condition, the peril of war and nuclear extermination, the ills of the flesh and the cares of the world — these in political macrocosm and personal microcosm

---

1. Karl Menninger, *Whatever Became of Sin?* (New York: Hawthorn, 1973).
2. As in William Wolf, *No Cross, No Crown* (Garden City, N.Y.: Doubleday, 1957), pp. 27-30.

are on the minds and hearts of the present generation. Faith communities respond accordingly, whether it be in the theodicy of a Harold Kushner *(When Bad Things Happen to Good People)* that strikes a responsive chord in a Boston suburb, or a liberation theology that energizes a base community in a Latin American barrio. Both the depth and degree of human peril and the seeming possibilities of historical promise, each tied up with advances in the artifacts of modernity that occasion fears and hopes or disseminate them globally, argue for bringing suffering and hope to the foreground of concern.[3]

Those who name the name of Jesus today will understand this question and engage it. They have a Deliverer who preaches good news to the poor, brings release to the captives, heals the sick, comforts the sorrowful, and blesses the peacemakers (Luke 4:17-21; Matt. 5:1-9). Out of thanksgiving they want to serve in the way he served those in need. Out of sobriety they know that if they pass by on the other side (Luke 10:29-37) or do not minister to the last and the least (Matt. 25:45), they must answer to a righteous God on the day of judgment. Further, if the technology of the time has raised sky-high the stakes of the

---

3. The growing literature on religious pluralism and the enlarging constituencies within both Protestant and Roman Catholic theology that question the scandal of particularity raise a fundamental challenge to the deeds/disclosure narrative. A measure of how far the conversation has moved in these circles in the past few decades is found in the titles of two definitive works: W. A. Visser 't Hooft's earlier and unambiguous *No Other Name* (Philadelphia: Westminster, 1963) and Paul Knitter's *No Other Name?* (Maryknoll, N.Y.: Orbis, 1985). The latter traces the qualification and finally erosion of particularist views in many forms of modern theology, defending a version of the same as "theocentric universalism."

By choosing "suffering and hope" as my themes, I do not confront the issues posed by religious pluralism as directly as do other apologetic ventures. Nonetheless, the claims to particularity integral to this chapter do radically call into question the assumptions of the various current pluralist theologians (Hick, Cobb, Pannikar, Dawe, W. C. Smith, H. Smith, Knitter, etc.). For a typology and critique of such options, see my "The Scandals of Particularity and Universality," *Mid-Stream* 22 (January 1983): 32-52; and S. Mark Heim, *Is Christ the Only Way?* (Valley Forge, Pa.: Judson, 1985).

human prospect, then Christians must read these signs of the times (Matt. 16:1-3) and speak as well as act accordingly. The good news is a good word to those in pain and poverty, as well as a good deed. So to the interlocutors: Christians strive to speak the language of hope to the hopeless, indeed a sober hope, cognizant of both God's promise and the powers that militate against it.

Yet what is first in one's consciousness is not the whole of the matter. In another scale of value, suffering and hope take their meaning from a larger frame of reference. What of the sin of the world before the holy love of God? What of the lethal factor that undermines efforts to overcome suffering and persists in the brightest of hopes for a livable world? Here evangelical faith must risk the angry retorts ("copping out"), the knowing smiles (of course, "the opiate of the people"), and furrowed brows ("You're pushing on the brake when you should be stepping on the gas"), and ask the embarrassing unasked question. The discussion of divine disclosure that follows assumes the importance of this unasked question of *sin and guilt,* even as it regards God's deeds to deliver human beings from these evils as the context for all others.

Evangelical witness is important here not only because it points to the obscured aspect of the gospel but also because this very pointing serves the cause of deliverance from oppression and hope in the midst of suffering. Those liberation movements and theologies of hope that do not know of the sin that persists in every achievement of justice and peace, a sin that continues to infect the very agents of liberation and reconciliation, render their own cause a profound disservice. The evidence of history as well as the deeper perception of the eye of faith disclose the stubbornness of sin and its results. Among those consequences are the illusion of the righteous who know nothing against themselves and thus fall prey to a self-righteous fury that tramples all opposition. The same moral shortsightedness is liable to a despair that, seeing the ambiguity in both the achievement and the achiever, loses all hope for historical advance and

91

flees the struggle for justice and peace. These twin perversions are all too evident today among those eager to correct flaws in their foes but not in themselves, as in the Manichaean politics of both the religious right and the religious left, and in the burnout or ahistorical spiritualism of former visionaries and revolutionaries.[4] The unwelcome word about sin and guilt before God must be on the lips of believers because this word is true, and because this truth really does make people free.

This discussion of God the Discloser seeks to be faithful to the fundamental issue of God's controversy with the world. At the same time one can describe that controversy in motifs and metaphors that relate to this time of suffering and hope. Here a narrative idiom seems particularly appropriate. A story is a plot with characters moving over time and place through conflict to resolution.[5] A dramatic mood captures both the faith and the facts of the era. Vision and light are themes that carry the accent of hope. They also can speak to the visual environment so characteristic of modern technology (as in "television"). To take seriously the suffering and hope of this age also means hearing the voice of the voiceless and honoring the presence of long-submerged constituencies in both culture and church — Third World peoples, racial and ethnic communities, women, the aged, the disabled, the poor. When evangelicals ignore representatives of these peoples and perspectives, they weaken their message to the post-Christian world. The same situation circumscribes my own efforts to be catholic. This situation does not mean capitulating before simplistic versions of the sociology of knowledge or the hermeneutics of suspicion (these notions receive a sharp challenge in a subsequent section). But both a genuine sensitivity to the marginal-

---

4. I have sought to identify the Manichaean and Zoroastrian tendencies of the religious right in *The Religious Right and Christian Faith* (Grand Rapids: Eerdmans, 1982), pp. 47-52, 84, and passim.

5. For an analysis of narrative theology and a typology of current expressions of it, see my "Narrative Theology: An Overview," *Interpretation* 37 (October 1983): 340-52.

ized and the call for a full-orbed understanding of faith, as in Paul's word to the Corinthian church (1 Cor. 12–14), constitute a forceful word to evangelicals complacent about their possession of the truth.

The modern quest for justice and peace, as well as the modern encounter with suffering, is radicalized when put in an evangelical framework with its place for the depth of sin. Thus the struggle for justice in the world confronts one also with a question of the justice of God. Before the cross of Christ the problem of human suffering becomes the anguish of God. So too other human quandaries are deepened when placed before God. Ignorance becomes error; and death, more profound than mortality, becomes separation from God. Christian faith calls into question the conventional wisdom of the world about these perennial questions. These realities take on this deepest meaning only at the point where God discloses ultimately who each person is and who he is, the place where everyone is known and all are forgiven. A proper evangelical witness is given from the foot of the cross.

The form of this testimony is that of narrative. Such a presentation of God's self-disclosure relates to contemporary sensibility, as suggested already, but it also has an honored history as a way of Christian communication. The first baptismal confessions of faith follow this structure, one preserved in the present Apostles' Creed and developed further in the Nicene Creed. Here the great drama means the acts of creation, reconciliation, and redemption, the missions of the triune God, and thus the unfolding of the economic Trinity grounded in the inner-trinitarian life of God. The trajectory of the narrative in one way or another is familiar in the loci of classical dogmatics and more recent systematic theologies.[6] It is also found in the

---

6. An example of classical dogmatics is Heinrich Heppe, *Reformed Dogmatics,* ed. Ernst Bizer, trans. G. T. Thomson (Grand Rapids: Baker, repr. 1978); for a more recent systematic theology see Carl Braaten and Robert Jenson, eds., *Christian Dogmatics,* vols. 1 and 2 (Philadelphia: Fortress, 1984).

order of Scripture itself as it runs from creation to consummation with its center point in Jesus Christ.[7]

THE NARRATIVE OF
RECONCILIATION AND REVELATION

The source of the narrative of faith is in the Godhead, lying in "God's wisdom, secret and hidden, which God decreed before the ages for our glory" (1 Cor. 2:7). This purpose one comes to know in Jesus Christ, the divine intention, vision, Word from the "beginning" now made flesh (John 1:1, 14). Taking a clue from Augustine's psychological analogy for the Trinity, one may say that this narrative is the account of how the Purposer exercises power to fulfill purpose.

The social analogy of the Trinity, a necessary companion to the psychological one that honors the inner-trinitarian life together, is an important part of God's self-disclosure. Revelation in the economy of God is the expression of the radical openness of the persons to one another in their common life. The coinherence of Father, Son, and Spirit is a "disclosive" transparency that sets the stage for the open secret to be revealed in God's history with humanity.

CREATION

God brings the world to be. Creation is a gift of the Creator. The stars and stones are rich in possibility, nature is blessed

---

7. James Orr went a step further and argued that the narrative of faith as found in Scripture and in books on systematic theology is reflected in the history of dogma, as each chapter in succession became the occasion for the notable controversies (*Progress of Dogma* [London: Hodder & Stoughton, 1901]). For an illuminating commentary on this point, see Peter Toon, *The Development of Doctrine in the Church* (Grand Rapids: Eerdmans, 1979), pp. 62-70.

(Gen. 1:3-24). "Being, as such, is good," as Augustine put it. The human being, finite creature like all others yet the crown of creation, is made in the divine image: in relationship, the apple of God's eye; in capacity, given a will, reason, and spirit able to answer the divine invitation (Gen. 1:26; 1 Cor. 12:7). Transnatural being, the realm of powers and principalities, is called to special ministration in giving glory to God (Mark 1:13; Eph. 6:12). Cosmologies explaining these miracles come and go, but the fundamental meaning of God's creative deed does not change. This creation launches the biblical narrative.[8]

Assertions about God's disclosure are integral to God's deed. Creation in its intended state reflects God, the divine society — humanity knows its Maker, nature lives in harmony, and the powers of this world stand poised to serve their Source. Thus the light of God shines upon everything and enlightens everyone coming into the world (John 1:9). This Light and Word that form and inform the world is Jesus Christ: "all things came into being through him, and without him not one thing came into being" (John 1:3). Creation as deed and disclosure is finally the work of the triune God, the purpose of God leaving its imprint by the power of God.[9] The implications of this work as general revelation and common grace in the world after the fall I explore in a later section.

FALL

"The world came into being through him; yet the world did not know him" (John 1:10b).[10] The world rebuffs the beckoning of

---

8. A passage of Scripture, John 1:1-18, which in short compass indicates this larger biblical arc, provides the framework for the following section.

9. I exposit this and other deeds and doctrines in the narrative in *The Christian Story*, vol. 1: *A Narrative Interpretation of Basic Christian Doctrine*, rev. ed. (Grand Rapids: Eerdmans, 1984), pp. 68-76. See also Robert Paul Roth, *The Theater of God: Story in Christian Doctrines* (Philadelphia: Fortress, 1985).

10. See my *Christian Story*, 1:56-58.

God. This is the second chapter in the Christian story, the turn away from the Light, the stumble and fall into the night. All across creation resistance arises to the purpose for which the world was made. Powers turn treacherous and become the occasion for assault and temptation; human nature accedes to beguilement, seeks to usurp the place of its Maker, sullies its image of special relationship and capacity, and expresses its rebellion in an apathy and arrogance commensurate with its creatureliness and image. Nature turns red in tooth and claw, the wolf devouring the lamb, the asp striking the child, the body in pain and toil, the earth groaning. So megalomania — self-idolatry — arises to thwart God's purpose. The world shakes its fist in the face of God. But the wages of sin is death. The night of judgment falls on the day of rebellion. On these sobering facts the Christian story turns.

That "the world did not know him" means not only "did not accept him" (John 1:11b) but also did not *perceive* him. To turn from the Light is to be in the night, no longer able to see the direction in which one must go, nor empowered to pursue the journey. Here are the fall's consequences for revelation. The purpose in "the starry heavens above and the moral law within" no longer sends clear messages to the human spirit. The disorder of creation, prey to the demonic powers, distorted further by the darkened lens of humanity, undercuts the created ability to perceive the will and way of God and the original capacity for positive response. Sin remains separation from God, the death of the vision and the demise of creation.

COVENANT

Yet "the light shines in the darkness, and the darkness did not overcome it" (John 1:5). This narrative concerns a stubborn God, long-suffering with a rebel world. So comes the chapter that occupies two-thirds of Scripture, the enlightening work of God among the people of Israel. Here Light takes form as the pillar of fire by night, leading the people of God to a new land and toward the day of the Lord (Exod. 13:22). In Exodus, God selects law, patriarch, prophet, priest, royalty, sage — a people — to see and know the will of God, the purpose of *shalom*. The love of God and neighbor for which the world was made is now etched on the two tables of "the law . . . given through Moses" (John 1:17). This covenant deed of God is a sign of the promise that the Purposer will not give up on the divine intention; it seals a people through whom that promise will be fulfilled.

Although a special shaft of light pierces the darkness to rest upon an elect people, even in a darkened world hints of its source and goal remain, and indeed enough of a residual radiance for the narrative to make its way. Where life is, there must be light (John 1:4), enough of the subdued spark in each human to discern those conditions which make life livable. Here is the elemental perception and power God gives to the divine image in human beings that is shattered but not destroyed. Not *the* Life and *the* Light, but life and light in a general revelation and a common grace. Keeping the promise of a Noachian covenant, a gracious Providence works to keep life human in its rudiments, though not in its fundaments (Rom. 1:19-20; 2:14-15; Acts 14:19).

Seers of a particular covenantal Light transmit and interpret the special deeds of God among the people of Israel. The disclosure that comes through this witness is gathered up in the prophetic testimony of the Hebrew Scriptures. What this work of the Spirit means in providing Scripture I explore in tandem with the New Testament witness to God's definitive deed. At this point in the narrative the prophetic-apostolic testimony to God's reconciling work means the inspiration of the Scriptures.

The covenant people of God prove to be as human as everyone else; no one loves the Light. But the purpose and promise will not be turned aside. The trajectory of the pillar of fire continues in one who comes from within this people, who "was not the light, but he came to testify to the light" (John 1:8). The vision will not die — the prophetic hope for the wolf and the lamb together, the child with its hand over the asp's nest, swords beaten into plowshares and spears into pruning hooks, each person under her or his own vine and fig tree — all this comes to the burning point in a messianic longing for the One who will not only see the Light but *be* the Light, not only reflect the glory but enflesh it.

JESUS CHRIST

Thus "the Word became flesh and lived among us, and we have seen his glory, the glory as of the Father's only Son, full of grace and truth" (John 1:14, NRSV margin). With this text one comes to the center of the Christian story, the decisive deed and disclosure on which the narrative turns.

The deed accomplished by the triune God in the person and work of the Son is incarnation and atonement. God reconciles the alienated parties to the divine purpose through the work done by the Word made flesh. Only the purpose to redeem with commensurate power to effect that redemption can bond what is estranged. The place fitting for such a reunion is the very world where rebellion has had its way. Therefore the chief actor in this drama is One, truly God and truly human, who can wage the war and bring about the peace that removes the dividing walls of hostility (Eph. 2:14). So the eternal Son of the Father comes to humanity, born in a crib, growing up as a carpenter, to liberate and reconcile. From what? For what?

These questions pose the issue of atonement, the at-one-ment of the estranged parties to God's purpose, the world of human nature, nature, and transnature. What is done and what is disclosed, reconciliation and revelation, act toward and speak to this bondage in which God's partners are held. This is the fundamental meaning of liberation to which all other derivative meanings point: Jesus Christ is the deliverer from the slavery to the no that creation says to its Creator. That no is made up of the sin to which humans are in bondage (and the law with which it is bound up), the evil to which the powers and principalities are captive, and the death that ends in separation from God and a loss of the wholeness that God intends for humanity. In short, that no spells suffering, ignorance, mortality, and guilt before God.

God opens the way toward atonement through the birth, life, death, and resurrection of Jesus Christ. At Bethlehem God enters the realm of rebellion. In Galilee Jesus lives out the *agape* of radical love to God and neighbor, mercy for the sinner, and justice for the oppressed, manifesting the perfection of obedience to the Father. He preaches the good news of the coming of *shalom,* the arrival of the kingdom where righteousness rules and God is all in all. He declares that it exists among them when he is near.

On Calvary the world does its worst to the incarnate God, demonstrating the depth of its hate toward that vision in the crucifixion of the Son. Yet the very cross of the world's rebellion and shame is refashioned into the instrument of reconciliation. Jesus Christ, fully God and fully human, takes into himself the punishment that the holy God exacts of sin, the final night of death and damnation. As Luther put it, at Golgotha the divine love receives the divine wrath through the vicarious work of Christ. The cross of divine vulnerability overcomes sin and its consequences. Easter morning secures and announces that victory. The resurrection of Jesus Christ from the dead demonstrates that this life and its climactic act have ended the bondage of sin, defeated evil, and overcome death. The death that Jesus conquers is the guilt and power of sin, the futility of suffering, the finality of mortality, and the blindness of fallen bondage. By the liberating work in Christ's birth, life, death, and resurrection, God has reconciled the world to the divine intention, offering life together with himself in faith, life with neighbor and nature in love, and hope for a future beyond suffering and mortality.

THE WRITTEN WORD

Because the intent of this chapter is to describe the divine self-disclosure, it is appropriate at this point to discuss the revelatory aspect of God's reconciling act. Disclosure is integral to the deed. The value of nineteenth-century theologies of *Heilsgeschichte* as well as of twentieth-century efforts to construct biblical theology is the positioning of reconciliation at the heart of the revelation from God. In the twentieth century, however, this emphasis has often entailed the reduction of the scriptural testimony about what those events mean to the status of a human witness devoid in itself of any revelatory weight. This reduction happened either through a denial of the doctrine of the inspiration of Scripture or by such a reinterpretation of it as to remove the prophetic-apostolic testimony from the revelatory arc.[11] The end point of this development appears in hermeneutical ventures that either blur the distinction between canon and noncanonical material,[12] or treat canonical interpretations of God's deeds as merely the first community reflection on the event, different only in degree from subsequent ecclesial interpretation.[13] By contrast, in the

---

11. For a view that joins an emphasis on God's deeds with confidence in the prophetic-apostolic testimony, see William J. Abraham, *The Divine Inspiration of Holy Scripture* (New York: Oxford University Press, 1981).

12. On the canonical rim, see various writings of James Barr: *The Scope and Authority of the Bible* (Philadelphia: Westminster, 1980); *Holy Scripture: Canon, Authority, Criticism* (Philadelphia: Westminster, 1983); *Beyond Fundamentalism: Biblical Foundations for Evangelical Christianity* (Philadelphia: Westminster, 1984). Note especially the important new defense of the canon in the works of Brevard Childs, *Old Testament Theology in a Canonical Context* (Philadelphia: Fortress, 1986); and *The New Testament as Canon: An Introduction* (Philadelphia: Fortress, 1985).

13. For a wide-ranging exposition of this view, see the two volumes of Edward Schillebeeckx, *Jesus: An Experiment in Christology,* trans. Hubert Hoskins (New York: Seabury, 1979), and *Christ: The Experience of Jesus as Lord,* trans. John Bowden (New York: Seabury, 1980). For a critique of Schillebeeckx, see my "Bones Strong and Weak in the Skeletal Structure of Schillebeeckx's Christology," *Journal of Ecumenical Studies* 21 (Spring 1984): 248-77.

view of divine disclosure I have taken, the interpretation is inextricable from the deed. Thus inspiration as well as incarnation (and atonement) constitute the revelatory moment.[14]

This commitment to the cognitive weight of Scripture is a crucial evangelical witness in theology today. A doctrine of inspiration means that the Bible is not only the occasion for meeting (Barth's address of the Word, Brunner's personal encounter, Bultmann's existential decision, and the current variations on these themes — Scripture as word-event, performative communication, symbolic disclosure, the language game of the community, the rendering of an agent, the telling of stories, etc.) but also makes universal truth claims.[15] Although the prophetic-apostolic testimony is rich in expressive and evocative language, it constantly makes statements to which one must respond yes or no. Because these propositions concern life-and-death matters, they are more properly called affirmations. In any case, one can reduce revelation neither to the event as such nor to the reception of it by the engaged reader or hearer; it entails as well trustworthy language with its ontological referents. For this reason a sound understanding of inspiration is fundamental to a doctrine of revelation.

That inspiration is integral to revelation is crucial to evangelical witness. Evangelicals also agree on *why* such inspiration is necessary; they contend for its role in making propositional/ affirmational truth claims of a universal nature. They evidently agree even on *what* form this disclosure takes: verbal inspiration means the inbreathing of the Spirit into the recipients of inspiration, stirring the author and bestirring thoughts appropriate to the divine intent. But it also includes a breathing out of the words employed to express the insights given. (As Austin Farrer has argued, form cannot be separated from matter in the reve-

---

14. A move in this direction can be found in P. J. Achtemeier, *The Inspiration of Scripture: Problems and Proposals* (Philadelphia: Westminster, 1980).

15. See chapter 3 above for elaboration of this point.

latory process any more than it can in aesthetic creation.)[16] Just *how* the association of words with the Word takes place is the much-disputed question among evangelicals today.

In passing one may note the diversity of these different evangelical views, which I have discussed in chapter 1: inerrancy, which includes ultra-inerrancy, transmissive inerrancy, trajectory inerrancy, and intentional inerrancy; and infallibility, with its subcategories — unitive, essentialist, and christocentric.

Alongside these evangelical views of biblical inspiration stand the other modern positions on the authority of Scripture. (1) Some may take an ecclesial view of the text: a teaching office or tradition mediates the authority of the Bible. (2) Some insist that the deeds of God rather than assertions about them constitute revelation, as in the various traditions of *heilsgeschichtliche* or biblical theology. (3) For others a christological actualism in its various forms or an historical Jesus define the meaning of the Bible. (4) Still others hold that an experiential framework — rational, moral, aesthetic, or religious — either poses the critical questions to the text or determines the significance of it. Although some of these models of revelation exist in combination with evangelical positions, they stand outside the evangelical doctrine of inspiration as I have defined it here.

Evangelicals searching for a proper word to their post-Christian world might well ask this question: Does some common understanding of the how of inspiration bind the variety of evangelical perspectives together? I believe there is such a common understanding. The unifying point has to do with the working assumptions of most, if not all, evangelical expositors of Scripture. Now and then it surfaces as an "of course," which happens, for example, in Carl Henry's encyclopedic defense of a trajectory view of inerrancy. While making this defense Henry alludes to the heart of the matter in a brief summary that moves from the eternal purposes of God through creation, fall, the call

---

16. Austin Farrer, *The Glass of Vision* (Westminster, Md.: Dacre, 1948), pp. 43-57.

of Israel, the incarnation and atonement, the birth of the church, and the coming of salvation, to the resolution of all things at the end time.[17] The nonnegotiables of evangelical thinking on revelation are found right here, in the fundamentals. The locus classicus of inspiration means what it says, and no more: "All Scripture is inspired by God and is useful for teaching, for reproof, for correction, and for training in righteousness" (2 Tim. 3:16). Scripture is of the Spirit because it teaches these truths, it tells this story of the reconciling will and work of God. What believers have taken to be the narrative of faith, its ideas and its images, its affirmations and its idiom, is God-breathed.

Inspiration in this narrative sense means that a community of those who witness this action in one of its phases captures the overarching plot conceived in eternity and played out in the rough-and-tumble of God's engagement with a rebel creation. These seers understand it, record it, and order it canonically. The Holy Spirit so worked in this journey that the textual result is a trustworthy account of the divine intention and action. Indeed, the defining metaphors and motifs, stories and symbols in which these prophets and apostles cast their visions and affirmations, as inspired, are the Christian's code language, a guidebook of terms, a reference point for all communication and any translation of faith. Christians recognize this fact by weekly recourse in worship to the words of this Book. So too does a wider community tacitly acknowledge that same fact in its return ever again to the biblical pages as resources for the arts. This understanding of the inspiration of Scripture seems to be the functional presupposition of an evangelical perspective, whatever the differences in its outworking. The premise explicitly underlies my interpretation of God's disclosure.

---

17. Carl F. H. Henry, *God, Revelation and Authority,* 6 vols. (Waco: Word, 1976–83), 4:467-69.

CHURCH

Although the fundamental deed of reconciliation is accomplished at the center of God's history with humanity, there remains the application of the benefits of Christ's work, the narrative movement from the Already to the Not Yet, from firstfruits of the new season to harvesttime. This movement constitutes the concluding chapters of the Story: the birth of the church, the flow of the streams of salvation, and the consummation of all things. By following the biblical narrative one moves from the resurrection to the record of ensuing events and thus to the ascension of Christ (Acts 1) and the birth of the church (Acts 2).

The biblical imagery of light persists and provides a potent interpretive tool for visual and visionary times. The New Testament portrays the rising of the horizon Light of Easter to its meridian in the ascent of the Son to the right hand of the Father's glory, there to rule in his own glorified humanity. But this is no tale of abstract regency — "He's got the whole world in his hand." The manifestation of that rule is the release of the power of God's victorious purpose among humanity. So comes the descent of the Spirit of the Son of God as the tongues of Pentecostal fire.

The flames that kindled a new community also cast light that shows the new way. The deed of new birth is accompanied by a disclosure of new sight. The church is the people of God who are hearers and tellers of the deeds that have been done. They also point to the visions of what will be seen (Acts 2:17-18).

The revelatory characteristic of the church, with its new sight, is its gift of illumination, which is not the same as inspiration. Inspiration is the power the Spirit gave to eyewitnesses of God's defining deeds in order to identify these actions and disclose their inner meaning (an identification and perception that binds the church forever). Illumination is the power of the Spirit given over time in this community born at Pentecost to understand the inspired biblical story. The Spirit enjoys the mandate to interpret Scripture aright within the particularity of a time and place. Illumination is the church's light on the biblical map for its journey in the world. An exploration of the meaning of illumination in turn leads to some of the intense debates in hermeneutics today.

Illumination possesses two dimensions in its capacity to empower the church to steward the good news: it must be both faithful and fruitful. Faithful stewardship means that God gives the church the responsibility of interpreting the Scriptures and also provides means for that task. Somewhere within the church the gospel will always receive trustworthy proclamation. Fruitful stewardship means that the church is everywhere commissioned to translate the faith into terms connecting it with the issues and idiom where it lives. This aspect also carries the promise that the Spirit will somewhere be present in the church to make good this fruitfulness. The promise of faithfulness and fruitfulness constitutes the indefectibility of the church. The gift and demand of transparency to the Light are the joy and burden of good stewardship.

The weakness of the church is its difficulty in keeping these twin characteristics of illumination together. Some construe the Spirit's commission to be that of preserving the purity of the gospel in its original code language. Others understand the charge to mean the task of contemporizing the faith in the language and thought forms of modern settings. Standing alone, each of these perspectives is an inadequate understanding of ecclesial illumination. On the one hand, one must hear the good news to rejoice in it, hence telling the Story in a tongue unknown to the hearers does not edify (1 Cor. 14:2-25). On the other hand, an eagerness to be heard, understood, and accepted sometimes prompts the church to transform the message rather than translate it, editing out claims offensive to the ear of hearers. Depending on the temptation and challenge, the church may sometimes consider it more important to attend to the text (in periods of acculturation and accommodation), or at other times to the context (periods of retreat and repristination).[18] But finally the Spirit's promise of illumination is bound up with both text and context and their right interrelationship.

The full light of disclosure to a community occurs when the evangel hits home in the time and place to which it is addressed, when the text meets, illumines, and transforms the context. Why is the context a partner in this engagement? Why is it not enough for the text with its inherent power to confront and overcome the hearer regardless of the nature of the setting or of one's understanding of it? In a discussion of authority and revelation, this hermeneutical question is the counterpart to questions about the relationship of the human to the divine in Christology, ecclesiology, sacramentology, and soteriology. On the one hand, Docetic inclinations, which accord only a seeming reality to the context, or Monophysite tendencies, which undercut the significance of the context in order to exalt the divinity of the text, are a constant temptation to those who perceive themselves as guardians of the divine initiative. In this case loyalty to the text may prompt defenders to obscure the role of the human context, a particular temptation of evangelicals concerned to honor the biblical word. On the other hand, an Ebionite cum Nestorian inclination, a tendency to overstress the humanity of Scripture, attends much contemporary theology that has either newly discovered the impact of context or that carries forward a long tradition that has argued for the relevance of faith to culture.

Advocates of these views use one or another category from culture to make the faith indigenous, whether political framework, economic theory, cultural premise, psychological construct, religious sensibility, or philosophical conceptuality. The result leaves the text overwhelmed by the context. When this

---

18. In the United Church of Christ, with which I am associated, the commitment to "relevance" regularly imperils theological identity. Hence the concerned efforts in the UCC to get its doctrinal bearings. See, e.g., "Letter to Our Brothers and Sisters in Christ," from the 1984 Craigville Colloquy, *Keeping You Posted,* June 15, 1984.

happens faith is nothing more than the ideology of the moment dressed out in the language of piety. The most dangerous form of this hermeneutical illusion occurs when its adherents pay exaggerated homage to the text and make much of their suspicion of contextualization, but for all that, impart covertly a secular premise into the meaning of the text so that the modern assumption controls its interpretation.[19]

The process of translating the Scriptures provides some clues concerning the proper relationship between text and context. Thus the translator has several options. He or she may employ either a literal equivalent or a paraphrase, or conclude that neither will do and seek an alternative. The former preserves the words of the old text in a new language but may fail to convey its intention. The latter, seeking contemporaneity, may do so by reading the framework and values of the new land and language into the text, thereby violating its intended meaning. Rejecting both approaches, many translators venture a dynamic equivalence that takes into account contextual factors by the use of another idiom, but this contextual idiom is engaged as a junior partner in the dialogue. The intention of the original text, established through rigorous analysis of its meaning and pursued by close conformity to its linguistic contours, is the clear reference point for translation.[20] Revelatory illumination happens in the communication of the gospel when translators seek this kind of faithful and fruitful communication.

These reflections carry one into the debates on the hermeneutical circle. As an evangelical I assert the legitimacy of the circulation between text and context for the purpose of seeking a dynamic equivalence that ends in meaningful and true interpretation. In terms of final accountability (in contrast to the assertion of dynamism that the hermeneutical circle successfully

---

19. I have argued this point relative to political fundamentalism in *Religious Right and Christian Faith*.

20. For a discussion of these issues see D. A. Carson, ed., *Biblical Interpretation and the Church* (Exeter: Paternoster, 1984).

underscores), however, the image of a hermeneutical arrow is more apt. The contextual translation of the good news must always be accountable to the text. That text is the checkpoint for all contextualization and indigenization. One of the crucial roles that the evangelical community plays within the church is its witness to this final accountability.

The sociology of knowledge poses another controversial question in this area: How can the text be normative in this dialogue with its context when that text is always "my text" or "your text," its reading controlled by one particular social location, value system, or framework of meaning? Such a perspectivalist critique assumes that only those who share a given social location or commitment can talk to one another or have access to ultimate truth.[21] Here is a post-Christian challenge of major proportions. These assertions have just enough truth to make this position attractive within and beyond the church, because it challenges two simple assumptions about the accessibility of the text, and it does seek to honor the practical commitment that must accompany any faithful reading of the Bible. Yet there are dire consequences if this view prevails.

The truth in the perspectival analysis is related to one's overall understanding of revelation as a narrative. Human formulations of faith are truly en route, and therefore vulnerable to finitude and sin. As such they are indeed *human* affirmations about the gospel; they fall short of ultimacy; they offer insight, not sight; they are subject to enrichment and correction. Thus one must be properly self-critical of tendencies to intrude one's own agenda into the exposition of the Scriptures. The error in the perspectival view is that a radical perspectivalism disqualifies its own position as a serious partner in theological conversation. If its judgment is true, then the assertion of its own view itself

---

21. For the employment of this kind of sociology of knowledge in criticizing the aforementioned Craigville Letter, see Alfred Krass, "Evangelism, Social Action and the Craigville Colloquy," in *Seventh Angel* 1, no. 4 (September 1984): 22-23.

becomes perspectival, a weapon in the defense of its own social location and therefore no claim to universal truth.[22] Or if its view is an honest assertion of what is believed to be so, which one is to take with due seriousness, then it exempts itself from its own perspectival premise. As such, it must acknowledge that to do so in one case makes it legitimate for others to do so in their cases; what's sauce for the goose is sauce for the gander. One has no logical grounds, therefore, to deny others the right to struggle out of the mire of distortive perspectives or the hope that others can approach that goal.

A further objection to the conventional orthodoxy provided by the sociology of knowledge is that to make perspectivalism the criterion for adjudicating issues of revelation and authority is to allow the context to control the text. A view shaped by culture with its own intellectual and social history (from Karl Marx to Peter Berger, and from proletarian cadres to university departments of sociology) becomes the magisterium for interpreting Scripture and gospel. The sociology of knowledge determines the theology of knowledge. Evangelical Christians must firmly resist this reversal.

To resist, however, is not to reject its valuable lessons. Evangelicals must be prepared to honor the sovereignty and mystery of God. They must not presume to have penetrated the ultimate reaches of divine wisdom. Further, evangelicals, who should have a sharp eye for the work of sin — especially when it is cloaked in the garment of piety — should be glad to receive criticism about their own formulations. Thus evangelicals should offer a provisional welcome to the hermeneutics of suspicion. In the same way they may embrace the role of sociology as a human science enlightening the articulation of the good news, thereby recognizing context as the human underside of God's revelatory work. Yet a dialogue with context is not surrender to it: it is an engagement so that the gospel may stand forth in all its clarity and power.

---

22. A refrain in Carl Henry. See, e.g., *God, Revelation and Authority,* 1:96-111.

Still another factor in assessing the significance of perspectivalism is its effect on the life of the Christian community. On the one hand, to assert the significance of social location does give voice to marginalized constituencies and has enabled voiceless peoples to make their contribution to the catholicity of the church and the faith. Further, such constituencies have brought critical issues to the community's attention. On the other hand, pressed to its logical end, the doctrinal use of perspective in matters of authority and revelation means the Balkanization of the church (or, in more contemporary idiom, its Beirutization). If all perceptions of the text and the gospel are legitimate only because they are construed from social contexts, then no rationale or hope exists for sharing views across the barricades of social warfare. The only way one can understand what another is saying is to take up a stance within the other's camp, to capitulate to the commitments of a given locale. Or, if the boundaries are drawn by sex, race, ethnicity, class, and age, one cannot even make this transition, and one is thrown back behind the barricades.

This is a very different picture of the Body of Christ than that painted by Paul in 1 Corinthians. There, to be sure, Paul acknowledged socially rooted particularities and checked claims by any one party in the church to speak for the whole of the Body. But Paul also acknowledged the different gifts of different parts of the church, and he expressed confidence that mutual enrichment among these different parts is possible by the Spirit's work. Thus Paul urged the *agape,* or love, of 1 Corinthians 13 upon the parts of the Body in order to move beyond the boundaries of ecclesial locations and the varieties of different gifts to a mutual interpenetration and enrichment.

The Pauline counsel contains a lesson for those who claim too much for their parochial, partial perspectives, as well as for those with a hermeneutics of suspicion who have disavowed particularism but advocate their own privileged perspective as ruling out all others. Although the text of Scripture is subject to one's skewed perception, and although it does not deliver the ultimate vision of the kingdom, it is not inaccessible to the community. Therefore it can and must function as a reference and judge of one's efforts at contextualization. The lasting gift of the sociology of knowledge is to reinforce the traditional Christian assertion that the discernment of the meaning of the text is related to the wholeness of perception within the community. Christians discern its meaning when they seek it *together*, enriched by the varieties of perspective that constitute the Body of Christ.[23]

I need to say one more thing concerning questions of text and context, this time from the fuller perspective of the narrative of faith. By acknowledging the role of context in the revelatory process, I have assumed the continuous presence of creation, both its possibilities and its limitations, in the work of the Spirit. To speak of the illumination of the gospel in each new age and place is to say that God lets the narrative go forward into these ranges of being, and therefore Christians must take seriously the creation environment. Particular times and places provide the occasions for the articulation of the gospel just as the Word was made flesh in a crib and a carpenter shop. The task of Bible translation is important simply because the human linguistic context is an ever-present reality for an historic and incarnate faith.

Yet this underpinning of creation is no neutral terrain. It too bears the imprint of the story of salvation, its night and its light. These factors determine the priorities and functions of text and context. Because creation is fallen, context cannot control text. The bondage of the world means that the Light of God does not suffuse its exterior manifestations or automatically give spiritual sight to those who live in the world. By natural light the purpose of God is not self-evident. This is the reason why Christian faith is narrative. The fallen condition of the world moves God to reclaim it for the divine intention. The narrative of how God has done this reclamation makes up the good news and comes to humanity in the inspired canonical writings.

---

23. See my *Christian Story,* 1:248-49.

However benighted humans are by nature, God "has not left himself without a witness" (Acts 14:17a) in this fallen world. The divine purpose has moved the world as a covenant partner in its own journey, even apart from the special story of covenant history. To preserve the world from destroying itself by sin, the power of God gives enough clues to the purpose of God in creation to make and keep life human. These clues are the general disclosures of truth, beauty, and goodness that accomplish this purpose — universal revelation. In the incarnation and atonement Jesus Christ takes possession of what is his own, as the Logos of creation is now joined to the accomplished purpose. Thus the signs imparted to the world in creation now repossessed by their source at the center of history come to the church from culture as a vehicle for communicating the gospel to that culture.

This process of appropriation is manifest in various ways in the witness and theological work of the church. Thus the church uses a principle of coherent communication, the universal logic of the universal Logos, to interpret the Logos incarnate. So, too, elementary moral perceptions that make life livable are, in the proper setting, the avenue through which the hidden Christ comes to feed the hungry, clothe the naked, do justice, and make peace (Matt. 25:35-40). The graces of the Spirit of the Son at work in creation, fallen though the world is, offer reference points for the interpretation of the Bible. This is the normative reason for attention to context. In a given context the text honors the working of the incognito Christ, but always determines and defines the perception of that working by the norm of special revelation, Christ revealed in Scripture.

SALVATION

In the story of the events surrounding the birth of the church in the book of Acts, the invitation to faith comes after the preaching of the gospel. "Peter said to them, 'Repent, and be baptized every one of you in the name of Jesus Christ so that your sins may be forgiven; and you will receive the gift of the Holy Spirit. . . . Save yourselves from this corrupt generation'" (2:38, 40). And again after Peter's second homily, "Repent therefore, and turn to God so that your sins may be wiped away, that times of refreshing may come from the presence of the Lord" (3:19-20). The result? "And day by day the Lord added to their number those who were being saved" (2:47b).

Here is the deed of God in which grace works faith in those answering the divine beckoning. The Spirit takes the benefits of Christ's reconciling work and brings pardon *for* the believer and then power *in* the believer. This is salvation from sin and guilt by grace through faith. To God be the glory!

The Spirit, following the course of a grace that works faith, busy in love and energized by hope, brings light as well as life, indeed life through light. Faith arises because the Spirit opens the eye of faith to see the Light. Revelation is intertwined with redemption.

In the personal appropriation of the gospel, illumination becomes the concentrated ray that falls upon this life. The one who receives the good news with an authentic yes is given an understanding of the gospel, sound knowledge *(notitia),* the power to decide for it *(assensus),* and the power to trust in it *(fiducia).* This enlightenment and empowerment by the noetic and fiducial work of the Holy Spirit opens the eye of faith. Thus revelation reaches its personal destination, turning those made for the vision and service of God toward that end. The redeeming work of Christ, a work that particularizes the benefits of reconciliation, convicts and converts, and so gives personal insight, sight into the purpose of God in a darkened world — illumination of the inner eye of faith.

The configuration of means and ends, ecclesial and personal illumination in this phase of revelation, receives a dramatic exposition in the book of Acts. Thus Peter receives the gift of faithful illumination in his early sermons, which are a trustworthy accounting of the Christian narrative, with its origins in the eternal counsel of God, its enactment in creation and covenant, with the covenant community tiptoeing toward the fulfillment of Israel's hope. This hope comes in the life, death, and resurrection of Jesus Christ, so signaled by the pouring out of the Spirit in the new age in which Christ rules over all things, gathering a people to himself by the cleansing of sin through water and word, and pointing to a final day of the Lord (2:16-36; 3:11-26).

This is not an abstract tale, for the whole account is couched in the idiom and related to the issues of Peter's hearers who are of Israel. Thus Peter calls on Joel as a witness (2:17-21), David steps forward to give his testimony (2:25-28, 34-35), so too Moses (3:22-23), Abraham (3:25), Samuel, and all the prophets (3:24). Here Peter marks the particulars of Israel's encounter with Christ, and he draws the hopes of Israel into view. All this is the indigenizing, or contextualizing, of the good news, especially so in this case because this people is itself a very chapter of the Story. Yet in the larger sense this is the way illumination always happens, when text is brought into living relation to context. Here is a model of how illumination happens when the church offers its faithful account of the good news and its fruitful contextualization.

One sees the personal consequences of Spirit-empowered communication in the revelatory consequences of salvation. Fires are lit from this Light: "So those who welcomed his message were baptized, and that day about three thousand persons were added" (Acts 2:41). More: "They devoted themselves to the apostles' teaching and fellowship, to the breaking of bread and the prayers" (2:42). Furthermore: "Awe came upon everyone, because many wonders and signs were being done by the apostles. All who believed were together and had all things in common; they would sell their possessions and goods and distribute the proceeds to all, as any had need" (2:43-45). The early church enjoyed knowledge and courage that confused the powers and principalities of the day with truth and boldness. "When they had prayed, the place in which they were gathered

114

together was shaken; and they were all filled with the Holy Spirit and spoke the word of God with boldness" (4:31). Here was power and light, illumination in its fullest meaning, the application of the benefits of Christ, in community and persons, in church and in believer.

CONSUMMATION

The final chapter of the narrative points toward the consummation of the divine intention, the fulfillment of God's promise, the maturation of the Not Yet developing in the womb of the Already, incarnation and atonement. Because this event is yet to be, one trusts the biblical seers in their assertions about its approach and in their characterizations of its nature. The prophetic-apostolic testimony of the end gives a large place to the figural mode appropriate to the mystery of the Not Yet. Here are stained-glass images that give enough light, shape, and color to serve the purposes of discernment, yet that also encourage modesty about one's understanding of what lies beyond. What God grants in the visions of the end couched in the symbols of this world is the knowledge of the resurrection of the dead, the return of Christ, the final judgment, and the coming of everlasting life in its personal, social, and cosmic plenitude (1 Cor. 15; John 5:28-29; 1 Thess. 4:16; 1 Cor. 4:5; Rev. 20:12; Matt. 25:31-46; 10:28; Luke 16:19-31; John 5:25-29; 2 Thess. 1:9; Heb. 6:8; 9:27; Deut. 14:10-11; Matt. 5:8; Rev. 21:24; 5:13). What God grants to the prophets and to believers today, in this time between the times, is an assurance of this ultimate fruition, done so through signs of the kingdom given in history, as well as by bonding the justified and the sanctified, when they die, with the age to come (Luke 8:52; 1 Cor. 15:20; 2 Pet. 3:4; John 3:36; 5:24; 6:40; Luke 16:19-31; 23:43; Rev. 6:9; Rom. 8:35-39).

The doctrine of revelation accompanies Christian teaching about the final act of reconciliation, reaching thereby its own point of culmination. In the end, when God is all in all and the kingdom comes, the eye of faith becomes the eye of sight: "now we see in a mirror, dimly, but then we will see face to face. Now I know only in part; then I will know fully" (1 Cor. 13:12). Illumination as insight is turned into illumination as sight, the full disclosure of who God is and what God does.

Revelation in this ultimate sense is knowing God as one is known. "Blessed are the pure in heart, for they will see God," said Jesus (Matt. 5:8). The vision of God is the revelatory promise. John portrays this beatific vision in the richest of images: "There in heaven stood a throne, with one seated on the throne! And the one seated there looks like jasper and carnelian, and around the throne is a rainbow that looks like an emerald" (Rev. 4:2-3). Now the long-blind eyes are opened and behold this ineffable Light. Humans face the One from whom they had turned, so that they may live and love in communion with God.

To see the Envisioner is to see also the Vision, to know its suffering and its victory: "I saw between the throne and the four living creatures . . . a Lamb standing as if it had been slaughtered" (Rev. 5:6). To see by the Spirit the Father and the Son is to exult, "You are worthy, our Lord and God, to receive glory and honor and power. . . . Worthy is the Lamb that was slaughtered to receive power and wealth and wisdom and might and honor and glory and blessing!" (4:11; 5:12). To see the Light is to celebrate. The joy of thanksgiving, portended in eucharistic worship, is the service of worship and praise that issues from seeing.

Seeing the Light is seeing *by* the Light as well. The biblical portraiture of fulfillment has a horizontal as well as a vertical dimension. One sees in the Light of the glory of God the brothers and sisters in Christ. The estranged will dwell in unity: "The nations will walk by its light, and the kings of the earth will bring their glory into it" (Rev. 21:24). Revelation describes the Vision given to humanity not only in interpersonal metaphors of life together in joy and love, but also in social and political images. The powers as well as persons of this world will come together, give obedience and praise to their Maker and Redeemer, and become agents of reconciliation instead of alienation. "[He] showed me the holy city Jerusalem coming down out of heaven from God. It has the glory of God and a radiance like a very rare jewel, like jasper, clear as crystal" (21:10-11).

In its vision of things to come, the Apocalypse places "living creatures" around the throne of God. John declares, "I saw a new heaven and a new earth" (Rev. 21:1), a revivified nature that includes crystal waters, abundant crops, and flourishing forests whose "leaves . . . are for the healing of the nations" (22:2). Thus the New Testament continues and completes the prophetic vision of *shalom* in nature in which the wolf and the lamb lie down together, the child is a friend of the snake, and the desert blooms. The creation no longer groans but rejoices: "I heard every creature in heaven and on earth and under the earth and in the sea, and all that is in them, singing, 'To the one seated on the throne and to the Lamb be blessing and honor and glory and might forever and ever!'" (5:13).

The disclosure fulfilled, the deeds done, these are the things for which hope yearns and to which faith points; and these are the visions that love serves. Eschatology is inseparable from ethics. Similarly, testimony about God's disclosure is inextricably linked with deeds and words of mercy and justice in this time of suffering and hope.[24]

CONCLUSION: REVELATION'S GOOD NEWS OF GOD

In a play the characters are fully developed only when the action is completed. So too in the divine drama, God's final self-disclosure comes when humanity meets its Maker face-to-face. Yet the miracle of revelation is that the eye of faith has been given a glimpse of that encounter here and now, albeit "through

---

24. See ibid.

a glass, dimly." I have traced how this disclosure takes place in the narrative: from the *impartation* of universal revelation distorted by humanity's stumble and fall, through the central actions of the *election* of Israel and the *incarnation* of the Word, witnessed to in the *inspiration* of biblical seers, to the *illumination* of these disclosures in the life and testimony of the Christian community. Who has emerged as the chief Figure in the point-counterpoint of this action, and what has been unveiled? These are matters of theology (in its more restricted sense). The doctrine of God, therefore, is the final meaning of the revelatory journey, and I place it accordingly in this conclusion.

The Trinity

The course taken by God's revelatory arc influenced the development of the Christian doctrine of God. The earliest thought on the pattern of God's disclosure in the writings of Ignatius, Irenaeus, Hippolytus, and Tertullian took the form of an economic trinitarianism. These theologians held that an understanding of God was built up from the unfolding of the three acts of the divine drama, three stages in the great narrative. Steeped in the heritage of Israel, and knowing that they had to do with One who entered into covenant, the patristic writers and early creeds spoke of the "Maker of heaven and earth" who providentially drew the world toward its destination. With their decisive point of orientation being the deed of God in Christ, Christian interpreters knew their understanding of God could not be exhausted by simple descriptions of "the Father Almighty" but must entail a richness of being commensurate with this subsequent act: the Father has a Son. Then the sweep of events from this turning point in the life, death, and resurrection of Jesus Christ — the coming to be of the church, the forgiveness of sins, and the consummation of all things — reveals the age of the Paraclete. Here is the Spirit who proceeds from the Father through the Son.

In the biblical accounts of these three great acts, one God

118

is at work. Yet this same recital describes Father, Son, and Spirit as personal centers of action. Each, as such, is fully God, not fragmentary aspects or partial sequences of deity, or masks behind which some fourth unknown reality dwells. Economic description requires ontological distinctions — immanent trinitarian interrelationships as well as narrative development *ad extra*. Yet here one does not have polytheism, an association of independent deities, but a coinherence of the persons constituting the One who is the "Source, Guide, and Goal of all that is — to him be glory for ever!" (Rom. 11:36, New English Bible). Such a mystery of diversity in unity is the doctrine of the divine triad.

Attributes in Action

Into this trinitarian structure is poured the content of Christian belief about the character of God. A narrative perspective brings the communicable attributes to the fore. So, too, it shepherds the incommunicable attributes, which often stray into the hinterlands of philosophical speculation, toward the fields of divine action. The language of narrative participates in the two-sided, Already–Not Yet character of its trajectory. The prolepsis in Jesus Christ provides enough proximity to the realm of God to render language trustworthy, yet enough distance from the luminous end to discourage claims to replicate the discourse of eternity. Doctrinal terminology is therefore neither equivocal nor univocal but analogical.

The Story tells of a relentless, long-suffering pursuit of the unswerving purpose to bring all things together, a purpose accomplished against formidable resistance. At the heart of it are two manifest qualities, inseparably joined: holiness and love. God *is* holy love.

God is holy. The narrative from beginning to end is God's, not humanity's. As Source, Guide, and Goal, God deserves all the glory. The sorrow of the tale is humanity's determined effort to usurp the divine sovereignty. The human incapacity to carry out this devious intent demonstrates the majesty of God. The justice and judgment of God are the sharp edge of a holiness exercised against rebellion. That same majesty in its positive expression is the power to fulfill the promise of redemption.

God is love. The way and the end of divine sovereignty confute the world's fallen perspective on power. The goal of its use is not mindless obeisance to its raw exercise, but a Life with life in freedom and peace. This *shalom* of the prophet and of the kingdom of Christ comports with the way God wages the battle against the enemy. "Christ reigns from the cross." The implacable tread of the Hound is the sound of suffering. As Easter follows Good Friday, so the eschatological victory finally overcomes the no of the world, because "God's weakness is stronger than human strength" (1 Cor. 1:25). Love is holy even as holiness is loving.

A special word to the current generation may be found in this partnership of holiness and love. Those in this age who experience suffering while questing in hope can understand a word of *holy* love that speaks of a majesty that has vanquished evil and death. Knowing nothing against themselves ("Whatever became of sin?"), only by special grace can they know of a mercy that has overcome sin and guilt — a holy love.

God, who purposes and acts as holy love, is nothing less than personal. As humans are subjects of self-awareness and choosing, so God is subject. In narrative terms, "personal" means that God is Author and chief Actor in this analogical sense. At the beginning, middle, and end of the Story is the good and majestic will and work of the personal God.

Attributes of Implication

In a narrative framework one may view the qualities of deity sometimes called incommunicable or nonmoral as efforts to express dimensions of personal holy love active or implied in the history of God with humanity. One must hold tenaciously the twin qualities of holiness and love in their inseparable union in order to avoid the distortions that often appear in the doctrine of God when one or the other is eliminated or subordinated.

One can interpret the familiar "omni's" of God (i.e., omnipresence, omnipotence, omniscience) through a narrative understanding of holiness and love. To say that God is omnipotent in the context of the divine working along the time line of the Christian narrative is to say that God has the power to fulfill his chosen purpose. Such a power includes the power of self-restraint; it allows a real drama of invitation, rejection, and resistance to unfold; yet it also bespeaks a power of persistence that stubbornly endures until victory is won. Thus the vulnerability at the heart of the Story refutes human conceptions about the nature of power, because it manifests the power of powerlessness.

God is omniscient and omnipresent in like manner, knowing all that needs to be known to achieve the divine ends, and being wherever the Presence is required to accomplish that goal.

As utterly free and sovereign, the God of biblical history is self-existent, underived, the Source. As such, God is infinite, beyond and independent of all finitude, not part of or coextensive with the world. So, too, God is eternal, not constrained by time, beyond time and therefore before and after it. But the God of this transtemporal and transspatial holiness is a loving One who chooses to be with humanity — a Transcendence that risks immanence within temporality and spatiality — in it, with it, under it, while not being of it. So the amazing Story goes, shattering conventional wisdom about what infinity, eternity, and aseity are thought to be.

So too the divine immutability. Although the Greek philosopher, reflecting the mind of human experience, could not but think of divine majesty as impassible — incapable of suffering, invulnerable — the good news of God is a countervision of responsiveness, vulnerability, and readiness for long-suffering. Yet God is immutable in the way the Story reconstrues that unchangeableness in its own terms. God's purpose "to reconcile to himself all things" (Col. 1:20) is utterly unchanging, and the persistence of God in pursuing that purpose is undeviating.

121

The God of holy love revealed through the journey with humanity to the end, and shown to humanity in the central Light that illumines the whole track of history, transvalues all the values humans bring to theology proper. In God's dealings with humanity one is turned around in mind as well as in heart. Here, as in all doctrinal affirmations, one finds the way by the light of revelation, and beyond it, to the one "immortal, invisible, God only wise, in light inaccessible hid from our eyes."[25]

25. Walter C. Smith, "Immortal, Invisible, God Only Wise" (1867).

NARRATIVE THEOLOGY
IN EVANGELICAL PERSPECTIVE

OBSERVATIONS on the many meanings of "narrative" are a commonplace of narratology, and with reason. The variety of disciplines and fields of interest from which commentary on it now rises is striking, as is the diversity of points of view within each discipline and field. The extent to which the various perspectives have or have not taken one another into account makes a good story in itself.

Narrative theology, a subset of the larger narrative discussion, has the same variety and diversity. With it has come a predictable interest in sorting out its types and models. A current typology is the division of narrative theology into the views of Hans Frei and Paul Ricoeur — "biblical narrative" and "story theology," "pure narrative" and "impure narrative" — or against the background of larger questions of theological method, the cultural-linguistic vs. the experiential-expressivist approaches (also identified as the "post-liberal" and "revisionist" options).[1] One of the characteristics of current typology

---

1. On these kinds of distinctions see Gary Comstock, "Two Types of Narrative Theology," *Journal of the American Academy of Religion* 55, no. 4 (Winter 1987): 687-717; and Mark Ellingsen, *The Integrity of Biblical Narrative* (Minneapolis: Fortress, 1990), pp. 53-61. On the distinction as it relates to larger questions of theological method, see William Placher, *Unapologetic Theology* (Louisville: Westminster, 1989), passim. (I am grateful to Timothy Peebles, Todd Lake, and Elmer Colyer, students at Andover Newton,

making — including this one — is the absence of a tradition that has been the mother of narrative sensibility for large sections of the nineteenth- and twentieth-century church. I refer to "evangelical narrative." One of the ironies of this absence, incidentally, is the prominent role C. S. Lewis, a mentor to many evangelicals, plays in the larger literary discussion of narrative.

The missing evangelical voice impoverishes the current theological conversation about narrative. This circumstance may soon change; evangelicals are clearing their throats and raising their hands. Their number includes the essentially critical interventions of Carl Henry on current forms of narrative theology,[2] the yes and no reactions of Millard Erickson to the same,[3] the "perhaps, with alterations" assessments of Alister McGrath and I. M. Wallace,[4] and the approving responses of Mark Ellingsen and Clark Pinnock to one or another type.[5] Current evangelical commentary, along with the historic presence and practice of evangelical narrative, has gone largely unnoticed in the academic discussion of the subject.[6] One aim of this essay is to raise the evangelical decibel count so its voice will be heard. Another purpose is to examine specific features

---

for their testing of my ideas on these typologies and for their comments on other aspects of the subject matter in this essay.)

2. Carl F. H. Henry, "Narrative Theology: An Evangelical Appraisal," *Trinity Journal,* n.s., 8 (1987): 3-19.

3. Millard Erickson, "Narrative Theology: Translation or Transformation?" in *Festschrift: A Tribute to Dr. William Hordern,* ed. Walter Freitag (Saskatoon: University of Saskatchewan Press, 1985), pp. 30-34; and *The Word Became Flesh* (Grand Rapids: Baker, 1991), pp. 359-79.

4. Alister McGrath, "The Biography of God," *Christianity Today* 35, no. 8 (July 22, 1991): 22-24; and *The Genesis of Doctrine* (Oxford: Basil Blackwell, 1990), pp. 14-34, 52-65; I. M. Wallace, "The New Yale Theology," *Christian Scholar's Review* 17, no. 2 (December 1987): 154-70.

5. Ellingsen, *Integrity,* passim; and *The Evangelical Movement* (Minneapolis: Augsburg, 1988), pp. 364-88; Clark Pinnock, *Tracking the Maze* (San Francisco: Harper & Row, 1990), passim.

6. Hans Frei did respond to Carl Henry's views when the latter presented them to an evangelical gathering at Yale: "Response to 'Narrative Theology: An Evangelical Appraisal,' " *Trinity Journal,* n.s., 8 (1987): 21-24.

of evangelical narrative that can serve as a corrective to present views. Yet another purpose is to investigate places where evangelical narrative can learn from its conversation partners.

EVANGELICAL

In chapters 1 and 2 I have examined the meaning of "evangelical" and "evangelicalism,"[7] including the variety of subcommunities (from fundamentalists to ecumenical evangelicals), as well as the range of evangelical hermeneutics (various types of inerrancy and infallibility).[8] Each of the subcommunities is identifiable by its network of churches and para-churches, journals, publishing houses, educational institutions, advocacy movements, mailing lists, and so forth.

Nonetheless, there is fluidity, a mobility within and among the evangelical camps, and one may further subdivide the subcommunities. For example, one may divide fundamentalism between the political fundamentalism of the Christian Right and the apolitical posture of more traditional fundamentalists, or between apocalyptic fundamentalism (especially premillennialist, and within this "pretrib," "midtrib," and "posttrib") and nonapocalyptic fundamentalism (viz. postmillennial Reconstructionists). For all this diversity (regularly lost upon outside commentary, both secular and religious), the commonalities noted do give evangelicalism its identity and constitute the perspective from which I view narrative theology here.

---

7. See my article on "Evangelical, Evangelicalism," in *Westminster Dictionary of Christian Theology,* ed. Alan Richardson and John Bowden (Philadelphia: Westminster, 1983), pp. 191-92.

8. I explore these categories in *The Christian Story,* vol. 2: *Authority: Scripture in the Church for the World* (Grand Rapids: Eerdmans, 1987), pp. 61-73.

NARRATIVE THEOLOGY

Building toward a definition requires an initial distinction between a broader and narrower understanding of "narrative." In the most general sense, literary narrative is

> an account of events and participants moving over time and space, a recital with beginning and ending patterned by the narrator's principle of selection. . . . Narrative in the narrow sense [is] an account of characters and events in a plot moving over time and space through conflict toward resolution. While narrative broadly conceived includes history, as action patterned according to some interpretive horizon, the narrator in a *story* — the term to be used here for narrative in this narrow sense — plays a plotting role; the narrative defers to the intention of the author rather than the purposes of "ostensive reference" (Hans Frei). This does not mean that historical referents are excluded from the story, even crucial ones on which the tale turns, but rather that the coherence, meaning, and the direction of the events are acknowledged to be the expression of the narrator's vision. Pattern becomes plot, participants become characters, and movement has directionality through conflict toward resolution.[9]

Further, the elements of tension and surprise in the unfolding drama and the free play of the imagination in the recital have an evocative power unattainable by either bare chronicle or abstract analysis.

As I use the concept here, narrative *theology* is the discernment of a plot in the ways of God and the deployment of story as a means of describing it. One should note the variety encompassed in this idea and its current practice, ranging from narrative theologies that focus on personal or social stories, to those

---

9. Excerpted from my "Narrative Theology: An Overview," *Interpretation* 37, no. 4 (October 1983): 341.

whose subject matter is the study of Scripture's manifold tales, to those who are concerned about the overarching "cult epic" that gives the church its identity. How evangelical narrative does and does not fit into this wide-ranging conversation is the subject of inquiry here.

PERCEPTIONS OF EVANGELICAL NARRATIVE

Although references to the evangelical perspective on narrative are rare in the current discussion of narrative theology, two of the formative figures in its development have commented passingly upon it. Their perceptions provide an entry point.

Karl Barth speaks appreciatively of the lasting influence upon him of an evangelical narrativity:

> I must interpose at this point a small but sincerely grateful tribute. It is to a theologian who cannot be called great, but to whom I am greatly indebted. I refer to Abel Burckhardt, who a hundred years ago — a contemporary of the more famous Jacob Burkhardt — was the second pastor at the minster here in Basel. He composed and edited a collection of songs for children in the local district. This was the text-book in which, at the beginning of the last decade of the last century, I received my first theological instruction in a form appropriate to my then immaturity. And what made an indelible impression on me was the homely naturalness with which these very modest compositions spoke of the events of Christmas, Palm Sunday, Good Friday, Easter, the Ascension, Pentecost, as things which might take place any day in Basel or its environs like any other important happenings. . . . As these songs were sung in the everyday language we were then beginning to hear and speak, and as we joined in singing, we took our mother's hand, as it were, and went to the stall at Bethlehem, and to the streets of Jerusalem where, greeted by children of a similar age, the Saviour made His entry, and to

127

the dark hill of Golgotha, and as the sun rose to the garden of Joseph.[10]

Here a European pietism is remembered for its stewardship of biblical stories, especially so those that compose the New Testament portrait of Jesus. Barth rightly identifies the first characteristic of evangelical narrative to be discussed: the immersion in biblical stories. In passing, I note also his appreciation for the musical form in which evangelical narrative is often carried forward, a clue that I shall follow up.

Like Barth, Hans Frei alludes to an evangelical presence, though less charitably, in his account of the decline of biblical hermeneutics in eighteenth-century hermeneutics:

> Such sense of a narrative framework as continued to exist among religious . . . readers was now no longer chiefly that of providentially governed biblical history. In that scheme . . . every present moral and historical experience had been fitted into it by bestowing on the present experience a figural interpretation that adapted it into the governing biblical narrative. All this had now changed. Such narrative sense as remained in the reading of the Bible found the connective tissue which served simultaneously as its own effective thread to the present experience in the present history of the soul's conversion and perfection. . . . In evangelical piety [the] relation is reversed; the atoning death of Jesus is indeed real in its own right and both necessary and efficacious for the redemption of the sinner. Nonetheless, though real in his own right, the atoning Redeemer is at the same time a figure or type of the Christian's journey; for this is the narrative framework, the meaningful pattern within which alone the occurrence of the cross finds its

---

10. Karl Barth, *Church Dogmatics,* IV/2, trans. G. W. Bromiley, ed. Bromiley and T. F. Torrance (Edinburgh: T. & T. Clark, 1958), pp. 112-13. David Ford calls attention to this tribute in *Barth and God's Story* (Frankfurt am Main: Peter Lang, 1981), p. 16.

applicative sense. What is real, and what therefore the Christian really lives, is his own pilgrimage; and to its pattern he looks for the assurance that he is really living it.[11]

Frei finds narrative still at work, but it has been relocated from the Scriptures to the believer's spiritual journey. Bracketing an evaluation of Frei's judgment that personal appropriation constitutes relocation, one can surely assert that evangelicalism brings to the fore subjective soteriology, the personal "*application* of the benefits*" of the work of Christ. Here then is a second aspect of the evangelical story tradition, its *pro me* accent, the emphasis on "my story." Its background is the conversion experience and the continuing companionship of the believer with Christ.

A third feature of evangelical narrative is missing in both these characterizations: "the God Story," the encompassing biblical narrative. Evangelical theology and piety never lost this grounding in first things, the great narrative that runs from creation to consummation, with its center in the life, death, and resurrection of Jesus Christ. More often latent than patent in its piety, its lines are more clearly discernible in its formal theology. The emphasis upon and special interpretation of this macrostory, along with the already mentioned accent on biblical stories and existential appropriation of Story, constitute my subject matter here.

THE GOSPEL SONG AND EVANGELICAL STORY

Lex orandi, lex credendi. From the earliest centuries, doctrine came alive and was preserved in worship. The ways of worship included singing as well as praying.[12] In like manner, evangelical

---

11. Hans Frei, *The Eclipse of Biblical Narrative* (New Haven: Yale University Press, 1974), pp. 141-42.

12. An early Christian hymn, *Phos hilaron*, preserves the church's teaching about the unity of first and second persons of the Trinity:

Serene Light of the Holy Glory

hymnody gives one a view of evangelical theology. As Barth found in the pious hymns of Abel Burckhardt evidences of evangelical narrative, I shall turn to the gospel song. Indeed, the gospel song — music rising out of the matrix of, and written for participants in, evangelical piety — provides the data for tracking the three features of evangelical narrative I have identified.

In gospel songs from the late nineteenth century forward, with a bulge in the early decades of the twentieth century, both the word and the theme *story* appear with regularity. What Sunday school pupil, Sunday night service worshiper, or revival-born Christian can forget "We've a Story to Tell to the Nations," "I Love to Tell the Story," "Tell Me the Stories of Jesus," "Tell Me the Old, Old Story," "I Think When I Read That Sweet Story of Old"? A closer look at some of these songs, and those that may not use the story terms but still tell a tale, elucidates the topic at hand.

The most prominent feature of gospel song narratology is the note of *personal* story. Thus the practice of evangelical "testimony" happens in singing as well as saying. In its songs, the language of the soul's salvation story is everywhere: C. H. Morris's ("Mrs.") "Calvary" — "I love the story sweet and old, of Christ who died for me; the sweetest story ever told, of pardon bought on Calvary"; F. H. Rowley's "I will sing the wondrous story of the Christ who died for me. How he left his home in glory for the cross of Calvary"; Fanny Crosby's "Blessed Assurance," with its chorus line, "This is my story, this is my song, praising my Saviour all the day long"; James Rowe's "His Grace Is Satisfying Me" — "The story telling, His praises swelling, for grace is satisfying me" — and his "Everywhere I Go" — "The lost shall hear the story of my Saviour's love for me." Other

Of the Father Everlasting
Jesus Christ.

On this and the use of light imagery in doctrine see Jaroslav Pelikan, *The Light of the World* (New York: Harper & Brothers, 1962), p. 31 and passim.

songs, some without the language of story as well as those with it, include these: "Wounded for Me," "He Lifted Me," "Jesus Loves Even Me." . . .

Along with the subjectivity of evangelical piety is its commitment to Scripture, a second feature of evangelical narrative. Thus the entreaty to "tell me the stories of *Jesus* . . ." and the telling of them, and other stories as well, in the songs themselves: Catherine Hankey's "I love to tell the story of unseen things above, of Jesus and his glory, of Jesus and his love"; Jemima Luke's "I think when I read that story of old when Jesus was here among men, how he called little children as lambs to his fold. I should like to have been with them then"; Fanny Crosby's "Tell me the story of Jesus, write on my heart every word. Tell me the story most precious, sweetest that ever was heard"; Charlotte Homer's "Awakening Chorus" — "Awake and sing the blessed story . . . the Lord Jesus reigns and sin is backward hurled" (women storytellers are prominent throughout the gospel song tradition); A. H. Ackley's "Let God use you to tell the old, old story . . . some heart needs a friend like Jesus, some sin-sick soul that stumbles alone"; A. P. Cobb's "Do you know the story that the wise men heard as they journeyed afar?" The stories range throughout the Bible, as in Carl Boberg's "How Great Thou Art" — "O Lord, My God, when I in awesome wonder consider all the worlds thy hands have made. . . . And when I think that God his Son not sparing sent him to die, I scarce can take it in." African-American gospel songs — "slave songs," "spirituals" — are especially focused on biblical stories, with all their powerful implications for present circumstances: "Go Down, Moses"; "Joshua Fit the Battle of Jericho"; "Go Tell It on the Mountain"; "My Lord Delivered Po' Daniel"; "Mary Don't You Weep"; "Jesus Walked on the Water and so Raised the Dead"; "Were You There When They Crucified My Lord?"

Latent in the individual stories told is a larger plot. The tale of creation, the fall, the covenant with Noah, God's election of Israel, the coming and redemptive deed of Jesus Christ, the birth of the church, the salvation of souls and sometimes of society, the hope for the final resolution in the end times — all this is the big Story. The overarching tale makes its presence felt from time to time in the gospel song: so Arthur Spooner's eschatological "Sometime, Somewhere" — "Sometime, somewhere, over the hill-tops of glory, shine the fair streets of gold; wonderful, wonderful story, never has half been told." The full sweep of the Story is found in the title, verses, and refrain of the well-known hymn "We've a Story to Tell to the Nations." At its center is the chapter on which the evangelical tale turns: "The Lord who . . . hath sent us His Son to save us . . . who the path of sorrow has trod. . . ." God's saving deed in Christ is set within a history of alienation that moves toward final reconciliation, as in the summary themes of the refrain: "For the darkness shall turn to dawning, and the dawning to noonday bright. And Christ's great kingdom shall come on earth, the kingdom of love and light."

I must admit that it is much harder to find the overarching biblical narrative in the gospel song, because the mood of testifying puts the personal and the specific tales of Scripture to the fore. Hence the themes picked up by Barth and Frei. Nevertheless, the big Story is integral to evangelical faith and is presupposed in its piety. For rendering explicit what is implicit in the gospel song, the systematics tradition of evangelical theology is revealing. A review of standard textbooks shows that evangelical theologians follow the familiar loci: after prolegomena come God/Trinity, creation, fall, Christology, soteriology, ecclesiology, eschatology.[13] These are expositions of the doctrines that rise from the narrative sequence in both Scripture and the ancient creeds. In the former case, the Story runs from Genesis to Revelation (so the 1909 multivolumed evangelical work, *The*

---

13. As in the older systematics works of Charles Hodge, *Systematic Theology;* Augustus Strong, *Systematic Theology;* Edgar Young Mullins, *The Christian Religion in its Doctrinal Expression;* and the current ones of Millard Erickson, *Christian Theology;* James Leo Garrett, *Systematic Theology;* and Gordon Lewis and Bruce Demarest, *Integrative Theology.*

Bible and its Story: Taught by One Thousand Picture Lessons). In the latter — the Apostles' and Nicene creeds — the drama moves from the mission of the Father in creation (paragraph 1, act I), to the mission of the Son (paragraph 2, act II), to the mission of the Spirit (paragraph 3, act III).

As Peter Toon points out,[14] Scottish divine James Orr (1844–1913) went a step further in discerning the overall narrative pattern in evangelical faith:

> What a singular *parallel* there is between the historical course of dogma, on the one hand, and the scientific order of the text-books on systematic theology on the other. . . . [After prolegomena] follow the great divisions of the theological system — Theology proper, or the doctrine of God; Anthropology, or the doctrine of man, including sin (sometimes a separate division); Christology, or the doctrine of the Person of Christ; Soteriology (Objective), or the doctrine of the work of Christ, especially the Atonement; Subjective Soteriology, or the doctrine of the application of redemption (Justification, Regeneration, etc.); finally, Eschatology, or the doctrine of the last things.[15]

As Toon points out, the analogy is somewhat forced (it leaves out the doctrine of the church and the place of Israel, and is only one possible reading of the history of doctrinal distillation). Nevertheless, it exemplifies the working assumption of evangelical theology regarding the sequence of the loci and an imaginative proposal that the narrative of divine deeds is repeated in the history of doctrine.

Carl Henry, today's best-known evangelical theologian, has written a six-volume work on what he calls "religious epistemology," *God, Revelation and Authority*. In fact, it is a

---

14. Peter Toon, *The Development of Doctrine in the Church* (Grand Rapids: Eerdmans, 1979), pp. 62-70.
15. Quoted in ibid., p. 67.

systematics that covers the loci, albeit with the problematic of revelation/authority as the organizing principle. At a crucial juncture in the argument, Henry reflects on the skeletal structure of Scripture. It turns out to be the Story — albeit with Henry-like accents:

> The unity of the Bible is not to be found in its literary genres nor in its human writers. It is found in the message and meaning of the book, namely, that the living sovereign God stands at the beginning of the universe — man and the worlds — as Creator and Governor, and at the end of history as final Judge; that he made mankind in his likeness for moral rectitude and spiritual fellowship and service; that human revolt precipitated disastrous consequences for humanity and the cosmos; that the manifested mercy of God, extended first to the Hebrews, proffers the only prospect of salvation; that the divine promise of deliverance, disclosed in the course of Hebrew redemptive history to the prophets, finds its fulfillment in Jesus of Nazareth; that the incarnation, crucifixion and resurrection of the Logos of God mark the beginnings of the new and final age; that the church is a new society of regenerate persons of all races and nations over whom Christ presently rules; that the history of mankind has a dual track, issuing in final and irreversible doom for the impenitent and in eternal blessing for the righteous; that Christ will return in awesome vindication of the holy will of God, to judge men and nations, and will in the resurrection of the dead conform the people of God to his moral image; that the benefits of redemption will embrace all creation both in a final subordination of evil and of the wicked, and in the eternal vindication of righteousness.[16]

Thus the third feature of evangelical narrative is latent in its hymnody and patent in its systematic theology. Together these

---

16. Carl F. H. Henry, *God, Revelation and Authority,* 6 vols. (Waco: Word, 1976–83), 4:468.

themes provide a working definition: Evangelical narrative is the linkage of the Christian Story to the believer's story through biblical stories. It is the Christian faith lived at the juncture of personal, ecclesial, and biblical narrative.

How then does this definition and how do these refrains relate to the current discussion of narrative theology?

EVANGELICAL STORY
AND NARRATIVE THEOLOGY

First, my story, biblical stories, the great Story — the three dimensions of evangelical narrative — bear a marked resemblance to three types of current narrative theology. I identify these types as *life story, canonical stories,* and *community story.*[17]

The life-story model is a response to what William Doty describes as "the cloture of science, the emptiness of mass-speak . . . the tyranny of definitions and dogma."[18] Theologies of this stripe challenge modern captivity to the cerebral, rationalistic, and technocratic, call upon both individuals and victim communities to resist oppressive structures and authoritarian systems by honoring and telling their own stories, personal or collective, and reread or redo Christian faith in the context of experiential narrative.[19] For some, retrieval of narrative identity means recovery of the very narrative shape of human existence.[20] Narrative theology so conceived not only urges the

---

17. See my "Narrative Theology," pp. 343-51.

18. William G. Doty, "The Stories of Our Times," in *Religion as Story,* ed. James B. Wiggins (New York: Harper & Row, 1975), p. 94.

19. See Wiggins, *Religion as Story,* passim; Lonnis Kliever, *The Sheltered Spectrum* (Atlanta: John Knox, 1981); John Navone and Thomas Cooper, *Tellers of the Word* (New York: LeJacq, 1981); Johan Baptist Metz, *Faith in History,* trans. David Smith (New York: Seabury, 1980); and Robert McAfee Brown, "My Story and 'The Story,'" *Theology Today* 22 (July 1975): 166-73.

20. Stephen Crites, "The Narrative Quality of Experience," *Journal of the American Academy of Religion* 39, no. 3 (September 1971): 291-311. For Roman Catholic and Reformation variations on the experience cum faith

telling of personal and social tales, but also probes autobiography and biography for their revelatory significance.[21]

A second constellation of narrative theologies is found in the field of biblical studies. Here the special dynamisms of scriptural story are explored: the creation of an alternative world into which the reader is drawn;[22] the honoring of ambiguity, complexity, indeterminacy;[23] the construction of imaginative cumulative narratives;[24] the expressive and transformative power of story, especially parable.[25] Features of the life-story model reappear in the last version, which holds the biblical stories to be polyvalent in meaning with a richness commensurate with myriad life situations. Thus the Bible comes alive as I let it "look me in the eye."[26]

Community story is a third type distinguished by its view of narrative as the tale that gives unity to Scripture and also shapes ecclesial identity. It is accessed, or speaks its own Word, only within its rightful hermeneutical community, the church. This biblical cum community narrative may be the overarching Story that runs from Genesis to Revelation, or the central story within it — the life, death, and resurrection of Jesus Christ. To tell this Story is to assure its faithful proclamation in the teaching

---

themes, see also John S. Dunne, *A Search for God in Time and Memory* (Notre Dame: University of Notre Dame Press, 1977); and Robert Paul Roth, *The Theater of God: Story in Christian Doctrines* (Philadelphia: Fortress, 1985).

21. James McLendon, Jr., *Theology as Biography* (Nashville: Abingdon, 1974).

22. Erich Auerbach, *Mimesis: The Representations of Reality in Western Literature,* trans. Willard R. Trask (Princeton: Princeton University Press, 1953).

23. Robert Alter, *The Art of Biblical Narrative* (New York: Basic Books, 1985).

24. James Barr, "Some Thoughts on Narrative, Myth and Incarnation," in *God Incarnate: Story and Belief,* ed. A. E. Harvey (London: SPCK, 1981), pp. 14-23.

25. John Dominic Crossan, *The Dark Interval* (Niles, Ill.: Argus Communications, 1975).

26. As Amos Wilder puts it. See his *Jesus' Parables and the War of Myths* (Philadelphia: Fortress, 1982).

and preaching of the church; to embody it in its worship, prayer, and praise; and to conform the behavior of the community to it, resisting all efforts to displace it by the culture's agendas. I shall give attention to one version of community story that developed in the Frei-Lindbeck tradition.

Evangelical narrative can enter into fruitful encounter with each of these constituencies. As the conversation develops, it has a word to speak and also one to hear. It is helpful to eavesdrop on the exchange.

LIFE STORY AND EVANGELICAL NARRATIVE

The *pro me* character of evangelical narrative suggests its readiness to affirm and appropriate aspects of personal life-story narrative theology. Giving one's personal testimony is in the family of storytelling that includes such diverse progeny as the therapy that requires the sharing of one's journey in addiction and the feminism that asserts the dignity of women by refusal to allow the oppressors' categories to define reality. In principle, evangelicals should be ready to acknowledge these siblings, although they may more readily welcome the therapeutics of the former than the politics of the latter, to judge by the fare on the shelves of Christian bookstores. Indeed, one could make a case that the twelve-step version of storytelling is traceable to evangelical roots by way of the pietism of the former's Oxford group lineage. Ownership of origins apart, a doctrine of general revelation usually associated with evangelicalism can provide a warrant for acknowledging these secular graces.

Evangelical narrative will be critical, however, of any point of view that rests its narrative case with celebrations of affect (autobiography or biography), or reads the Christian Story as a species of the genus (universal experiential story). Biblical narrative has an integrity of its own and cannot be absorbed into human experience as such. Although Christian faith and personal journey are inseparable, they are also distinguishable.

137

One is "redemption accomplished" and the other is "redemption applied."[27] Behind this fundamental distinction lies the evangelical assessment of the human condition, fallen and therefore both soteriologically and epistemologically wanting. Only the person and work of Christ can make possible the soul's saving story. An evangelical no must be spoken to construals that reduce narrative theology to life stories of one kind or another.

The strengths of evangelical narrative carry with them related weaknesses. The tradition of personal testimony does not easily lend itself to social, indeed, sociological, awarenesses and actions. Personal piety can fall prey to a pietism innocent of corporate and systemic realities. Evangelicalism, with significant exceptions past and present, has too often left it to others to call to account tyrannical social systems and do the difficult long-term work of organizing power to contest privilege. Its individualistic tendencies need to be challenged by the advocates of "social life story." ("Justice and peace" evangelicals who carry forward a long minority tradition of social witness are proof that this kind of expanded vision is possible.)

Evangelicalism's sometime absorption in personal story also needs to be regularly reminded that Christian narrative has to do first and foremost with the *God* Story — indeed its own working assumption. Hence the custodians of the community story, with their emphasis on the defining deeds of God, have a word to speak here as well. The "I, me, and mine" so prominent in gospel songs in general, and story hymnody in particular, can be the sign of a narcissistic piety if not held firmly in relationship to what God has done, is doing, and will do.

---

27. As in John Murray, *Redemption: Accomplished and Applied* (Grand Rapids: Eerdmans, 1955, repr. 1980).

CANONICAL STORIES
AND EVANGELICAL NARRATIVE

Evangelicalism challenges reductionist tendencies in literary-critical, critical-consciousness, and historical-critical readings of the canonical stories.

Evangelicals contend that scriptural stories mean just what they say. Hence "plain meaning" becomes a working principle of interpretation in association with "the analogy of faith" — clearer texts in canonical context clarifying murkier ones. One can identify evangelical hermeneutical commitments here as the "common sense" and the "canonical sense" of a biblical story.[28] The former means reading Scripture as one would a news report — or an essay arguing the literary-critical, historical-critical, or critical-consciousness points of view: word in sentence, sentence in paragraph, paragraph in the next defining literary unit, and so on. The latter means that what is discerned as the apparent meaning coheres with, and is illumined by, comparable Scripture and by the overall pattern of canonical teaching.

Narrative theologies that look to Scripture essentially for reinforcement of political, social, or economic agendas — usually on the grounds of a hermeneutics of suspicion that holds that texts are always read and, indeed, written perspectively by the wielders of power — eliminate the authorial intention of the story proper (the common sense) and the Authorial intention of the story discernible within the overall biblical pattern of teaching (the canonical sense). In the same way, narrative theologies that fix upon the evocative and expressive function of biblical stories, with their ethical and aesthetic fertility — often on the grounds of the inherent inaccessibility of textual intentions — regularly turn exegesis into eisegesis. Evangelicals bring to this encounter a doctrine of the inspiration of Scripture that compels respect for the authority of the intended meaning and resists captivity of the Bible to any extraneous program.

---

28. See my *Christian Story,* 2:160-70, 176-210, 254-340.

In both cases, ironies abound. Forms of narrative theology that reject evangelical allegiance to textual intentions as a dehistoricized, illusory objectivism insist upon equivalents to common and canonical senses in the act of publicly presenting their own hermeneutical theories. A serious textual argument for an historicist or a subjectivist perspective assumes that one can discuss publicly the intended meaning of the words and sentences employed.

Evangelical narrative also collides with a reduction of biblical stories to "the world in back of the text." The hermeneutic that delimits the meaning of Scripture to "the assured results of historical criticism" turns the Bible over to a new magisterium. The universality of access presupposed by the evangelical belief in perspicuity must challenge elitist exegesis. Further, the character of biblical literature is self-involving, and as such requires the *pro me* encounter to which an evangelical hermeneutic is also committed and for which no historical-critical approach, standing alone, is adequate.

Although evangelical narrative has its just complaints against reductionist readings of biblical stories, it also has things to hear from these sources. An application of evangelicalism's own acknowledgment of human finitude and sin, on the one hand, and the majesty and mystery of God, on the other, should make for more restraint in claims about the ease with which one accesses the plain meaning of biblical stories. Thus critical scholarship rightly makes a contribution when it seeks to discover the literary or historical context, while being self-critical about its own ideological possibilities. It can thus enrich (*bene esse,* not *esse*) one's grasp of a text's meaning.[29] Also, a critical consciousness can alert one to the social location and vested interests that skew readings of what biblical stories appear to say or have been said to mean in evangelical exegesis. A corrective to this is a *community* reading of biblical texts, an ecumenical conversation

---

29. Ibid., pp. 170-76.

among the many parts and perspectives in the Body of Christ.[30] The unearthing of "hidden histories" and the finding of untold stories in Scripture by oppressed peoples are genuine gifts to be received. So, too, personal significances can be richer and more unpredictable than the standard framework of evangelical interiority allows. Thus canonical stories have a take as well as a give.

COMMUNITY STORY
AND EVANGELICAL NARRATIVE

In this category the big Story comes center stage. Here I give attention to the ways in which evangelical narrative is focused on both the comprehensive Story and its central chapter.

In recent years, the "Yale theology" has been a prominent exponent of the community model of narrative theology. Hans Frei's comparison of Scripture to a nineteenth-century realistic novel and George Lindbeck's argument for a cultural-linguistic understanding of Christian doctrine are standard features of its exposition. In both cases, "narrative" functions as a way of faithfulness to the Word, and a key to preserving the integrity of the Christian community. The biblical narrative creates a world of its own, one not knowable by, or translatable into, the culture's regnant assumptions, with the identity of its chief Character, the God incarnate in Jesus Christ, rendered only as the story unfolds. Its lineaments are discernible in the lore and life together of the Christian community and through the agency of its interpretive skills. Faithfulness entails loyalty to its language world and the behavior commensurate with it. Peril to the community, its charter, grammar, and conduct, comes from proposals to substitute experiences, concepts, methodologies, and moral norms alien to the Tale and its telling.

On the face of it, evangelical narrative has marked simi-

---

30. Ibid., pp. 166-70.

larities with this kind of community narratology: the concern for the integrity of the comprehensive Christian Story and its christological center; the wariness about external categories taking the gospel hostage; the retrieval of a commonsense reading of Scripture; the assertion of the unity of Scripture; the acknowledgment of the role of classical tradition in the formulation of faith. But the resources from culture upon which both Frei and Lindbeck draw to state the case for narrative — the nineteenth-century novel genre, cultural anthropology, and language theory — can play such a decisive role in the interpretation of Christian faith, and do so among some of its advocates, that fundamental assumptions of historic Christian belief can be either obfuscated or eliminated. One confronts here another irony: a point of view wary of standard apologetics, because of its tendency to accommodate to its culture, itself flirts with this same possibility. How is this so?

Does the espousal of the gospel as a narrative along the lines of a realistic novel require, as such, a reality that corresponds to it? Mark Ellingsen, an interpreter of this version of narrative theology, says: "As preachers and teachers, when reading and telling biblical stories, our first responsibility is to expound them with the same literary style and imagination with which they were written. . . . There is no insistence as an article of faith or presupposition that the biblical accounts must have happened."[31] Ellingsen's judgment reflects Hans Frei's insistence upon the distinction between the "history-like" accounts of the realistic novel and historical writing accountable to "ostensive" referents. If one presses this principle to its limit, key events in the history of Israel, Jesus Christ, and the church would not be empirically necessary for the overall narrative to serve its function of assuring the integrity of the message and defining the boundaries of Christian community. In principle, the nonnecessity of ontological correspondence would include metaphysical

31. Ellingsen, *Integrity,* p. 23.

as well as physical referents. Does a narrative theology so conceived *require* that the chief Character in the Story correspond to the One who is and does?

Parallel to the logical nonnecessity of physical or metaphysical referents in the Frei tradition of narrative theology is the implication in Lindbeck's version of the Yale theology that "propositions" with their entailment of objective truth claims represent an alternative view of doctrine to the proffered cultural-linguistic framework. Thus Roman Catholic theologian Avery Dulles, with similar interests on this point as evangelical theology, observes: "For me, the church's claim to impose a doctrine in the name of revelation implies a claim of conformity to the real order, rather than a mere claim or power to regulate language."[32]

Evangelical theology sharply opposes any understanding of narrative theology that does not require the correspondence of the chapters in the Christian Story to "the real order." The Story is true to life as well as true for believers. As I. M. Wallace states it:

> Clearly, the Yale theologians . . . are not threatened by the "scandal of particularity" characteristic of the biblical texts and Christian doctrines (e.g. the belief that Jesus Christ is the Son of God). But what truth-claims, if any, do such faith-specific statements make? Can we ever say that such claims are statements about the world "out there" beyond the church's "in here" appropriation of its founding persons and events? Is theological discourse something more than a *witness* which instantiates certain grammatical rules (Lindbeck, Holmer), something more than a literary *interpretation* of biblical stories (Frei)? Does not theology also make *assertions* that refer *extra nos* to realities that exist independently of this grammar and these stories?[33]

---

32. Avery Dulles, "Observations on George Lindbeck's *The Nature of Doctrine*" (paper given at the Divinity School, Yale University, Sept. 14, 1984), p. 10.

33. Wallace, "New Yale Theology," p. 167.

One must make an important distinction here between both Lindbeck's and Frei's own use of the cultural-linguistic model of doctrine and the requirements of the model as such. Bruce Marshall has shown that Lindbeck's "postliberal" understanding of doctrine does not exclude propositional truth claims.[34] That is, the way correspondence truth claims for doctrine/story are warranted is by coherence with the "web" of Christian belief and behavior. Lindbeck agrees with Marshall's interpretation, commending him for saying it better than he succeeded in doing in *The Nature of Doctrine*.[35]

In his exchange with Carl Henry about the ontological touchstones of Scripture, Frei questions Henry's "clear and distinct ideas" about both physical and metaphysical truth but does affirm key christological referents:

> "Reference" is a difficult thing to get hold of even though one wants to refer. . . . I did not mean to deny reference at all, as Henry worries I do. . . . I don't think any of us want to. . . . Of course, I believe in the "historical reality" of Christ's death and resurrection, if those are the categories we employ. . . . If I am asked to speak in the language of factuality, then I would say, yes, in those terms, I have to speak of an empty tomb. In those terms I have to speak of a literal resurrection. But [with this qualification] I think those terms are not privileged theory-neutral, trans-cultural, an ingredient in the structure of the human mind and of reality always and everywhere for me, as I think they are for Dr. Henry.[36]

Usage made of the interpretive categories aside, even by their initiators, an evangelical critique of this type of narrative

---

34. Bruce Marshall, "Aquinas as a Post-Liberal Theologian," *Thomist* 53, no. 1 (July 1989): 353-402.

35. George Lindbeck, "Response to Bruce Marshall," *Thomist* 53, no. 1 (July 1989): 403-6.

36. Hans Frei, "Response to 'Narrative Theology: An Evangelical Appraisal,'" pp. 23-24.

theology questions the logic of a perspective that does not require ontological truth claims for the decisive historical and transcendent referents in its Story.

Evangelicalism has its own limitations in its deployment of features of community narrative. The often hidden character of the overarching biblical narrative invites misunderstanding. Its lower profile may have to do with these factors:

1. The entry point to faith for evangelicals is Christian experience, a "heart strangely warmed." Thus the personal appropriation of the gospel becomes paramount. It is a short step from this to the anthropomorphism about which Frei complains.

2. Suspicions about the role of tradition in evangelicalism mean that the resource role of the church in identifying the essentials of evangelical faith can become neglected. In the community model of narrative theology, the church plays an active part in discerning and carrying forward the centralities through its confessions of faith and liturgical traditions. Thus the big Story is embedded in the classical creeds, the lectionary readings of the church year, and the sacramental life (e.g., the eucharistic prayer in ecumenical liturgies, an act of thanksgiving that takes the worshiper from creation to Christ to consummation).

3. When evangelical theologians speak about "the basics," they often do so in strict propositional form. Thus what is historically "an unfolding drama"[37] is discursively organized and methodically classified. Evangelical insistence that revelation is what God says as well as what God does is a crucial point being made here. But although propositions are necessary, they are not sufficient. When the Epic of God is "pinned and classified like a butterfly in a collector's case" (J. B. Metz), the narrative quality of faith is dissolved into a proposition*ism*.

In each of these respects, evangelicalism's case for narrative would be strengthened by insights garnered from advocates of community narrative.

---

37. See Bernhard W. Anderson, *The Unfolding Drama of the Bible* (Philadelphia: Fortress, 1988).

CONCLUSION

For all its limitations, evangelical narrative has a corrective word to speak to the narrative theologies on the present scene. More than that, its attempt to hold together the three features of personal story, biblical stories, and the macrostory contrasts with the reductionist tendencies found in each of these types. A Christian story worth telling is an encompassing one that rises out of Scripture's intentions as interpreted and lived out by a faithful church and personally appropriated by the believer. May the evangelical voice be heard and its presence welcomed at the table of today's raconteurs.

THE PLACE OF ISRAEL
IN CHRISTIAN FAITH

HAS the church replaced Israel in the drama of redemption?
Have the chosen people been superseded with the coming of
Christ? Are replacement and supersessionist views in Christian
theology the cause of anti-Semitism and its most horrifying
result, the Holocaust? If the covenant with Israel continues after
Christ, does that include the promise of ancestral lands? Where
does the uprising of the Palestinian people (the *Intifada*) fit into
the purposes of God for the Jewish people?

Wrenching theological questions underlie the political issues in the Middle East and interfaith matters very close to
home. Pastors and congregations face them daily with Jewish
(and Arab) neighbors. Theologians have agonized over them in
a rash of volumes since World War II that could fill a library,
and official church bodies have produced their own shelf of
studies and statements. What follows, initially, is a survey of the
range of opinion on the subject (which some call "Israelology")
within the Christian community today. Because caricatures
abound, I try to identify the variety of points of view, which are
often highly nuanced. The organizing principle is the issue of
"supersessionism vs. antisupersessionism," as much of the current debate describes it. Following this review, I take a position
— an "evangelical antisupersessionism" that attempts to learn
from the current debate and exegete Paul's struggle with the
subject in Romans 9–11. As such, it is my tribute to Klaus

147

Bockmuehl's evangelical passion and commitment to biblical authority.

SUPERSESSIONIST PERSPECTIVES

Retributive Replacement View

The Church Is Israel Now is the title of a book distributed by the reconstructionist movement of J. H. Rushdoony. It asserts: "When the Israelites obeyed God, God loved them, but when they turned from him, he hated them, stripping them of their Israelite status. After centuries of Israelite rebellion against God, culminating in their rejection of Jesus the Messiah, the titles, attributes and blessings of Israel were transferred to all who accept Jesus Christ as Lord and Savior, and to no one else, regardless of Abrahamic descent. The Church is Israel now."[1] This assertion of the displacement of Israel by the church baldly states the supersessionist premise: the covenant with Israel has been abrogated by the coming of Christ and the birth of the church. Here the author goes further in a declaration of the divine "hate" for a disobedient Israel, one that carries with it the implication that God cursed Jews for rejecting Christ.

The retributive replacement view holds that the rejection of Christ both eliminates Israel from God's covenant love and provokes divine retribution. Thus in this view the history of Israel's suffering is the result of its refusal to accept Christ as its Lord. Such a view also gives tacit, if not explicit, licence to humans to be an agency of the divine retribution. The later Luther's two-hundred-page diatribe against the Jews and his "seven steps" for their silencing, dispossession, exile, and the burning of their synagogues and prayer books are an outworking of the retributive premise. Nazis employed these writings in

---

1. Charles D. Provan, *The Church Is Israel Now* (Vallecito, Calif.: Ross House Books, 1987), back cover.

their own programs. (The early Luther had very different views.)[2] Retributive replacement theology has regularly provided the justification for anti-Semitic acts that extend to Klan reprisals and the Holocaust. The churches, including the reconstructionist movement, regularly deny the logic of humans implementing the divine wrath, although they see the suffering of Jews at the hands of others as divine retribution.[3]

This view places no theological significance on the present state of Israel, because the church as a "spiritual Israel" has no geographic or ethnic location.

Nonretributive Replacement View

A softer version of replacement characterizes much formal supersessionist thinking today, and has done so also in historic Christian theology. In this case, the focus is on the unique act of God in Christ, rather than the displacement of Israel by the church. It stresses the singular person of Christ, truly human, truly God, truly one, as in the Chalcedonian formula, and the unique atoning work, especially as it is effected in the death and resurrection of Christ. This "once-happened" person and work inaugurates the new age, although one may find anticipations of it in Israel's covenant. But the new covenant displaces the old covenant.

Who would not want to live in the light of the new age? How can Christians not determinedly share the salvation found "in no other name"? So reasons this moderate replacement view; accordingly, its adherents are moved to share the news with all, Jews included. This view has no active theories about the fate in store for Jews who rejected Christ, or who now stand outside the Christian faith, except the assumption of the destiny assumed for all estranged from God.

---

2. See Eric Gritsch and Marc Tanenbaum, *Luther and the Jews* (New York: Lutheran Council in the USA, 1983), passim.

3. Jerry Falwell, *Listen America!* (Garden City, N.Y.: Doubleday, 1980), pp. 93-98.

Along with the absence of a theory of Israel's destiny between the times, this view makes no assertion of God's special
curse on Israel and no commission to carry out a presumed
divine retribution. Indeed, those who hold this view are sad
about anti-Semitism and make some effort to deal with it at a
moral level. But they have little zeal to examine the contribution
of sacred texts or inherited theology to latent or patent anti-
Semitism, and they do not inquire about the relation of abro-
gation views to anti-Semitism or the Holocaust.

Given the strong christocentricity and soteric intent, they
do not emphasize land issues or give any theological significance
to the present state of Israel.

Modified Replacement View

The impact of the massive literature on antisupersessionism,[4] a
raised awareness of the horrors of the Holocaust and continuing
anti-Semitism, and the struggle to form and sustain the state of
Israel have contributed to the modification of a replacement
position. It strives to be sensitive to these developments yet
incorporates them into a supersessionist position, enlarging the
place of Israel on the one hand, yet sharpening the focus of the
christological commitment and its soteriological implications on
the other hand.

This modified replacement view finds a continuing place
for Jewish identity after Christ by stressing the role of the
Hebrew Scriptures in Christian faith, the right of Messianic Jews
to incorporate their heritage into their Christian profession, a
strong commitment to fight anti-Semitism and anti-Judaism, the
making of common social cause between Christians and Jews,
the legitimacy of dialogue between Christians and Jews (and

---

4. For a detailed bibliography of books and articles on antisupersessionism see Michael B. McGarry, *Christology After Auschwitz* (New York: Paulist,
1977). A bibliography of books and articles from 1977 to 1989 can be
obtained from me.

those of other faiths), and the endorsement of the Jewish "quest for a homeland with secure borders and just peace."[5] But it makes these points against the background of explicitly asserting the sole sufficiency of Christ as the way God reconciles the world, and faith in Christ as the only way of salvation. Shaped by an evangelical ethos, this modified replacement view stresses evangelism.

Responding to antisupersessionist criticism of traditional teaching, this view explicitly denies that contemporary Judaism is a continuation of the Abrahamic faith of ancient Israel, that the covenantal privilege of Israel, whatever its benefits before Christ, depends retroactively on the sacrifice of Christ, and that no personal salvation is available within Judaism today. Further, it accents the evangelistic call to convert Jews to Christ, including the legitimacy of special evangelistic efforts toward Jews. Thus it endorses Messianic Judaism as an extension of its commitment to Christian particularity.

Its relationship to land issues is limited to the right of Israel to secure borders and the counsel that this right should not "constitute oppression of people-groups or individuals."[6]

Messianic Replacement View

"Jews for Jesus" is a phrase that stirs passions among both critics and supporters. The phenomenon of Messianic Judaism in recent times has created a supersessionist view that does not easily fit into standard categories. It is represented by Jews who have converted to Christian faith but who want to retain their Jewish identity, incorporating customs and rituals from their heritage into their worship and practice.

Messianic Judaism comprises believers — Jews by ethnicity

---

5. Consultation on the Gospel and the Jewish People, *The Willowbank Declaration on the Christian Gospel and the Jewish People* (Wheaton, Ill.: World Evangelical Fellowship, 1989), p. 6.
6. Ibid.

but not always with a history of practicing Judaism — who have declared Christ as the fulfillment of Jewish hope. Coming to Christian faith, often in a conversion experience, means that Christian particularity is a decisive feature of this view. What is believed true for Messianic Jews is believed necessary for all other Jews as well. Thus they mount a specific campaign to make "Jews for Jesus."

Yet this view has antisupersessionist features; it maintains the continuing validity of the Jewish heritage in some respects. This view not only affirms ethnic identity but also incorporates some religious practices of the Jewish people into Christian worship. Further, some Messianic Jews see the present state of Israel as part of the divine plan.

This view is more Jewish than other forms of replacement theology, hence its position this far along on the continuum. Yet its zealous efforts to convert other Jews to Christian faith make it more actively supersessionist.

Christological Election View

The profundity and complexity of Karl Barth's thought on this as well as on other topics make it difficult to summarize in brief compass. But his christological election view has been very influential in ecumenical circles.

The people of Israel enjoy an "eternal election" in this view. Regardless of their "disobedience" in ancient history, and their rejection of Christ, God maintains them in a special elective grace. Manifestation of that election is the role they play vis-à-vis the church. God has elected one community for special service, and that community is made up of both Israel and the church. In an extensive exegesis of Romans 9–11 Barth argues that (1) God chose Israel as the organ of reconciliation by the coming of the Son in "Jesus the Jew." (2) The church and the synagogue are in symbiotic relationship because *(a)* without the disobedience of Israel the gospel would not have gone out to the Gentiles. *(b)* The disobedience of Israel is a witness to the electing love of God, which continues even in the face of disobedience. *(c)* Israel's service is to reflect the divine judgment. (3) The alienation of Jews from God is only temporary; in the end "all Israel will be saved."[7]

The church has a mandate to share its knowledge of the reconciling work of God in Christ with all, including Jews. Mission is "vocation," however, not the bringing of salvation. Only God in the divine freedom can finally say who is included in the end, although Christians have a right to hope for universal salvation, Jews included.

ANTISUPERSESSIONIST PERSPECTIVES

Dispensationalism

Some of the ideas found in post-Holocaust antisupersessionism are anticipated in the theology of dispensationalism developed by John Nelson Darby (1800–1882) and widely disseminated in the Scofield Reference Bible (1902–1909). Dispensationalism holds that the coming of Christ has not abrogated the covenant with Israel. It contends that God continues to have a special place for the Jewish people, both in human history and beyond it. Yet these beliefs are housed in a very traditional, particularist theology, and are based on an inerrantist view of Scripture.

Today's dispensationalists (whose ideas can be found in the writings of Hal Lindsey and in the teachings of many of the television evangelists, particularly Jerry Falwell) declare that in the present sixth period of the divine plan — the church and the Holy Spirit — a new phase of God's unconditional love for the Jews is taking place, signalled by the creation of the state of

---

7. Karl Barth, *Church Dogmatics*, II/2, trans. G. W. Bromiley, et al., ed. Bromiley and T. F. Torrance (Edinburgh: T. & T. Clark, 1957), pp. 195-305; IV/1, trans. Bromiley, ed. Bromiley and Torrance (1956), pp. 20-35, 36; IV/2, trans. Bromiley, ed. Bromiley and Torrance (1958), pp. 761-66, 768-71.

Israel in 1948. The present nation of Israel is now the focal point for climactic events that will usher in the end of the world (rapture, seven years of tribulation, millennium, etc.). As the land of the chosen people of God, under assault by the powers of evil, it deserves the support of Christian believers, including political and military support (and for some the repossession of the Dome of the Rock where the new temple of God will be built). This kind of antisupersessionism therefore entails a strong land interest and political commitment.

Dispensationalist eschatology includes the continuing covenant with Israel, one that grants to it the restoration of its ancestral land in the coming peaceable kingdom on earth (after the battle of Armageddon) of one thousand years. But the *eternal* destiny of Jews rests on their conversion to Christ in a kingdom that has no end, one that follows the last uprising and defeat of Satan at the close of the millennium.

In spite of the christocentric theology and expectation of the ultimate conversion of Jews (including the setting up by Pat Robertson of a Middle Eastern television station in order to preach Christ to the Jews before the end events), the dispensationalists' political support of the state of Israel has evoked a positive response to today's political fundamentalists by leaders in the state of Israel.

One People View

Markus Barth has carried forward Karl Barth's view, developing some and minimizing other aspects of a christological election view. By extensive exegesis he makes the case that the Jews are humanity's representative people and Christians the naturalized citizens of the Israel of God. "Jesus the Jew" is focal in this representation, the only Jew raised from the dead, enacting and disclosing justification and sanctification for all people.

After Christ, Jews continue to be the chosen people with a mission for all time. Thus "Gentile Christians are relieved of the illusion that the Jews are now the abandoned and lost ones,

154

and that it is up to us to convert them. After Auschwitz and the early church-supported pogroms our only task is to be penitent and let ourselves be converted."[8]

As part (with Jews) of "the one people of God on earth," Christians are called to be in solidarity with Jews in their suffering and in their leadership in the struggles for justice in the world. Although he does not develop a theology of the land, Markus Barth does assert that "After Auschwitz the Jews have a rational and moral right to a state of their own."[9] With a strong sense of the Palestinian cause, however, he asserts that the state of Israel must be founded on the biblical vision of peace and righteousness, with its right to exist being conditional on the vocation of Israel to grant equality to other inhabitants in the land.

Paradoxical View

The horror of the Holocaust, the continuing and growing anti-Semitism, the establishment of the state of Israel, the realization of the linkage between anti-Judaism and anti-Semitism in Christian history and Christian texts have eventuated in much soul-searching in the churches since World War II. A massive literature on the theological aspects of Jewish-Christian relations and the appearance of church statements confessing Christian sins of commission and omission have also called for a theological self-examination of supersessionism. A refrain in church statements has been the rejection of replacement assumptions found in the first five views in the spectrum. In the words of the United Church of Christ General Synod statement of 1987: "God's covenant with the Jewish people has not been rescinded or abrogated by God,

---

8. Markus Barth, *Jesus the Jew,* trans. Frederick Prussner (Atlanta: John Knox, 1978), p. 94. The One People view has its roots in the "one covenant" theology of Heinrich Bullinger. For its exposition and related themes in Reformed theology see Alan P. Sell, ed., *Reformed Theology and the Jewish People* (Geneva: World Alliance of Reformed Churches, 1986), pp. 8ff. and passim.

9. Ibid., p. 39.

but remains in full force." Although ecumenical and denominational statements reject supersessionism, at the same time they presume, and often assert, the classical Christian teachings about the Trinity and the unique person and work of Christ, with their particularist premises: the eternal second person of the Trinity enfleshed in Jesus of Nazareth and the reconciliation of God and the world accomplished in the life, death, and resurrection of Jesus Christ. To make sure this universal significance of the incarnation and the atonement was not ignored, the assembly discussion added to the 1987 Presbyterian Study Document this christological clarification: "At the same time we can never forget that we stand in a covenant established by Jesus Christ (Hebrews 8) and that faithfulness to that covenant requires us to call *all* women and men to faith in Jesus Christ."[10]

How can one assert an affirmation of the uniquely reconciling work of Christ and its universal call to saving faith at the same time that one maintains the continuing covenant of God with Israel? Subsequent views attempt to speak to this question or abandon the double affirmation. The paradoxical view does not. It leaves open the question of how both can be asserted and thus fits the standard definition of a theological paradox: the assertion of mutually contradictory positions on the basis of facts or faith. Critics accuse the paradoxical view of logical incoherence and of unmatured theological investigation.[11]

This view often, but not always, entails land issues, argued more on moral grounds — Israel has the right to a state with defensible borders after Auschwitz — but it also increasingly accents the just administration of that state with due regard for Palestinian rights as a response to the *Intifada*.

---

10. 1987 General Assembly, Presbyterian Church (U.S.A.), *A Theological Understanding of the Relationship Between Christians and Jews* (A Paper Commended to the Church for Study and Reflection), p. 9.

11. For a record of many of the official church statements that reflect this paradoxical view see World Council of Churches, *The Theology of the Churches and the Jewish People: Statements by the World Council of Churches and its Member Churches* (Geneva: WCC Publications, 1988).

Eschatological View

The eschatological view goes further than standard church statements in affirming that the Abrahamic faith *before* Christ (acknowledged as "saving" by traditional theology, as in patristic thought and the Westminster Confession) continues *after* Christ. Following an Eastern tradition that interprets the Apostles' Creed teaching of the descent of Christ into the place of the dead and exegetes 1 Peter 3 and 4 accordingly, it extends the eschatological encounter (limited before to the faithful in the Hebrew Bible) to all of Abrahamic faith in any time and place: Jews will there meet Christ, the source of saving Abrahamic faith, even as many Jews hold to an eschatological verification of Judaism's beliefs.

This view asserts the importance of communicating Christian faith to all, and therefore does not exclude Jews from the church's call to share its message. But it appropriates Karl Barth's missiology of "vocation" with respect only to the covenant people (in contrast to Barth's universal application), holding that "naming the Name" is knowledge of a salvation already accomplished by the grace of Abrahamic faith.

The eschatological view affirms the legitimacy of the state of Israel on moral grounds. It views the people of Israel as the covenanted keeper of the vision of *shalom,* a special conscience of the human community, and as such requiring space for that stewardship against the world's assaults. Yet it holds Israel accountable to its own vision in its treatment of the Palestinian people and views the *Intifada* as part of God's continuing covenantal history, calling Israel to account for that stewardship. As God's custodian of this vision, Christians will keep company with Jews who are regularly at the forefront of the struggles for justice and peace in this nation.[12]

---

12. For a current exposition of this view see my *Theology and Culture Newsletter,* no. 27 (Mimeograph, 1988).

157

Dual (Double) Covenant View

This position solves the logical puzzle posed by the paradoxical view by declaring for two distinct saving relationships. Thus God establishes an irrevocable covenant with Jews in a line from Abraham-Moses-David to believing Jews today. Jews are blessed by God to the extent that they are faithful to this special covenant. For Gentiles, however, God has established a second covenant in Jesus Christ. Indeed, Israel's call to be a light to the nations is carried out beyond the people of Israel by Christ and by the mission of the church.

Because Jews find their right relationship to God through their own covenant, one should not propagate Christian faith among them. Dialogue between Christians and Jews is appropriate, but Christians are called to share their faith only with Gentiles.

Both Jews and Christians in the dual covenant are "partners in waiting" for the *eschaton*. Christian theologies of hope and the associated critique of realized eschatologies are in debt to Judaism for correcting a traditional overemphasis on the incarnation and the consequent elimination of the Not Yet aspect of Christian faith. But Jews and Christians wait with different perceptions of the significance of Jesus and different understandings of the extent to which the coming kingdom has already broken in. Thus the dual covenant view has a future-oriented note and a similarity, by implication, to the eschatological view in the verification of respective truth claims.

The dual covenant view is often associated with strong assertions of the legitimacy of the state of Israel, yet there is a stress as well on the standards of justice for that state, and a needed sense of the rights of the Palestinian people.

Midrashic View

Paul van Buren has sought to rethink Christian faith in its entirety from within the framework of a radical antisupersessionism. In three volumes of a projected four-volume series he has focused on "Israel's God" as the reference point for interpreting Christology and the whole orb of Christian belief. Accordingly, he identifies the Hebrew Bible as "Scripture" and the New Testament as "Apostolic Writings," prompting my identification of this view as "midrashic." Christian text and teaching are exposition (midrash) of the revelatory acts of Israel's God, attested in Scripture, and also continuing in the *post Christum* destiny of Israel, including the history of anti-Semitism and anti-Judaism, Christianity's complicity in the same, the Holocaust, and the creation of the state of Israel.

Testimony to Israel's God active in the long history of the Jewish people is the lens through which van Buren views Christian text and teaching. Thus classical understandings about the deity of Christ, the Trinity, the reconciling work of Christ, and salvation by grace through faith in Christ must all be judged as supersessionist. Their particularism violates the regency of Israel's God and, as such, has laid the groundwork for the history of anti-Judaism and anti-Semitism. Although Christians must be faithful to their "story," especially the resurrection of Christ, all doctrine must pass muster before the discernment of the work and intent of Yahweh in holy history. Van Buren interprets the Christian and Jewish stories as community "language-games" rather than propositional truth claims.

As the history of God with Israel continues to the present, the birth of the state of Israel is a disclosure event. It gives theological warrant to the nation's land claims, and strong support for the state of Israel accompanies the midrashic view. Because the *Intifada* has taken place within this same revelatory history, the logic of the midrashic view includes it but has yet to clarify its significance. (In contrast, some current Jewish theology urges a step beyond the Holocaust theology of Fackenheim, Wiesel, Greenberg, and Rubinstein — on which van Buren draws — to "deabsolutizing" the state of Israel.)[13]

---

13. Paul van Buren works out his position in *Discerning the Way* (New York: Seabury, 1980); and *Christ in Context* (San Francisco: Harper & Row,

Moral Pluralism View

A raised awareness of the multiplicity of religious options and Kantian doubt about the accessibility of ontological truth have helped to create a relativist view of Jewish-Christian theological issues. One cannot know whose god is real, and it is better that way, because religious truth claims create imperialism and fanaticism. What one believes is what best serves one's individual spiritual and social needs: "different strokes for different folks." Nonetheless, one must give due regard to the needs of others, hence the limits of legitimate belief are set by whether a view infringes on the rights of others. Religious belief is what is true "for me," though morally responsibly so — what speaks to my needs yet is sensitive to the circumstances and needs of others. This view may entail a belief in a transcendent God who chooses to manifest truth and salvation in multiple ways or may espouse a common core experience of the holy or moral intuition.

Jewish-Christian discussion gives this pluralist view corporate expression. By their particular history, Jews find serviceable a set of beliefs expressed in their lore and ritual life. Christians have their own symbols and convictions growing out of Israel's history, but draw as well on a Jesus tradition. Each must go its own way — "do its own thing" — because one cannot know what is ultimately true in matters religious, or because the universal Deity gives access to the holy through a variety of social circumstances. But the view of the world that each tradition takes must meet the test of just treatment of others. Supersessionist Christian theology, with its particularist truth claims, has contributed to anti-Semitism and finally the Holocaust. Jewish particularism is also suspect in view of its elimination of the tribes that lived in the promised land and its treatment of the Palestinian people.

1988). For a critique of Holocaust theology see Marc H. Ellis, *Toward a Jewish Theology of Liberation: The Uprising and the Future* (Maryknoll, N.Y.: Orbis, 1989), pp. 111-36.

With moral constraints on religious belief, proponents of this view can strongly support the state of Israel as the right response to the Holocaust and as a safe haven for Jews in a hostile world. But they can also support the Palestinian cause on the grounds of Israel's assault on the poor of the Third World.

Cultural-Linguistic View

One could locate this view at different points on the spectrum, depending on its interpretation. As understood by some of its advocates, doctrine constitutes the rules of speech in religious communities. Doctrines are not propositions that make objective truth claims. Christian and Jewish worldviews are stories that constitute each community and determine its attitude and behavior. They describe neither external reality nor Reality. The experiences one has — including religious experiences — are the result, not the root, of one's cultural and linguistic frameworks.

In another form, this view does make propositional truth claims but justifies them by their coherence with the story and its behavioral expectations. In yet another variation, it holds that doctrines do constitute a community's language world, but they are judgments of faith rather than knowledge, verifiable only eschatologically.[14]

---

14. George Lindbeck is associated with the cultural-linguistic interpretation of doctrine. His articulation of it in *The Nature of Doctrine* (Philadelphia: Westminster, 1984) has prompted the criticism by Colman E. O'Neill ("The Rule Theory of Doctrine and Propositional Truth," *Thomist* 49, no. 3 [1985]: 417-42) and others that Lindbeck does not make correspondence truth claims for the doctrinal rules of the Christian community. But Bruce Marshall's important study of Lindbeck's theses ("Aquinas as a Post-Liberal Theologian," *Thomist* 53, no. 3 [1989]: 353-402) argues persuasively that he does. In a response to Marshall's essay, Lindbeck agrees with Marshall's analysis. Lindbeck's view of the relation of Israel to Christ approximates the One People view here described ("The Story-Shaped Church: Critical Exegesis and Theological Interpretation," in *Scriptural Authority and Narrative Interpretation*, ed. Garrett Green [Philadelphia: Fortress, 1987], pp. 161-78). For an eschatologically verified cultural-linguistic view, see Ronald Thiemann, *Revelation and Theol-*

Whether or not propositional truth claims are made, the cultural-linguistic view also lends itself to either more conservative or more radical positions on the relation of the covenants of Israel and Christ. From a conservative position, it can distinguish sharply between Jewish and Christian perspectives. To be what it is, a community must be loyal to this "construal," worship in this idiom and not another, and act ethically in accord with its story. Christians have their construal and commitment, and Jews have theirs. One cannot accommodate the other. From a more radical position, this view can lend itself to great flexibility on the ground that language changes and so too does a religious community's idiom and identity, with ever-new adaptation to fresh settings.

If a cultural-linguistic view makes no propositional claims, it also makes no salvation claims, and hence has no evangelism mandate toward Jews or others. Again, if this view makes no correspondence truth claims on issues of land, it has no stake in either the state of Israel or the Palestinian cause. Usually, however, norms of justice go with the Christian community's story, and these are brought into play. They can move either toward a moral justification for the state of Israel based on the Holocaust or toward a moral repudiation of such claims based on solidarity with the Palestinian poor.

EVANGELICAL ANTISUPERSESSIONISM

Can one learn from the various points of view described yet challenge their shortcomings? What follows is a proposal based on an interpretation of Paul's struggle with these issues in Romans 9–11, read canonically.

1. "All Israel will be saved . . . for the gifts and the calling of God are irrevocable" (Rom. 11:26, 29). These are two of fourteen references in Romans 9–11 to the positive role and

_____

ogy: *The Gospel as Narrated Promise* (Notre Dame: University of Notre Dame Press, 1989).

destiny of Israel in the purpose of God. (Other themes vis-à-vis Israel: the urging of Gentiles to value their engrafting, chap. 12; the hardening and disobedience of Israel, chap. 9; affirmation of a remnant in Israel who received Christ, among them Paul, chap. 4; etc.)' As a major theme in these chapters, consonant with canonical accents, the irrevocability of the covenant, including the promise of salvation for "all Israel," is a fundamental New Testament teaching.

2. From the same chapters: "If you confess with your lips that Jesus is Lord and believe in your heart that God raised him from the dead, you will be saved. . . . And how are they to believe in one of whom they have never heard? . . . 'How beautiful are the feet of those who bring good news!' " (10:9, 14b, 15b). This scandal of particularity, repeated hundreds of times throughout the New Testament, is also integral to Christian teaching.[15] The affirmation of christological singularity, the new covenant/New Testament in Jesus Christ, is a Christian nonnegotiable.

3. The partnership of new and old covenants is not an innovation. The covenant with Abraham does not eliminate the covenant with Noah. The covenant with Moses does not revoke the covenant with Abraham. Each new chapter in the great Story incorporates the earlier ones. This is a canonical refrain. The difficult question is *how* the covenants with Abraham, Moses, and David continue in the time of the new covenant in Christ. A minimalist view is content to assert the partnership and not explore it further. But this view ignores Paul's profound struggle with the question and too quickly settles for what appears to be a flat contradiction.

4. How does Israel's covenant continue *after* the unique deed of God in Christ? Christians believe that in Christ's life, death, and resurrection the powers of sin, evil, and death were finally defeated. Paul's effort to hold together both the continu-

---

15. I have argued this point in *The Christian Story,* vol. 2: *Authority: Scripture in the Church for the World* (Grand Rapids: Eerdmans, 1987), pp. 254-340.

ing old and the new covenant, read canonically, can be understood this way:

a. Israel plays a unique role in the salvation story. "To them belong the adoption, the glory, the covenants, the giving of the law, the worship, and the promises. . . . And from them, according to their flesh, comes the Messiah" (Rom. 9:4, 5). Indeed, Abraham is "the father of faith," and those who are his true children in Israel before Christ are "saved" — albeit by the retroactive "application of the benefits of Christ," as the traditional teaching has it. Yet Paul extends this special claim *forward,* as well as backward. Thus the future tense: "All Israel *will* be saved." One must read the "all," however, in the light of Paul's statement that "not all Israelites truly belong to Israel" (9:6b). Only those of true Abrahamic faith are heirs. By implication, those in the future (after Christ) who stand in this faithful line constitute "all Israel." Whoever has Abrahamic faith, then and *now,* has saving faith.

b. Yet how can Paul say this if a *knowledge* of Christ is the need and goal of all humanity? This knowledge entails a *confession* of Christ in the "heart" and with the "lips."

Some resources from the early church fathers, and from Karl Barth, help here. Interpreting the descent of Christ to the place of the dead on Good Friday, the church fathers believed that the faithful in Israel before Christ were confronted by him in his descent into death, evoking confession of Christ as the fulfillment of their proleptic faith.[16] In a complementary line of thought, Barth held that *all* humanity died and rose again in Christ. Christian mission tells the world what it does not yet know about its already reconciled life in the new age. Pressing the fathers' insight beyond Good Friday, and limiting Barth's neo-universalism to the Israel of Romans 11, points to an eschatological encounter of Christ with all those of Abrahamic faith. Those redeemed in that faith come to know the Reconciler,

---

16. See 1 Peter 3 and 4, the Apostles' Creed, etc., discussed in my *Christian Story,* 2:288-92.

Jesus Christ. In this way both the christological centralities and the irrevocable covenant with Israel are affirmed.

c. Another consideration is closely related to Paul's own personal journey. "I myself am an Israelite, a descendant of Abraham" (Rom. 11:1b). Before the Damascus road, Paul was no Abrahamic believer, but a devotee of the law, one who "did not strive for it on the basis of faith, but as if it were based on works" (9:32a). Yet there was hope even for this person, "chiefest of sinners," saved by grace through faith in Christ. He puzzled over why only a "remnant" in Israel so responded, but he went on to urge the proclamation of faith to Jews as well as Gentiles. With him, and those few who believed, faith is not only noetic (as in point b) but also fiducial, a saving faith contingent on the knowledge of Christ. Might Paul's "all Israel" also include those zealous for the law who must also first meet Christ — in time or eternity — as Paul did on the Damascus road, to learn of the gracious faith that saves? Did Paul have a special place in his heart for others, like himself, whose ardor for God proved to be the first step on the path from works to faith?

Antisupersessionism as just described does not forbid sharing the gospel with Jewish people. Indeed, exclusion is a subtle form of discrimination, denying to Jews what Christians believe to be their own most precious gift. *How* one carries out this nonexclusionary mission mandate, while honoring the continuing covenant of God with Israel, is not clear. What is clear is that targeting Jews for evangelism, on the grounds that they will not be saved without Christian ministrations, appears to conflict with Paul's judgments in Romans 11.

5. Paul struggles mightily with how the continuing covenant with Israel worked *collectively*, as well as personally. He does so with an eye on symbiosis: what happens to Israel affects the church in a salutary way.

One sign of the symbiotic relation today is Israel's custodianship of basic codes of human life together. The heirs of Amos and Isaiah are regularly found in the front ranks of causes of

165

justice and peace. As Reinhold Niebuhr observed, one soon learns that one can count on Jews in the community as allies in the struggles for humanization. Indeed, the witness of Israel reminds the church of its own historical commitments, and often saves it from Marcionite temptations to write off the Hebrew Bible and overspiritualize the gospel. As a special community of conscience to both church and world, Israel reminds Christians, "It is not you that support the root, but the root that supports you" (Rom. 11:18).

6. Does a continuing covenant entail the promise of land? Many Jews are more interested in what Christians have to say on this subject than on the strictly theological questions addressed above. Christian Zionism notwithstanding, one finds no direct biblical warrants for the reacquisition of the soil of ancient Israel. Nor can one have any straight-line theological endorsement of the modern state of Israel. The uncritical identification of the will of God with human institutions violates the divine sovereignty. The Romans passage does not link the continuing covenant and a future nation-state.

But an excessive disjunction between land and covenant is not in order, either, for the following reasons:

a. The God of Abraham and Sarah, the same God incarnate in Jesus Christ, is One who lives and acts in human history, and thus is active in human political moil and toil.

b. The hardships of the people of Israel over time are directly related to its stewardship of God's Torah. As conscience of the human community, this people evokes the hostility of a fallen creation. Thus space is needed to assure its continued witness — geography "with defensible borders" — especially in the face of the twentieth-century record of hate toward the bearers of the prophetic tradition.

c. Geographic stewardship is inseparable from the covenant mandate: a land flowing with the milk and honey of the Law and the Prophets. The most painful testing place for such a model of *shalom* in the late twentieth century is in the Fertile Crescent, where marching armies from north and south have

166

ever and again challenged this vision, and from whose womb three great religions, all proclaiming *shalom*, were born. Here is an opportunity for the state of Israel to be what it is, the world's community of conscience, demonstrating what life together can mean. No realization of this vision is possible without the partnership of the Palestinian people. What more dramatic witness could there be to a political life together in this time than such a "light to the nations"?

CONCLUSION

The conversation on the place of Israel in Christian faith — both the ecumenical exchange and the internal evangelical dialogue — is far from over. Critical to its advance is an understanding of the range of alternatives. So too is a close reading, and canonical interpretation, of the relevant biblical texts. This essay is a contribution to both these tasks.

GIANTS IN THE LAND

CARL F. H. HENRY,
ECUMENICALLY CONSIDERED[*]

IF the twentieth-century "evangelical renaissance"[1] in North America has produced a Michelangelo, that exemplar is surely Carl Henry. Premier theologian, key figure in its formative institutions, chief public interpreter of its ways, and critic of its wanderings, this renaissance man has left his mark on an epoch. Yet there is no Sistine Chapel or public piazza on the American scene where all can view these works of genius. Religious pluralism and parochialism are such that a Henry can write an encyclopedic six-volume work on epistemology that will go unreviewed in major journals of academia, or he can lecture across the continent and around the world but be known only on the circuit of evangelical para-institutions. Durability and impact count, however, especially in a pragmatic culture. As evangelical presence is now widely felt throughout American society and its churches, its intellectual leaders are getting a hearing. In this company Henry has no peer.

Carl Ferdinand Howard Henry was born of immigrant parents, Karl F. and Johanna (Vaethroeder), in New York City,

---

*"Ecumenically considered" in this chapter has more to do with the capacity of an evangelical ecumenical to set forth with fairness another point of view than with presenting a critique — the charge given by the editors of *A Handbook of Christian Theologians,* in which this essay first appeared.

1. As identified by Donald Bloesch in *The Evangelical Renaissance* (Grand Rapids: Eerdmans, 1973).

January 22, 1913, and raised on Long Island in Central Islip, New York. After baptism and confirmation in an Episcopal congregation to which religiously indifferent parents sent their children, Henry became a teenage church dropout. Equipped with some sportswriting skills learned in high school, he took a job upon graduation as a reporter for the *Islip Press,* moving later to an editorship at the *Smithtown Star* and from there to the *Port Jefferson Town Echo,* as well as serving as a regional reporter for the *New York Tribune.*

On June 10, 1933, a three-hour conversation with a friend eventuated in a personal experience of conversion and evangelical commitment and in his subsequent immersion and membership in a Baptist congregation on Long Island. This new stance of faith had vocational implications. Henry considered how best he could serve his Lord, and in 1935 he entered Wheaton College in Illinois, the "evangelical Harvard." He received both his A.B. and M.A. from that institution and chose to go on to Northern Baptist Seminary in Chicago, declining an offer to take an influential post at the Moody Bible Institute in public relations. He was ordained in 1941 and served as student pastor in the Humboldt Park Baptist Church, and for a short time as interim pastor at First Baptist Church of Elmhurst, but his academic gifts were taking him toward another form of ministry. Completing doctoral work at Northern Baptist Seminary (Th.D.), he was invited to teach philosophy and religion at his alma mater, where he eventually became a full professor. His agile and disciplined mind set high standards for the students, who esteemed him as a person of warmth and brilliance, and indeed a terror in his examination expectations.[2] During this period Henry was active as one of the organizers of the National Association of Evangelicals (1943), writing for its organ, *United Evangelical*

---

2. When teacher evaluation forms were introduced at Eastern Baptist Theological Seminary, Henry received the highest rating as "the best prepared and most stimulating teacher." Letter from Thorwald W. Bender to author, February 2, 1984.

Action, and was instrumental in creating its Commission on Social Ethics. In 1940, while in Chicago, Henry married Helga Bender, whom he had met at Wheaton; from their lifelong felicitous union came two children, Paul Brentwood and Carol Jennifer.

In these early years of academic preparation and teaching, Henry found time to write *The Pacific Garden Mission: A Doorway to Heaven* (1941) and *Successful Church Publicity* (1942). In 1947 his first major work was published, *The Uneasy Conscience of Modern Fundamentalism.* In this seventy-five-page tract — "the manifesto of neo-evangelicalism," according to Dirk Jellema — Henry criticizes the separatist tendencies of rigid orthodoxies on the one hand, and their lack of social ethics on the other.

In 1947 Henry was invited to serve on the first faculty of the newly founded Fuller Theological Seminary in Pasadena, California, created to provide evangelical congregations with a learned ministry. Although he previously declined a seminary presidency and deanship, he was drawn to Fuller because of its special academic goals and promise. He began his work there not only as a professor of philosophy and theology but also served, for the first year of the institution's existence, as acting dean. The intellectual stimulation of colleagues and students at Fuller, and the opportunities for research and writing, made these years happy ones. During that time a prolific writing career developed, giving voice to the burgeoning evangelical movement. In rapid succession a series of doctrinal works came from his pen, including *Remaking the Modern Mind* (1948), *Giving a Reason for Our Hope* (1949), *The Protestant Dilemma* (1949), *Notes on the Doctrine of God* (1949), *Fifty Years of Protestant Theology* (1950), *The Drift of Western Thought* (1951), and *Glimpses of a Sacred Land* (1953). His published dissertation (Ph.D., Boston University, 1949), entitled *Personal Idealism and Strong's Theology* (1951), marked him as a constructive critic of Augustus Hopkins Strong, the most influential theologian in the American Baptist Convention. In 1957 his first major book in a field in which he began to specialize — ethics — was published, *Chris-*

tian Personal Ethics, as well as his *Evangelical Responsibility in Contemporary Theology.* In these varied works in theology, philosophy, and ethics, Henry's concern for the rational articulation and defense of faith became increasingly manifest.

Henry had captured the attention of key evangelical figures, and in 1955 and 1956, when Billy Graham and L. Nelson Bell were forming a new journal, they asked him as an architect of evangelical theology to give *Christianity Today* editorial leadership. Accepting the invitation, he took a leave from Fuller (one extended by faculty and administration for three succeeding years), making a permanent commitment to the enterprise in 1959. During his twelve-year tenure as editor-in-chief, Henry — and the staff he gathered around him — established *Christianity Today* as the most influential organ of American evangelicalism, with a paid circulation of 170,000.

Through the writers Henry assembled and the magazine's new coverage and commentary, a "new evangelicalism" emerged, one that expressed unswerving commitment to evangelical distinctives yet sought to show their relevance to contemporary social issues and to demonstrate the intellectual viability of evangelical faith. In his editorial leadership Henry aimed to reduce the partisanships that historically divided evangelicals; he encouraged movement on a common front. For example, his recommendation for an evangelism effort in the United States subsequently issued in the national endeavor called "Key 73." This ecumenical evangelicalism took form in the World Congress on Evangelism in 1966 in Berlin; it was sponsored by *Christianity Today* and chaired by Henry, with Billy Graham as honorary chairman. Another expression of the concern for evangelical collegiality was a series of symposia gathered and edited by Henry, including *Contemporary Evangelical Thought* (1957), *Revelation and the Bible* (1959), *The Biblical Expositor* (3 vols.; 1960), *Basic Christian Doctrines* (1962), *Christian Faith and Modern Theology* (1964), *Jesus of Nazareth: Saviour and Lord* (1966), and *Fundamentals of the Faith* (1969).

In 1968 Henry acceded to the wishes of a group in the

executive committee of *Christianity Today*'s board of directors to step down as editor, that group seeking tighter control of the contents and stance of the magazine. Henry departed for a period to Cambridge, England, to begin his massive work on the doctrine of God. He returned to become professor-at-large at Eastern Baptist Theological Seminary in Philadelphia until 1974, when he began devoting most of his time to writing and lecturing. In 1968 he also helped organize the Institute for Advanced Christian Studies, a mobile think tank of evangelical scholars seeking to relate Christian faith to the intellectual disciplines. In 1982 the group launched a major venture with the William B. Eerdmans Publishing Company: a series of volumes by distinguished philosophers, historians, scientists, and others on the relation of rational faith to modernity.

In 1974 Henry became a lecturer for World Vision, Inc., an evangelical social service agency, and thus an itinerant who, as he expressed it himself, "flew some 2 million miles by air, lecturing, preaching and teaching, wearing a suit bought in Majorca, a beret from Spain, shoes resoled in Korea, carrying a Bible rebound in the Philippines, and meeting people everywhere who scarcely suspect what God can do for the individual whose mind and heart have been stretched by the good news of the Gospel." Henry had become a kind of world evangelist — "the thinking man's Billy Graham," as he is sometimes called.

Although at home most of all in the world of words and books, Henry has had a rich history of human relationships — family, friends, colleagues, and, yes, enemies, too. Helga, his "good and godly" spouse, has been at his side in all his ventures, a companion of mind and heart, as have been his two children, who continue the family's evangelical commitments.[3] Gordon Clark, philosopher and theologian, is Henry's chief intellectual mentor both in the thirst for ideas and in the specifics of the history of philosophy. Yet Edgar Brightman, a personalist philos-

---

3. His son, Paul Henry, has written *Politics for Evangelicals* (Philadelphia: Judson, 1974).

opher of a very different theological perspective with whom he did doctoral studies at Boston University, has left an impression on him because of his intellectual rigor and fairness of spirit. Cornelius Van Til and Edward Carnell, the latter a colleague at Fuller, were reinforcing influences in their evangelical orthodoxy (respectively, presuppositionalist and apologist). W. Harry Jellema, former Indiana University teacher, also shaped his thinking. Billy Graham, who visited him at Pasadena to urge him to become editor of *Christianity Today,* has been a close friend and coworker. So, too, has been Everett Harrison, former professor of New Testament at Fuller. Laity in the evangelical movement have meant much to Henry, including lifelong friendships with A. Lewis Shingler of Pasadena; Cleo Shook, formerly of the U.S. AID program; and Richard Ostling, religion editor of *Time,* who served as *Christianity Today*'s news editor during a portion of Henry's tenure. Leadership in the American Theological Society, including its presidency in 1981, and movement among the establishment have also brought friends in those circles.

Theological combat as well as parochialism within both the liberal and evangelical communities have left their mark on Henry's life. Often treated as an outsider in denominational and ecumenical circles, Henry was given token time on assembly agendas or accorded at best a marginal relationship to the working life of the institutions of mainline Christianity. His awkward departure from the editorship of *Christianity Today,* including the removal of his column, "Footnotes," and the dropping of his name from the masthead during a succeeding editorship, has left wounds. Although Henry is a polemicist for his point of view, he is also a gentle man and does not respond in kind to personal affront. More and more his generosity of spirit and ecumenical evangelicalism are ready to honor "each soldier where he fights well."[4] Thus the ardor and range of his thought, as well as his human decency, have over time won the

---

4. Letter to author, February 8, 1984.

respect of friend and foe, securing for him a front-rank place in world evangelicalism and American Christianity; he is a "maker of the modern theological mind."[5]

REVELATION AND AUTHORITY

In his various roles as teacher, writer, editor, initiator, and organizer, Henry manifests an arrowlike purpose: the rational articulation and defense of Christian faith.[6] As dogmatic theologian, he seeks to render intelligible the fundamentals of the gospel in the face of intellectual confusions within Christian theology; and as apologetic theologian, he aims to demonstrate its intellectual superiority over competing worldviews.[7] Henry is a communicator who sees his task as clarifying the identity of the Christian religion while manifesting its profundity in the contest with current alternatives. Thus his theological work is marked by frequent juxtapositions between core belief and what he holds to be distortions of it or challenges to it. Hence I pay attention to these competing views, most of which are to the left of Henry.[8] In these exchanges, the contours of his own position are sharpened.

As a newspaperman, Henry knew that information gather-

---

5. See Bob E. Patterson's excellent study, *Carl F. H. Henry,* in the series Makers of the Modern Theological Mind (Waco: Word, 1983).

6. Longtime friend Everett Harrison remarks that one of Henry's favorite phrases is "to strike a blow for the faith." Letter to author, February 19, 1984.

7. The line between dogmatics and apologetics is never sharp for Henry, because clarifying confusions within has to do with the invasion of alien themes from without.

8. Because modernity's challenge is the historical context in which Henry does his work, the left gets much of the criticism. But his influential early volume, *The Uneasy Conscience of Modern Fundamentalism* (Grand Rapids: Eerdmans, 1947), is evangelical self-criticism regarding the lack of social relevance. "Evangelicalism" and "fundamentalism" were synonymous for him at this stage — he pled for a "progressive fundamentalism" — but he used "fundamentalism" in a more critical sense in *Evangelical Responsibility in Contemporary Theology* (Grand Rapids: Eerdmans, 1957), where he associated it with a narrow-spirited polemicism.

ing required reliable sources, and in his subsequent work of theological communication, soundness at the source of disclosure became of decisive importance. Very early he made the point that the questions of authority and revelation are the commanding theological issues of the time.[9] His six-volume *God, Revelation and Authority* shows an investment of energy commensurate with this lifelong conviction; indeed, "in every church epoch it is the fate of the Bible that decides the fate of Christianity."[10] Thus the reliability of where we go to find out what is ultimately so is basic for interpreting faith. To this subject of the authority of Scripture, and its underlying premise of divine revelation, I now turn, giving attention to its critical themes: inspiration, inerrancy, illumination, and their relation to reason.

The Authority of Scripture

For the believer, God is the "fontal authority" (P. T. Forsyth), but the flow from that fountain is the authority issue in theology, the question of palpable mediate authority (I, IV). That access point for Henry is the Scripture of the Old and New Testaments. Therein God has disclosed the divine purpose; in this Word the rational Logos has unveiled the divine being and doing. What information God wants humanity to have is given in the original (inerrant) writings as those are conveyed in the doctrinally sound (infallible) copies and reliable translations that are available (IV). Thus the Bible's authority rests on God's revelatory action, deeds done and meanings conveyed in the trustworthy propositions of the prophetic-apostolic testimony (IV).

---

9. At mid-century he asserted that "the pivot . . . is the question of revelation . . . and with it an adequate objective authority" (*The Protestant Dilemma* [Grand Rapids: Eerdmans, 1949], pp. 39, 56).

10. Carl Henry, *God, Revelation and Authority* (Waco: Word, 1976–83), IV:380, hereafter cited as *GRA*. In some instances, only the volume number(s) are included in the text as roman numerals enclosed in parentheses. Vols. I and II were published in 1976, vols. III and IV in 1979, vol. V in 1982, and vol. VI in 1983.

Why does one need this special revelation? Because reason in revolt obscures the communication between God and human beings that marked the origins of history in paradise and even continued in the sullied but surviving image of God in humanity (II, IV, V). This general revelation of God in nature and history, perceived by the real but dimmed light of reason and conscience, does render one accountable for disobedience and makes one open to something more, but does not give saving knowledge. Moreover, it does not make a natural theology possible (I, II, III, IV, VI). The light that comes to dispel the darkness shines in the incarnate Word and is transmitted in the "epistemic Word," the Scriptures (IV). As the deposit of God's revealed truths, the Bible has unrivaled authority.

The authority of Scripture is put in question by naturalisms, ancient and modern, which turn to human experience and its wisdom to legitimate their worldviews. In the modern setting the heirs of the Renaissance and Enlightenment dominate Western culture with their antisupernaturalist ontology and humanist value systems.[11] That regency is also challenged by forms of Christian theology that allow the world's agenda to compromise biblical authority with philosophical, moral, social, economic, aesthetic, affective, and spiritual experiences or constructs, dictating the meaning of theological assertions (IV).

The Inspiration of Scripture

The authority of Scripture is secured by the plenary verbal inspiration of the originals (or autographs). This "God-breathed" quality is attested in its own words: "All scripture is inspired by God" (2 Tim. 3:16).[12] The Holy Spirit has worked

---

11. From early, middle, through later writings, Henry challenges naturalism. See comments in *Uneasy Conscience,* p. 70 and passim; *Remaking the Modern Mind* (Grand Rapids: Eerdmans, 1946), pp. 264ff.; *Protestant Dilemma,* pp. 23ff.; through editorials in *Christianity Today;* to the essay "The Crisis of Modern Learning," *This World* no. 7 (Winter 1984): 95-105. See *GRA,* I:17-30, 135-51; IV:10ff.

12. See *GRA,* IV:129-61, for exposition and related texts.

in and through the biblical authors in such a manner that their words are guided ("breathed-out") to their proper end (IV). That does not mean the dictation of a heavenly text to earthly amanuenses, a view associated more with the Koran or Book of Mormon (IV). Biblical inspiration honors the particularity of human agency, which is evident from the different vocabulary ranges, styles, and cultural idioms of the authors, as well as their manifest struggle and personal journey (IV, VI). Inspiration means the ever-present concursive operation of the Holy Spirit in the writing process and the superintendence of the same, so that what is produced is always what God intends and as such is errorless. To the last point I shall return, but first one very important feature of the how of revelation must be identified. Carl Henry is a determined defender of propositional revelation — "revealed shareable propositional truths" (I, III).

As noted in chapter 4, propositions are sentences to which the responses yes or no are appropriate. A theological proposition makes claims about particular subjects: who God is; what God has done, is doing, and will do; who humans are; what humans are to do; and what humans will be. In Henry's view, one cannot construe these assertions as reliable unless they are "univocal," rather than "equivocal" (contradictory) or "analogical" (saying what they are like rather than what they are), statements.[13] A long-standing tradition in philosophy and theology, influenced by Kant, has shaped current nonevangelical faith and thought, a tradition that Henry believes casts epistemological doubt on all statements made in Scripture and derivative doctrinal reflection. Of particular concern to him are those commendable efforts at biblical retrieval that undercut their possible contribution by ambiguity about their cognitive weight. Here Karl Barth and neoorthodoxy in general come under heavy criticism. Henry believes that the interpretation of Scripture as

---

13. On the unremitting attack on analogy and the defense of univocal propositions, see *GRA*, II:53-54; III:362-66; IV:117-21; V:86-88, 261-62, 355-56.

"witness" to revelation rather than revelation itself, or revelation as an "event" rather than the communication of revealed truths, loses God's self-disclosure in the mists of human subjectivity. Henry seeks to preserve the rationality of the Bible, which in this case means the revelatory deliverance of knowledge about God in intelligible sentences.[14]

One must also assert the propositional status of revelation against the widespread contemporary assumption of cultural relativity, which claims that biblical statements are so wed to their historical context that abiding transcultural truth is not possible. This assumption declares that readers are so rooted in their own culture that they cannot understand what is said in Scripture, which can hardly be relevant to another time with its own contextual issues and sensibilities. "No flashpoint of contemporary religious dialogue bears more critically than this upon the significance of the Christian faith."[15] Although acknowledging the "culture-relatedness" of biblical writers in the sense that they borrow the idiom of their time to make their point, Henry believes that the revelatory assertions made in Scripture have a fixed, transcultural meaning extractable by grammatical-historical analysis. The biblical author was not so bound by the premises of that day, nor is the believer by those of this one, that truth-bearing propositions cannot be carried over time and space from source to receiver, giving trustworthy, unchanging, intelligible information, "abiding instruction" (I, III, IV, V).

Plenary verbal inspiration is an understanding of the divine self-disclosure as the very speaking of God, the revelation of truth

---

14. Henry's engagement with the thought of Barth is intensive and extensive. Acknowledging that Barth does speak of the cognitive weight of biblical assertions, Henry believes that the location of that truth claim by him in the moment of revelatory encounter and the distinction of Barth's theology between the Word and the biblical words undercut their propositional status and thus the truth claim of Christian faith. For his struggle with Barth on this issue see GRA, I:203-12; II:40-41, 143-47, 158-62; III:224-29; IV:148-61, 174-92, 196-200, 257-71, 298-303; V:39, 53, 97, 299, 366-70.

15. GRA, V:398.

in "conceptual-verbal" form (III). The Bible is the epistemic Word even as Jesus Christ is the incarnate Word, and Christianity is a book religion (III, IV). Yet one cannot forget its incarnational center and historical character, because God "shows" as well as "speaks." Although the divine speech interprets the divine deeds, the heart of the inscripturated truth is a record of God's activity, a narrative that runs from creation to consummation with its turning point in the life, death, resurrection, and ascension of Jesus Christ.[16] In particular, Henry returns time and again to the words and work of Christ and thus places a strong christological norm at the center of his authority structure (II, III). This structure is not one that juxtaposes an incarnate Word to the written Word, but one in which the latter comes to plenitude and clarity of meaning in the former (III, IV).

Although Henry shares with twentieth-century salvation history theologians this attention to the deeds of God and to the christological center, he takes pains to distinguish his view from those who would (1) reduce the Bible to the recounting of divine deeds, (2) polarize Jesus Christ with scriptural teaching considered less worthy, (3) understand the prophetic and apostolic interpretation of the deeds of God as only human formulations secondary in significance to the deeds, (4) isolate some deeds and interpretation as a trustworthy core with an errant context, or (5) argue for a canon within the canon (II, III, IV). Revelation is the whole cloth of the Bible, not a red thread within it, albeit set forth progressively in the historical flow of the Bible (II, III).

The Inerrancy of Scripture

Implicit in claims to biblical authority, and a logical inference from verbal inspiration, is the teaching of biblical inerrancy. Can

---

16. From time to time Henry sets out simply and forcefully the highlights of the Christian narrative. See especially *GRA*, IV:468-69; also I:34; V:15-16, 54.

God lie or the Spirit inspire error? Can the Bible be authoritative as an inspired literary deposit if it appears to be a broken and erroneous testimony? In addition to these considerations, Henry declares that the text itself witnesses to Christ's own assurance of the reliability of the Hebrew Bible, because he quotes it with confidence (II, IV, V). Further, the spirit and form of the "thus saith the Lord" declarations that pervade Scripture argue for its errorlessness. Alternative views of limited or partial inerrancy are either contradictory or an invitation to a slippery slope, the end of which is the rejection of biblical authority (IV). Thus by biblical warrant and rational argument, Henry sees inerrancy as integral to the meaning of authority.

What is inerrancy? This teaching asserts that the autographs are safeguarded from error in whatever they teach as doctrine — not only in theological and moral matters but also in scientific, historical, and geographical ones. As already noted, this does not mean the dictation of a text but the superintendence of it with allowances for authorial individuality and historical context. The latter includes a respect for literary genre, and thus the refusal to impose standards of modern historiography on poetic license or oriental hyperbole, latitude in the traditions of citation (as is shown in the quotations of the Hebrew Bible in the New Testament), the employment of metaphor (the "sun rising" was not a scientific statement then nor is it one now), the ways of ancient numerology (divergent estimates reflecting the practice of generalization), and so on (IV).

When logical or factual contradictions appear to persist, what then? Some can be attributed to transmission frailties, as noted regularly by ancient exegetes who presupposed an errorless text. Other challenges at this level that assume the finality of empirical data which seem to contradict the biblical chronicle are methodologically ambiguous, because all empirical tests must be tentative (I, III, IV). Still other problems require patience, with the assumption that the biblical record will be validated at some future time, as newer archaeological discoveries tend to corroborate (IV).

In these matters, one must distinguish the infallibility of received copies from the inerrancy of inaccessible autographs. In the former case, the errorless potency of the original persists even in semantic details, and the power of Providence continues to secure them. Approved copies, therefore, are not error-prone, nor is their doctrinal and moral teaching in doubt. Because truth is carried not by isolated words but by propositions or sentences, one can assert the doctrinal reliability of the copies even with the linguistic and factual inaccuracies that are discernible along the edges of the documents (IV).

Whenever one questions inerrancy, one either undercuts or puts in serious jeopardy the Bible's authority, as is the case with views like the following: (1) Neo-Protestant views assert the authority of the Bible, but either *(a)* deny its cognitive status by holding Scripture to be the occasion for encounter or existential decision, or to be only functionally authoritative through its performative language; *(b)* construe Scripture as a witness to events rather than a deposit of trustworthy propositions; *(c)* treat the Bible as a compendium of ideas or images; *(d)* consider the Bible to be vast scriptural authority in a canon within a canon — Jesus Christ, or Jesus recovered by historical scholarship, or a motif such as justification, covenant, liberation, and so forth; or *(e)* read a sociological theory, philosophical system, or political program into the Scriptures (I, IV, V). (2) Traditional Roman Catholic views declare for inerrancy but assert the magisterium to be the key to its meaning (IV). (3) Neo-Catholic views seek to relate the magisterium to contemporary experience and in that fusion look for a canon within a canon (IV). (4) Evangelical views *(a)* claim limited inerrancy for doctrines and morals or soteric knowledge but withhold confidence in matters of science and history; *(b)* construe the Bible essentially as a vehicle of conversion; or *(c)* allow claims to the present work of the Spirit in charismatic sensibility to exercise authority over the inspired text (III, IV).

In the case of evangelicals whose limited inerrancy views are "unstable" and invite deterioration of the Bible's authority,

Henry believes that efforts at rational persuasion are more in order than recrimination, crusades, and accusations of apostasy (IV). Further, "unbalanced preoccupation with inerrancy" is a costly evangelical diversion. To Henry, "the mark of New Testament authenticity is first and foremost proclamation of the crucified and risen Jesus as the indispensable and irreplaceable heart of the Christian message."[17]

Related to the issue of inerrancy is the function of biblical scholarship. Henry's exegetical emphasis is on historical-grammatical work with texts, seeking the intended common-sense meaning, with obscure texts illumined by clear ones (the "analogy of faith"), and assuming the unity of Scripture, providing the horizon that renders the Bible its own best interpreter (II, IV). In contrast to those who indict the historical-critical method as such, Henry affirms its limited usefulness (Jonah could be a theological tale, not an empirical narrative, although arguments for either are not conclusive), as long as one detaches from it the antisupernaturalist premises that have often controlled such inquiry. Henry is firmly committed to textual criticism, because proximity to the autographs, and thus the distinction of superior from inferior texts, is a desideratum (IV).

The Illumination of Scripture

Although individuals who use the rational faculty available to them by virtue of the *imago Dei* can understand Scripture, the Word reaches its proper end of changing heart and mind only in persons moved by the fiducial work of the Holy Spirit. The Spirit's gift of illumination is a regeneration that sets the soul on fire at the beginning of the journey of faith. The Spirit brings a new birth that takes the believer into a framework of faith which affects how those who espouse inerrancy read the Bible. This new disposition carries with it the assumption, the

---

17. *GRA*, IV:365.

"epistemic axiom," that Scripture will tell the truth and that the use of reason will confirm it (II). As believers read Scripture, the Holy Spirit guides them to its truth and enlivens its truth, as well as convicts and converts (II, IV). But faith so illumined must be rational. Epistemologically this is a "moderate presuppositionalism," which returns one full circle to the authority of Scripture, because for Henry the work of the Spirit — not reason — establishes Scripture's authority in a believer. Yet reason plays a very important role in Henry's theology.

Reason

For Henry reason is grounded in the very being of God, the eternal Logos. Therefore he is deeply concerned about the anti-intellectual currents of the times (III, V). His view of human nature holds that the fall has not so impaired the image of God in humans that reason is disqualified in the discernment of ultimate truth.[18] Thus the believer must "be ready to make your defense . . . for the hope that is in you" (1 Pet. 3:15). Although the believer comes to faith by regeneration (the new birth by the work of the Spirit), those converted are called to give reasons for faith and to assess and challenge the rationality of alternative views. Reason — the mind's grappling with evidence, the use of ordered thought and obedience to the laws of logic — expresses itself in Christian apologetics. Apologetics seeks to show, on the one hand, that attacks on Christian faith are unpersuasive and alternatives to Christian belief are contradictory or inadequate, and, on the other hand, that Christian faith is a coherent and consistent view (I). Indeed, reason is a test of truth, because the claims of Christian faith must be subject themselves to the laws of logic (I, IV). In the ordinary course of living, as well as in the practice of intellectual disciplines, human beings cannot function without rational norms and attention to evidence (I,

---

18. Indeed, "the Fall conditions man's will more pervasively than his reason" (*GRA*, I:226).

III, IV). Henry's dialogue with alternative views comes down time and again to these tests: Is this position intellectually self-consistent? Does it at any point contradict itself?

An example of his employment of logic in disputation is his critique of theological relativism. How can an ideological relativist claim with a straight face the absolute truth of the assertion that all propositions are culturally relative? The premise of the argument denies its own exposition, or it exempts itself from its thesis and thus undercuts it (IV). Henry makes a similar charge against logical positivists who grant validity only to sentences with empirical warrants and thereby render nonsensical their own nonempirical premise (I, V). Thus Henry seeks to reduce to logical absurdity various opposing worldviews. Correspondingly, he challenges his critics to find inconsistency in his own understanding of Christian faith. Hence "logical consistency is a negative test and coherence a subordinate test" for religious truths.[19]

The concern for reason is reflected also in Henry's philosophical interest and competence. He believes that faith has its own ontology, one that must be in conversation with and critical of nonrevelational worldviews. The influence of Gordon Clark and Edgar Brightman is apparent here, as is a philosophical commitment that continues through his membership in the American Philosophical Association (I).

In all these matters, a discursive interpretation of Christian faith is to the fore, but it would be wrong to identify Henry simply as a rationalist. He contests evangelical positions that seek to validate Christian faith in toto by reason, and he also argues with others who think one can come to faith by reason. These limitations do not, of course, deny that the Holy Spirit uses reason as an instrument of persuasion. Henry believes that theology develops out of a fundamental framework of faith, a "revelational axiom" into which one is brought by an act of

---

19. *GRA*, I:232.

faith through the power of the Holy Spirit (I, II). Reason functions as partner in that act by clearing the ground of presumedly rational objections to faith, and after that act reason shows the logical warrants for faith.

GOD AND CHRISTIAN FAITH

Henry's massive volumes on revelation and authority are so designed that the content, as well as the method, of discerning truth is set forth. Under the word *God* in the title is found the outline of a full-scale dogmatics. Drawing on Henry's earlier writing as well as the subject material in his magnum opus, I identify briefly some of those doctrinal propositions.

The doctrine of God is to the foreground as the logical companion of the doctrine of revelation — the God who "stands" is the One who "speaks" and "shows." The deeds of that same God — as the One who "stoops" and "stays" — constitute the material for the traditional doctrines of creation, humanity, Christ, church, salvation, Providence, and the last things.

In a wide-ranging debate with philosophical and theological alternatives, classical and contemporary (such as Platonism, Aristotelianism, Scholasticism, positivism, personalism, existentialism, process thought), Henry argues the case for "evangelical theism" (V, VI). Unabashedly defending supernaturalism, Henry declares God to be the living, personal Spirit of the Bible, infinite, eternal, immutable, omniscient, omnipresent, omnipotent, foreordaining (election/divine decrees) as well as foreknowing, yet not in violation of human freedom (V, VI). Critical of liberal and neoorthodox theologians who focus too exclusively on divine love, Henry stresses the parity of divine righteousness and benevolence, with a concern that one not lose view of the sinner's accountability before the holiness of God (VI). The One with these attributes and perfections is the triune God, whose three persons, economic and immanent, express tripersonality in unipersonality. That only God knows the depths of the divine being, that human formulations do not "exhaustively" define that ultimate reality, does not preclude the knowability of God and the reliability of biblical teaching about the One Who Is (V).

Following the acts in the biblical drama, Henry turns to the doctrine of creation, developing it against the background of the revived creationist-evolutionist controversy of the 1980s. He expounds the well-known orthodox themes on the goodness but not the divinity of finite being (creation out of nothing), human nature as uniquely made in the image of God, with special attention to human rational and spiritual capacities and the creation of angels as "messengers of God." Henry examines evolutionist and young-earth scenarios of the world's origin and argues that the Genesis account does deal with the how as well as the what and why, interpreting the order of the days and the acts of God at each level to be theologically significant — although not so the length of the days, therefore leaving room for the results of careful geological research. In the same vein, he asserts the reality of a paradise before the fall and the historicity of the fall — that of Adam and Eve and Satan and the demonic legions — although he recognizes that one must honor the literary genre for what it is in the details, rather than forcing those details into the doctrine (VI).

Henry follows classical theology in the doctrine of the person of Christ, holding to Christ's deity, humanity, and unity. Continuing the current stress of Protestant orthodoxy on the virgin birth, the miracles of Christ, and the bodily resurrection, he argues against a view of natural law as a closed system. On the work of Christ, he continues the evangelical accent on Calvary and finds a central place for the penal substitutionary view of the atonement, yet not to the exclusion of the Galilean Christ, whose teaching figures prominently in his epistemology and ethics (II, III, VI). Here too is a strong emphasis on the uniqueness of Christ in the face of modern pluralism and its tendencies to relativize particularist truth claims (III, VI). In subjective soteriology, Henry continues the Protestant emphasis on salvation by grace through faith, stressing the personal experience of regeneration and the fruit it bears in a sanctified life and evangelistic commitment (VI). In a fashion commensurate with these soteriological themes, he understands the church as a regenerate community marked by baptismal profession at the age of accountability and showing signs of its faithfulness through witness in word and deed. Proclamation and defense of the gospel are its principal mission, but one that includes as well personal and social ethical concern carried out primarily by the Christian believer at work in the world.

Henry points to "the God who stays" as One whose providence watches over the world both in its microcosmic and in its macrocosmic circumstances, and who by the gift of faith and the ministry of prayer enables humans to face with trust and hope the enigma of evil. God leads the world to its completion and fulfillment when Christ personally returns to judge the living and the dead at the general resurrection, with the elect going to eternal bliss and the damned to their eternal destiny with Satan and his minions, as the kingdom comes and God unveils the divine glory (VI). Henry shuns making further eschatological details a test of Christian fellowship, although his own view is broadly premillennial.

ETHICS

Quoting Alvah Hovey approvingly, Henry says that "in the order of logical study, Christian ethics must follow Christian theology."[20] I honor that sequence here, although Henry's ethical concern is manifest wherever his theology is expounded. Indeed, ethics was the emphasis of his influential early book *The Uneasy Conscience of Modern Fundamentalism* and characterized his major intellectual effort, *Christian Personal Ethics*, until the launching of his 1978–83 project in a wider systematics.

---

20. *Christian Personal Ethics* (Grand Rapids: Eerdmans, 1957), p. 197.

Also, his editorship of *Baker's Dictionary of Christian Ethics* reflects the importance of this subject for him. The moral decay in culture and the inadequacy of secular moral theory, on the one hand, and the concern about unclarity in personal and social ethics in the churches, on the other, constitute the reference points for the development of his views.

In his textbook work on ethics (identified in the title as "personal ethics" but far more wide-ranging), Henry criticizes a variety of ancient and contemporary theories — naturalisms, idealisms, existentialisms — and finds that these "speculative ethics" divorced from revelation are too much prey to the human revolt against God and thus mired in relativity and sterility. Respecting the potential of moral sensitivity in all humans through the continued but distorted image of God, he believes that one must enrich and redirect these impulses by an understanding of "the good as the will of the Lord" given in Scripture.[21] At its center one finds the disclosure of *agape* in the person of Jesus Christ, where its embodiment and teaching provide the definitive moral norm. Yet one cannot juxtapose a christocentric perspective to the concern for law and justice in the Hebrew Bible and in the New Testament. Nor can one reduce it to the liberals' Jesus of history; it must be united with obedience to the crucified and risen Lord of apostolic testimony.[22] Thus "comprehensive moral principles," absolute in character, together with specific rules in some areas of application, and Christ as perfect exemplification, give guidance to the regenerate believer and also provide a rationally compelling model for the world at large.[23]

Social ethics for Henry means the relating of these biblical standards to human life in communities and institutions in which one must confront questions of justice, peace, order, law, and freedom without succumbing to such current ideologies as

---

21. Ibid., pp. 209-18.
22. Ibid., pp. 219-35, 327-418.
23. See also his critique of John Yoder's pacifism in *GRA*, IV:531-37.

191

Marxism and liberation theology (IV). Faulting fundamentalists past and present for their interiorizing of piety, he calls evangelicals to be the "vanguard" rather than the "rearguard" of efforts in society to make and keep life human.

But one should not mount the impact of the Christian community on society through the kind of social action that liberal and mainstream church bodies too often attempt: "The use of political compulsion to regenerate society is alien to both American politics and to the Protestant religious heritage."[24] The chief tasks of the church are preaching the gospel and carrying out evangelism. Through this mission, lives are changed and, in turn, make their social witness — one carried out through the ministry of the laity in their vocations and in terms of responsible Christian citizenship. Mission also can be exercised in the preaching and teaching of the church as it holds the state and other institutions accountable to transcendent reality. Para-church ministries of social service are natural avenues of Christian discipleship (World Vision, the largest evangelical social agency, and one with which Henry has long been affiliated, is a good example). The church in general and theology in particular seek to provide sound general principles from Scripture for the guidance of Christians living out their social commitment in the world, yet without prescribing or endorsing specific programs. The church endeavors to establish in its own household the practice of righteousness, serving thereby as a model for the larger community.

THEOLOGICAL ACHIEVEMENT

The conventional wisdom about the demise of theological giants in the latter half of the twentieth century invites some second thoughts. Indeed, the writing of Carl Henry has not received the

24. *Aspects of Christian Social Ethics* (Grand Rapids: Eerdmans, 1964), p. 144.

attention in the wider culture of a Barth, Niebuhr, or Tillich, nor has it influenced the broad sweep of Christian thought as have some of these earlier figures. But the extensive and formidable nature of Henry's systematic work has begun to evoke comparison with some of the century's notables. Like others of eminent stature, he speaks for a considerable constituency, an evangelical presence he has helped to shape and bring to self-awareness, and one that universally acknowledges him as its preeminent voice. As the evangelical community itself comes more and more to constitute the mainstream of North American church life and thought, an awareness is developing that other giants may be in the land.[25]

On the specifics of theological content, Henry's argument for the cognitive weight of biblical and theological assertions has had an influence both in and beyond evangelicalism. His stress on propositional revelation and his criticism of views that reduce faith to the experience of personal encounter or historical event, or reduce theological language to evocative or expressive functions, have earned considerable attention. His insistence that Christian faith makes universal truth claims as well as personal ones has become a force to be reckoned with in contemporary theological debate. Closely associated with this point is his defense of the metaphysical status of theological claims and his related espousal of the role of reason in theological discourse. The revived interest in apologetics among evangelicals is in no small measure due to Henry's practice of that art.[26]

The written Word makes its own way in the world but not without its chief expositors and protagonists. Henry has been

---

25. See Leslie R. Keylock, "Evangelical Protestants Take Over Center Field," *Publishers Weekly,* March 9, 1984, pp. 32-33. For my definition of *evangelical,* see my article on "Evangelical, Evangelicalism," in *Westminster Dictionary of Christian Theology,* ed. Alan Richardson and John Bowden (Philadelphia: Westminster, 1983), pp. 191-92; see also chap. 1 above. The name of Carl Henry appears more and more in the typologies of modern theology as representing a point of view and significant constituency. For example, see Avery Dulles, *Models of Revelation* (Garden City, N.Y.: Doubleday, 1983), pp. 37-41, 250-52.

26. See Patterson, *Carl F. H. Henry,* p. 9.

one of those, both giving expression to the recovery of concern for the Bible in the late twentieth century and contributing to it. Although his argument for inerrancy has had little influence beyond segments of evangelical thought and piety, his unflagging defense of biblical authority, including its inspiration and cognitive claims, has had significant impact. As it goes into translation in languages from German to Mandarin, his magnum opus promises to become the chief evangelical voice for biblical authority around the world for many years to come.

Although occupying the center only of his early intellectual endeavors, Henry's work in ethics has given a lasting bequest to the evangelical heritage. His effort to make an important place for social concern in evangelical thought and mission, including involvement with contemporary issues of justice, helped to change the direction of a movement. Further, Henry's early and continuing attention to personal ethics (which the church at large so easily lost from view in its concentration on macroquestions, and which modern relativisms eroded) anticipated and helped to inform the current concern with Christian norms for personal behavior.

In these and other areas, firmness of conviction marks Henry's achievement, which is nonetheless held together in a remarkable way with openness to dialogue and collegiality with others in the faith community who see things differently.

HENRY'S CRITICS

Because Henry has taken religious epistemology as the framework for his major systematic work, one can range his critics along a continuum of its options. To Henry's far left are those who assume that human experience, in one or another sense, is the source and norm of truth and as such tells one nothing of the God to whom Henry testifies. Naturalism in its various expressions accuses Henry of supernaturalist mythmaking that cannot stand up under the scrutiny of empirical and rational verification procedures or represents the ideology of the ruling classes and the escapist projection of a premodern subculture. Closer to the middle are critics who believe that one must relate universal human experience to the lore of faith in a critical fashion, and they fault Henry for overly exuberant claims about special revelation. Thus earlier liberals and neo-naturalists, and later process, secular, existentialist, and liberation theologians, declare that evangelical orthodoxy fails the tests put to it by the modern mind, the deepest human sensibilities, or the most rigorous moral imperatives. Still closer to the middle are those who share Henry's commitment to special revelation but hold that he has succumbed to an Enlightenment rationalism by construing it too exclusively in propositional terms. Others, even persons of similar evangelical persuasion, believe that Henry has not honored the Enlightenment contributions to critical scholarship in his determined defense of biblical inerrancy. To the right of Henry are fellow inerrantists who believe him to be too moderate in spirit and theology about matters of both orthodoxy and rationality. Further to the right are fundamentalists and the hyperorthodox who hold that he has accommodated to modernity, has combined faith with social ethics or with the wrong social ethics, or has given insufficient attention to apocalyptic or too much latitude to biblical criticism.

Henry's friendly critics in the ranks of a developing evangelical-ecumenical partnership pose the following kinds of questions:

1. Cannot one defend cognitive truth claims and propositional revelation with the recognition, at the same time, of *(a)* the analogical character of faith language with its overlap of identity but acknowledgment of divine mystery; *(b)* the enrichment and corrigibility of theological assertions as the Spirit lets "ever new light and truth break forth from God's Holy Word" and thus the development of doctrine; and *(c)* the inseparability of personal trust from the truth claims of faith *(fiducia* bonded to *assensus)* and thus the status of theological assertions as "affirmations" rather than "propositions"?

2. Can one grant an "epistemic Word" parity with the incarnate Word in such a way that the perfections of Christ's humanity appropriate to the latter are paralleled by claims for the perfections of human authorship in the former? Is the lordship of Christ over the Bible given due honor by a theory of inerrancy that links historical and scientific matters with the revelation of the eternal Word? Indeed, given the dispute among evangelicals about the meaning of the word *inerrancy,* can it function as a modern battle cry? Does the "domino theory," which sees the inevitability of doctrinal erosion in the wake of deviance on inerrancy, have the empirical and rational warrants befitting Henry's esteem of reason?

3. Should not the church have a higher profile in Henry's authority structure because *(a)* it functions covertly at various points as an instrument of Providence in the canonization and transmission process, as a resource in the identification of classical doctrine in Scripture, and as a principle of selection among doctrines in the case of teachings accented by evangelicals; and *(b)* Scripture testifies to the presence of the Spirit in the church, giving therein knowledge as well as power? Thus do the church and its traditions not serve as a guardian against the pick-and-choose temptations of biblical interpretation by functioning as ministerial while Scripture remains magisterial?

4. Does Henry give reason too prominent a place as an authority in one sense and too inadequate a place in another sense? The process of deductive reasoning is always in the hands of a finite and sinful reasoner and as such is subject to the limitations and agenda of the one doing the reasoning, making inordinate confidence in it suspect. As thought rising from a given time and place, although vulnerable to the same conditions of creation and the fall, reason may also propose contextual questions to and give fresh perspective on faith, serving thereby as a catalytic agent to a deeper understanding of the Bible and the gospel, although always under the norm of Scripture.

5. If the experience of today's human context — with special respect to the perils of nuclear war, economic justice,

and political tyranny — is accorded a catalytic role in the interpreting of Scripture, should not the biblical judgments on war and peace, solidarity with the poor, and liberation of the oppressed play a larger role in social ethics and in the mission of the church today?

CONCLUSION

Critical attention and the impressive proportions of the work I have examined give force to Henry biographer Bob E. Patterson's description of him as "the prime interpreter of evangelical theology, one of its leading theoreticians, and now in his seventies the unofficial spokesman for the entire tradition."[27] The test of time contributes as well to this judgment. In an era of transient theologies and the accommodation of faith to ideologies of both the right and the left, Henry has embodied his own ideal of consistency and has demonstrated an uncommon theological durability. Thus he has played a decisive role in making evangelical thought an articulate conversation partner in the theological dialogue of the twentieth century, as well as "striking a blow for the faith."

---

27. Ibid., p. 131.

DAVID TRACY,
EVANGELICALLY CONSIDERED

MARTIN Marty once described David Tracy as "the most original of today's Catholic theologians, and one with whom other theologians, Catholic and Protestant, have to reckon."[1] Evangelical Christians need to participate in the reckoning. Indeed, Tracy's recent writings indicate a readiness for this engagement.

Three features of Tracy's thought raise issues of special interest to evangelical theology. Each has to do with theological method: typology, correlation, and conversation.

TYPOLOGY

Typology is the attempt to classify all the options in a field of inquiry according to discernible major tendencies, with due allowance for nuances within, and mobility between and among, the designated types. Although not employing the language of typology, Tracy frequently uses this mode of analysis. For example, in *The Analogical Imagination* it appears in his classification of theological ventures according to their social location, constituency, and purpose: academic or fundamental theology,

---

1. Quoted in Eugene Kennedy, "A Dissenting Voice: Catholic Theologian David Tracy," *New York Times Magazine,* Nov. 9, 1986, p. 23.

systematic or church theology, and practical or political theology.[2] These are *descriptive* distinctions, albeit with a hint of normativity in the weight given throughout his writing to perspectives that rise from the polis and the academy and thus to fundamental and sociopolitical theology. In other work, however, Tracy's sifting and sorting have clear normative intent and corresponding implications for my topic.

In "On Naming the Present," Tracy organizes the current interpretations of the phenomenon of "modernity" according to their position as (1) the defenders of modernity, (2) the exponents of antimodernity, and (3) the advocates of postmodernity.[3] He finds these perspectives both within the wider culture and in various camps of Christian theology.

Tracy uses typology not only to get the lay of the theological land but also as a point of departure for his own reconstruction. Thus he often incorporates approved aspects of the types identified in the development of an alternative type. For example, in the matter of modernity he offers the reader a fourth option identified as "mystical-prophetic resistance and hope."[4]

In another essay he takes a similar tack in commenting on theological method: "Every great religion, Friedrich Heiler once observed, is comprised of three fundamental elements: the mystical, the institutional, and the intellectual. Only when all three are flourishing may the religion itself be said to flourish. However limited the applicability of Heiler's observations may be for other religious traditions, it remains, I believe, the most fruitful hypothesis for understanding the Roman Catholic tradition."[5] Here one can note both the striving for inclusivity through an

---

2. David Tracy, *The Analogical Imagination: Christian Theology and the Culture of Pluralism* (New York: Crossroad, 1981), pp. 3-98.

3. David Tracy, "On Naming the Present," in *On the Threshold of the Third Millennium,* Concilium, special issue, ed. Philip Hillyer (London: SCM; Philadelphia: Trinity Press International, 1990), pp. 66-85.

4. David Tracy, "The Uneasy Alliance Reconceived," *Theological Studies* 50 (1989): 548-70.

5. Ibid., p. 548.

appreciation of the values in the various types (an anticipation of the theme of "conversation" and with it a reworking of his Roman Catholic tradition in terms of a *catholicity* of approach to a topic) and a linkage of Christian faith to wider religious phenomena.

Typology can also function for Tracy in a more polemical fashion. This function is at work in his proposal (in alliance with Hans Küng) of "correlational" theology as a "new paradigm" that should replace — and is replacing — the obsolescent "classicist" paradigm.[6] Although Tracy seeks to honor the continuities and bring along the best of the old, reflecting therein the inclusive motif of general typological usage, the correlational option clearly wins out. I find the same juxtaposition between "us" and "them" — now even sharper — in Tracy's dismissal of fundamentalism in Christian theologies and other religious traditions.

Evangelical Response

As an evangelical *ecumenical,* I find Tracy a kindred soul in both his use of typology and his appropriation of it in order to set forth a more inclusive perspective on doctrine. In the first case, it reflects a willingness to listen to the range of voices in the Christian community on a subject of mutual concern. The model for that willingness is Paul's wise counsel to the partisans in the church at Corinth (1 Cor. 12–14) to honor all the parts of the Body. In the second instance, the challenge to reductionism, the absolutizing of partial truths, is faithful to classical Christian teaching from the early christological controversies forward. Thus all who honor the Scriptures and the church's struggles to see and proclaim the faith in its totality should give a firm yes to "catholicity."

As an *evangelical* ecumenical, however, I find Tracy's typology wanting. If this mode of analysis entails an exhaustive

---

6. Ibid.

review of current options and seeks from it a fuller alternative, then one must challenge the narrowness of the constructs, especially with regard to the exclusion of an evangelical option. But one must also challenge the benign neglect of other representatives of classical faith. This constricted horizon has a history.

In his first major work, *Blessed Rage for Order,* Tracy canvasses the "New Pluralism in Theology." Its range includes orthodox, liberal, neoorthodox, radical, and revisionist types.[7] One could not expect Tracy, writing in the early 1970s, to include in the orthodox option the then-developing Frei-Lindbeck retrieval position, of which he later takes cognizance (the Yale theology). But he limits the representatives of orthodoxy to "Denzinger-theologies" in his own tradition and the "sophisticated biblical theologies as the 'salvation history' approaches of Cullmann and others."[8] The evangelical option is invisible. Tracy does make passing reference to one representative in a footnote mentioning G. K. Berkouwer's *The Triumph of Grace in the Theology of Karl Barth,* "a critique of Barth from the 'orthodox' model."[9] But he does not *engage* evangelical thought, either as a subset of the orthodox model or as a type in its own right.

The pattern of exclusion continues in *The Analogical Imagination* and *Plurality and Ambiguity.* But a new category does appear in the latter volume: neoconservative. The term refers to a constituency that runs from the Ayatollah Khomeini through the Holy Office to Reverend Falwell and Rabbi Kehane, all representing "the worldwide neoconservative resurgence."[10] An "us and them" typology is at work here. "Fundamentalism" has become the term for the foe. Perhaps Tracy would subsume "evangelical" under Jerry Falwell, but one hopes not.

---

7. David Tracy, *Blessed Rage for Order: The New Pluralism in Theology* (New York: Seabury, 1975).

8. Ibid., p. 36.

9. Ibid., p. 97.

10. David Tracy, *Plurality and Ambiguity: Hermeneutics, Religion, Hope* (San Francisco: Harper & Row, 1987), p. 95.

Are there others in continuity with the old orthodox model? A new one does appear. The Yale theology has made its presence felt, one Tracy acknowledges to differ significantly from "the literalism and fundamentalism of religious dogmatists in all traditions."[11] He recognizes Hans Frei as a legitimate interlocutor and discusses him in several paragraphs. Tracy also refers to George Lindbeck's work in a footnote, and makes passing reference to "the resurgence of social-justice concerns in many evangelical theologies."[12] But Tracy says nothing more at this stage of his thought.

Tracy's more recent essays, however, suggest a change in his thought. In the typology organized around the theme of modernity, fundamentalism and neoconservatism are no longer synonymous but appear separately, both under the antimodernity category. The former is still the evil empire. In fundamentalism "all the ethical and political values of modernity (individual rights, pluralism, a democratic ethos, a trust in public reason) must be rejected at the very same time as technologised science and industrialism are embraced. . . . This rejection includes all theology which employs modern scientific methods (like historical criticism and ideology critique)."[13] Yes, there are reasons for its power and growth — its protest against the denial of tradition, community, ultimate meaning, and hope by the forces of modernity. But it is disqualified as a conversation partner: "It must be frankly, even bluntly, stated that religious fundamentalism cannot be taken as an intellectually serious theological option."[14]

The same does not apply to the neoconservatives. "The non-fundamentalist version of anti-modernity, on the other hand, merits not merely human but full intellectual respect . . . as in conservative evangelical but not fundamentalist Christians

---

11. Ibid., p. 101.
12. Ibid., p. 102.
13. Tracy, "On Naming the Present," p. 74.
14. Ibid., p. 75.

in the Americas, as in Roman Catholic traditional theologies as distinct from the traditionalism of Lefebvre, as in the great resurgence of Islamic thought as distinct from Khomeini, as in the retrieval of Jewish traditions across all the forms of Judaism."[15] Specifically, what Christian forms? "Honourable 'post-liberal' options: like the new Barthianism of the Yale school; the new sectarian insistence on pure witness of much Western Christian ethics . . . the great theology of retrieval of Hans Urs von Balthasar . . . the call to reaffirm Christian identity in the Roman Catholic theology of Ratzinger."[16]

Tracy has given the "honourable 'post-liberal' options" considerable attention in his current writing. Indeed, he has been convinced of "the value of the Frei-Lindbeck insistence upon the 'plain reading' of the common passion narrative,"[17] insofar as it casts light on "what Schubert Ogden has nicely named 'criteria of appropriateness.'"[18] Although acknowledging how central that plain sense should be for all Christian theology,[19] he believes the plain sense should also be "open both to further questioning of its coherence with the 'Jesus-kerygma' of the original apostolic witness as well as to further reflections on the theological implications of the diversity of readings of that plain sense in the New Testament itself and, indeed, in all biblically sound readings of the common narrative of the great Christian tradition."[20] Further, in contrast to the Frei-Lindbeck option, Tracy holds that "there must also be criteria of intelligibility or credibility for a full theological method."[21]

Does the christological and biblical "centrality" asserted

---

15. Ibid.

16. Ibid., pp. 75-76.

17. David Tracy, "On Reading the Scriptures Theologically," in *Theology and Dialogue: Essays in Conversation with George Lindbeck* (Notre Dame: University of Notre Dame Press, 1990), p. 36.

18. Ibid., p. 37.

19. Ibid., p. 35.

20. Ibid., p. 37.

21. Ibid., p. 36.

by the postliberal advocates here die the death of a thousand qualifications? I will return to this question in analyzing the role of Scripture in Tracy's method. For now, on matters of taxonomy, I look for engagement with the evangelical option. As already noted, he does mention it in a clause juxtaposing evangelicals to fundamentalists as part of "the neo-conservative revival . . . a profound and, in many ways, a heartening phenomenon."[22] Evangelicals get "honourable mention" but no attention.

There is a certain irony here. Not only does the evangelical model constitute a major alternative type, but some sociological indicators suggest that it is the working theology of many in the cultural situation to which a correlational theology must speak. For one, they make up one of the "street theologies" by which ordinary folk live.[23] Tracy calls one to pay attention to these grass-root phenomena: "There is perhaps no option more important for the intellectuals in [any] religion to reflect upon than the ordinary ways practiced by most members of the religion. . . . The religions are carried along at least as much by the vast undertow of ordinary people leading ordinary religious lives as by the classic prophets, mystics, and saints."[24] Without attention to this option in both its street and classroom expressions, the quest for inclusivity will fall short of its goal.

CORRELATION

"The classicist paradigm of theology is spent."[25] Working with Thomas Kuhn's much-discussed term,[26] Tracy believes that a

---

22. Tracy, "On Naming the Present," p. 75.

23. Tracy, *Plurality and Ambiguity*, p. 102.

24. Ibid., p. 96.

25. David Tracy, "Theological Method," in *Christian Theology: An Introduction to Its Traditions and Tasks,* ed. Peter C. Hodgson and Robert H. King, rev. and enl. ed. (Philadelphia: Fortress, 1985), p. 36.

26. One that itself may be a "spent force," having been adopted by

new theological paradigm is in the making. The volume *Paradigm Change in Theology,* with papers from a major conference on the subject edited and introduced by Tracy and Küng, tells the story.

What is the new paradigm that is on the way to replacing the old one — the fresh way of interpreting the theological task made necessary because of the manifest anomalies in the classicist framework? It is "the attempt to establish mutually critical correlations between an interpretation of the Christian tradition and an interpretation of contemporary experience."[27] Assumed here are two constants, which Tracy says Küng describes as " 'the present world of experience in all its ambivalence, contingency and change' and 'the Judaeo-Christian tradition which is ultimately based on the Christian message, the Gospel of Jesus Christ.' "[28]

In contrast to the classicist paradigm's assumption that the tradition is immediately accessible, a new historical consciousness makes moderns aware that the easily retrieved thing-in-itself is in fact an interpretation of it shaped by historical factors. Further, a hermeneutics of suspicion reminds one of how much race, class, sex, and other privileged groups' power interests have controlled both the original text and the history of its interpretation. For Tracy, to live and work out of the paradigm change means being clear about the process of interpretation itself. His reading and writing over the years have given much attention to the hermeneutical debates, especially those in the philosophical arena.

---

conservative political theorists and now the subject of satire — e.g., *Newsweek,* Dec. 17, 1990, p. 17: "Overheard: My theory on the word paradigm is that it's like an old dog. It drools on you, but you remember it. — Deputy Assistant to the President, on why his much discussed new domestic policy is called the New Paradigm."

27. David Tracy, "Hermeneutical Reflections in the New Paradigm," in *Paradigm Change in Theology: A Symposium for the Future,* trans. Margaret Kohl, ed. Hans Küng and David Tracy (New York: Crossroad, 1989), p. 35.

28. Ibid.

How can one — or even *can* one — be in communication with a text (for Tracy, especially a "classic" text) from which one is separated by distinctive contexts? If one is to "correlate" (Tillich) message and situation, one had better be able to engage the former and understand something of the latter.

On the one hand, Tracy knows the doubts now current about the simplistic Enlightenment assumption that one can understand a text by freeing oneself from biases — Gadamer's "prejudice against pre-judgements." On the other hand, Tracy still believes in the possibility and necessity of historical-critical inquiry, which honors "the liberating demand classically expressed by Kant as *aude sapere:* i.e., dare to think for yourself."[29] But the problem that makes the Enlightenment program a half-truth is the impossibility of jumping out of one's cultural skin: "No interpreter . . . is as purely autonomous as the Enlightenment model promised."[30] Pervasive inherited traditions live on in language and cultural frameworks. One cannot deny the social formation that affects the way one reads data. Furthermore, the hermeneuticians of suspicion have shown how standard construals of ancient texts, and the texts themselves, have been hostage to the power agendas of both their interpreters and their authors.

One uses critical tools to do the hard work of unmasking these captivities. Such exposure is a kind of therapy. Indeed, a refusal to go through the cleansing disciplines makes genuine conversation impossible.

> In the course of any conversation, if any one of us begins to suspect (the verb here is apt) that our conversation-partner is psychotic, we would be justified in suspending the conversation for the moment. . . . There can be no naive claims to immediacy nor to certainty. . . . For all is interpretation. . . . [We] need to give up the quest for an illusory ahistorical

---

29. Ibid., p. 38.
30. Ibid.

certainty [as with] neo-scholastics and all traditionalists and fundamentalists . . . returning to their untroubled and ahistorical fortresses.[31]

The task of correlation entails going as far as one can to retrieve critically the tradition, and to discern critically the shape of the historical context one is called to address. Given the culture-relative character of the seekers at both poles of the correlation, access to text and context demands a plenitude of perspectives. Because all theology is hermeneutical — an interpretation of the text and context — interchange is essential. Hence the importance of "conversation."

How mutually critical correlation functions in terms of a specific text I discuss in the next section. For now I concentrate on the larger theory, the "revised correlationist paradigm."

Evangelical Response

Evangelicals and proponents of the classicist (better, "classical") paradigm respond to Tracy's proposals in terms of some standard teachings of historic Christian faith. Based on these norms, some initial agreements are evident.

1. Human finitude. Human beings are made in the image of God. But at the same time they are creatures of time and space. This psychosomatic reality means that human thought is shaped by its physical and historical contingencies. Humans do not have a God's-eye view of things. Thus it comes as no surprise that finitude creeps into human perceptions and formulations. Based on this realism about the human condition, one has every reason to be self-critical about too-quick claims to have the thing-in-itself, whether that be the text or the context. An illustration of this self-criticism among even the most conservative of evangelicals is the determination to have the purest of original

---

31. Tracy, *Paradigm Change in Theology,* pp. 44, 462, 463, 465.

biblical texts, and hence, as Carl Henry notes, the zeal of these evangelicals for textual criticism — the quest for the autographs.[32]

2. Human sin. Evangelicals have a very sober view of the extent of the fall. The pervasiveness and depth of sin mean its presence, along with finitude, in all human perceptions and formulations. Evangelical faith entails sobriety about the sin at work in claims to truth, particularly those in which self-righteousness cloaks the will to power in the garments of piety, wisdom, or morality, evangelical self-righteousness included.[33]

Discoveries of finitude and sin at work in those who claim to master either the tradition or the situation are a late arrival at insights long held in the very classical paradigm considered obsolescent. But the issues around sin that need to be joined are (a) the classical and evangelical assertion that sin has met its match in Jesus Christ, and the epistemological consequences thereof, specifically the accessibility of revelation; and (b) the continuing seriousness of the effects of the fall on *general* human experience, and thus the brokenness of all claims to ultimate truth made by the culture's philosophies, sociologies, literary theories, and so forth.

3. Also in that classical paradigm is a commitment to the helpless and the hapless, which Tracy, acknowledging the contributions of liberation theology, sees as integral to the new paradigm. The "other" is ever present in Scripture, from the prophets' preferential option for the poor to the New Testament community's dignifying of society's rejects — the slave, the widow, the orphan, the woman, the stranger, the sick, the starving. Also to be found in this charter is the Corinthian call for a mutually corrective conversation within the Body of Christ.

----

32. Carl Henry, *God, Revelation and Authority*, 6 vols. (Waco: Word, 1976–83), 4:231-42.

33. A prime example of the failure to take evangelicalism's own doctrine of sin seriously is the Religious Right. See my *The Religious Right and Christian Faith* (Grand Rapids: Eerdmans, 1982), pp. 45-47.

But believers have a long way to go in appropriating these traditions and responding to these imperatives. To the charge that one has passed by on the other side of the "other," one can only reply, mea culpa.

A response to the correlational proposal requires a clarification. At times Tracy suggests that Christian theology is in practice always correlational, and the "new" aspect has to do with the acknowledgment of that fact and active pursuit of its implications. "In one sense, this hermeneutical formulation is simply a rendering explicit and deliberate of the fact which unites all forms of theology."[34] Indeed, classical theology has explicitly pursued this agenda, and evangelical theology in many places does so today as well. If correlation means the interpretation of faith in the idiom of its time and place, then such has been the practice from the Gospel of John's use of *logos* categories through the substance philosophy employed in Nicea's *homoousios* to the selective use of liberation postulates in the World Council of Churches' official statements. In evangelical circles, C. S. Lewis's apologetic has reached almost icon status.

David Wells has given programmatic exposition of this bipolarity: "It is the task of theology, then, to discover what God has said in and through Scripture and to clothe that in a conceptuality which is native to our own age. Scripture, at its *terminus a quo*, needs to be de-contextualized in order to grasp its transcultural content, and it needs to be re-contextualized in order that its content may be meshed with the cognitive assumptions and social patterns of our own time."[35] These are standard assertions of defenders of a classical paradigm. One cannot easily dismiss them as ahistorical naivetés.

But something more is going on in Tracy's version of the

---

34. Tracy, *Paradigm Change in Theology*, p. 462.
35. David F. Wells, "The Nature and Function of Theology," in *The Use of the Bible in Theology: Evangelical Options*, ed. Robert K. Johnston (Atlanta: John Knox, 1985), p. 177.

correlation model, and here one can note a distinct difference between his view and an evangelical perspective. It has to do with how these poles function in the dynamic between text and context. For Tracy the adjective *mutual* is crucial — "mutual correlation," and even "mutual transformation" as that pertains, for example, to "other classic religions . . . and classic secular, scientific and humanistic and post-humanistic world-views."[36] These mutually corrigible constants in Tracy's thought are weighted quite differently in the classic paradigm and its evangelical version: yes, a "hermeneutical circulation" that moves between text and context; no, not a "hermeneutical circle" with equal weight given to each pole, but a "hermeneutical arrow" with its normative tip, Scripture. All translation and interpretations proffered for the modern context must pass muster before the authority of Scripture. Scripture is the *source,* and the world of human experience is the *setting.* There are not *two* sources in mutual correlation.[37]

In Tracy's recent writing on the authority and interpretation of Scripture, one can draw similar conclusions about the normativity of Scripture for Tracy himself. In language reminiscent of Karl Barth, Tracy declares: "[Christian] revelation is the event of divine self-manifestation in the words of scripture. . . . The scripture remains the authoritative *normans non normata.*"[38] This contention sounds similar to Tracy's recent acknowledgment of the "centrality" of the passion narratives as highlighted in the Frei-Lindbeck proposals. Does either statement signify the theological normativity of a christologically read Scripture?

They would, according to an evangelically interpreted ecu-

---

36. Tracy, *Paradigm Change in Theology,* p. 43.

37. For an exposition of this idea see my *The Christian Story,* vol. 2: *Authority: Scripture in the Church for the World* (Grand Rapids: Eerdmans, 1987), pp. 341-50 and passim.

38. David Tracy, "The Word and Written Texts in the Hermeneutics of Christian Revelation," pp. 3, 7. Forthcoming.

menical faith, if "Jesus Christ" signified not only the New Testament narratives as such, or New Testament narratives as appropriated by or experienced in the Christian community, but New Testament narratives (against a Hebrew Bible background) with their *identifiable assertions* about who God is, who Christ is, what Christ does to reconcile God and the world, who humans are, and what humans are destined for. Some biblically warranted affirmations are integral to the meaning of Jesus Christ. The presence and authoritative status of these assertions are not clear from Tracy's hermeneutical principles or the conclusions he draws from them.

The "plain sense" of the narratives themselves must be questioned for their "coherence with the 'Jesus-kerygma' . . . the diversity of readings of that plain sense . . . and . . . all biblically sound readings of the common narrative of the great Christian tradition."[39] Tracy mentions in this connection a range of readings — Funk, Ricoeur, McFague, Crossan, Perrin, Eliade, Ogden — many of which would appear to be on a collision course with either the "plain sense" of defining narratives or implied defining assertions, even if they are understood in a community sense. Tracy is right that it is "theologically impoverishing" not to take into account this range of opinion and even a much greater range of the interpretation of texts, but coherence with them is something else again.

Two further qualifiers erode the stability of a christological cum biblical norm: First, the role of "intelligibility" in making theological judgments, "the need for the criteria of credibility along with the criteria of appropriateness."[40] Whatever the status of biblical authority, even if one could identify a set of normative biblical assertions derivative from the plain meaning of the narratives — ones that "should define but not confine the possible range of Christian construals" — their validity would

---

39. Tracy, "On Reading the Scriptures Theologically," p. 37.
40. Ibid., p. 60.

be subject to tests of cultural or philosophical intelligibility and adequacy. Delimiting the biblical *normans non normata* to the pole of "appropriateness" undermines its criteriological status.

Second, the association of the "plain sense" with "the obvious or direct sense of the text for the Christian community."[41] This *communal* understanding of "common sense" is an important corrective to the individualistic tendencies of traditional Protestant hermeneutics.[42] But the community sense is always itself accountable to something and Someone beyond it. The perspicuity of Scripture means that any given ecclesial reading is always corrigible by common sense or plain sense in its *widest* meaning — what a "careful reading" (Tracy here and there acknowledges just that) by any reader might yield. Also, as Barth has helped to clarify, common ecclesial or wider communal readings themselves always stand under a Word that God may choose to speak through Scripture, against these readings. Revisionist and postliberal theologies (and thus Tracy's recent positive response to Frei and Lindbeck on the "plain sense") must answer the evangelical question as to how the normativity of Scripture is still maintained when "Scripture-in-tradition" (Tracy's phrase) appears to vest final authority for its understanding in the Christian community.

The setting *does* have a significant role in this dynamism. It makes three contributions:

1. It provides the idiom in which the gospel speaks. Here the responsible translation of Scripture provides an analogy as it seeks to avoid both literal and paraphrastic options, attempting instead dynamic equivalence.

2. It poses questions to which the gospel must speak. In the present time the question of suffering and hope commands significance.[43]

---

41. Ibid., p. 38. Here Tracy cites Kathryn E. Tanner, "Theology and the Plain Sense," in *Scriptural Authority and Narrative Interpretation,* ed. Garrett Green (Philadelphia: Fortress, 1987), p. 63.

42. See my *Christian Story,* 2:160-70.

43. Ibid., pp. 233-43.

3. It functions catalytically to render patent meanings of the gospel that have been latent, contributing thereby to the development of doctrine.

Evangelical and classical understandings of correlation are grounded in a commensurate twofold doctrine of revelation: special and general revelation. General revelation, given to all humans in the state of universal sin through the covenant with Noah, allows humanity a dim awareness of the good, the true, and the beautiful and makes hearts restless for the Other — a flickering light given to keep the great Story moving forward. But this world of general revelation is, as Calvin put it, the *theater* of the divine glory, not the drama itself. Only in the singular deeds of God in Israel and finally in Jesus Christ — and in the inspired prophetic-apostolic testimony to them — is definitive disclosure given. Hence the primacy of special revelation.

The difference between the classical/evangelical paradigm of correlation and the revised correlation paradigm seems finally to rest on a difference in the doctrine of revelation. If there is absolute mutuality of criticism, then there is parity of disclosure. If parity, then the priority of special revelation is denied. How can this denial not mean an inordinate trust in the general state of human experience and wisdom, and a corresponding diminution of the unique deeds and disclosures of God?

One expected rejoinder to these criticisms is this: You are assuming an access to those definitive events through Scripture that one can no longer conceive in the postmodern world. One now knows about the chasm between the culture-relative biblical text and your culture-relative reading of it. Hence one can dismiss the classical paradigm as naive and ahistorical.

Again, the issue of revelation is at stake. To hold that God has acted disclosively in Jesus Christ means that nothing can stand in the way of the intended communication; an epistemological grace is present at this defining point. Postmodern denials of this access reduce Scripture to a species of the genus "text," which like any other text is closed off to moderns on historicist and suspicionist grounds. Thus one exercises a veto by principles of interpretation drawn from cultural sources. Functionally, this veto means not only the parity but also the priority of the situational pole of correlation. Epistemologically, it implies a serious reduction of the claims of special revelation found in Scripture and Christian tradition.

The Word of God is not the species of a universal genus defined by postmodernity, but its own genus. Access to the disclosure of the purposes of God is given by the power of God. Here is the ancient teaching of the Holy Spirit's work in the histories of Israel and Christ and their Spirit-inspired biblical interpreters, and one's illumination thereof by the internal testimony of the Holy Spirit. Although evangelicals debate, and the classical tradition debated, the extent and character of biblical inspiration, they share the common conviction that the authority of the Bible is grounded in the Holy Spirit's special gift of insight to the prophetic-apostolic witnesses. Further, the Spirit works in a confirmatory way — with biblical inspiration received by a present illumination — through the internal testimony of the Holy Spirit. However expressed — "the Word will do it," "the Spirit empowers," "grace abounds" — the integrity of this genus is affirmed in the classical/evangelical paradigm, constituting itself an anomaly in any proposed alternative paradigm.[44]

Short of the claims of special revelation, but also important, is the intelligibility of the text to all potential inquirers in or out of the trajectory of singular disclosure, a view identified in evangelical tradition as the "perspicuity of Scripture." Although some limit this intelligibility to the community of believers, I understand it here as a gift of common grace to all human beings, or the general revelation given in the Noachian covenant. As such, it maintains the existence of continuities across time and space. Thus the reader who is willing to undertake responsible exegesis

---

44. Ibid., pp. 347-50.

can discern the transcultural content of Scripture. Discernment is not the conviction that is given only by the mysteries of another grace, but it *is* something — "necessary but not sufficient." The belief in perspicuity so defined converges with hermeneutical theories and anthropological premises that affirm some measure of historical continuity and human commonality.

In the defense of both disclosive deed and common grace, evangelical hermeneutics is sensitive to any apparent constraints on the epistemological privilege of the Word incarnate, inspired, or illumined. Its challenge to the correlational paradigm is to show how that paradigm's inordinate reliance on creative cultural interpretations does not mute the Word.

CONVERSATION

The metaphor of "conversation" has a long intellectual history traceable to Plato's dialogues. Luther employed it in describing a means of grace in the congregation as the "mutual conversation and consolation" of the brothers and sisters. Hans-Georg Gadamer gave an imaginative turn to this figure of speech in his hermeneutical theory. Tracy has carried forward Gadamer's usage and widened its meaning.

For Tracy the word and concept function in two ways: as a method of interpreting texts, and as a mode of appropriating the Christian tradition. The word is drawn from interpersonal relationships, but Tracy, following Gadamer, applies it to the process of textual interpretation and then returns it to the interpersonal context in an ecclesial form. Issues of revelation and authority already canvassed come up again under this rubric.

Textual Conversation

As noted, Tracy's problematic is the cultural distance between a classic text and the reader today. The chasm is the result of a development beginning with seventeenth-century science and the eighteenth-century Enlightenment, continuing in the rise of nineteenth-century historical consciousness and the hermeneuticians of suspicion of that century and of the twentieth (Marx, Freud, Nietzsche, and their followers), and climaxed by today's liberation movements and the raised awareness of world religions. Thus interpreters see the ancient text as enclosed by its historical context, and modern readers by the modern context, with both evidencing power agendas that one must unmask.

What then can one gain from encounter with an ancient text? Tracy wants to avoid, on the one hand, a simplistic claim to retrieval (the plans of both antimodernity and modernity), and, on the other hand, a despair over any contact with it and thus recourse to playful self-edification (as in postmodernity). He turns to Gadamer for help, specifically to "the game of conversation." That is, one's meeting with the text is like entry into the to-and-fro of a game. One is taken out of the normal processes of self-consciousness and caught up in the dynamisms of play. Conversation with a text begins when the world one brings to the text — one's preunderstandings and prejudgments — are nudged, pushed off balance, provoked, intrigued, questioned. Thus the "excess of meaning" in a classic text does its work of resisting the interpretive framework one is tempted to impose upon it.

This jarring and jolting reaches a point of special richness when one hears the text's existential questions as one's own questions (e.g., universal "limit questions" like "finitude or fault . . . meaning and trust")[45] and attends to its subject matter as worthy of consideration. At this luminous moment, "interpretation-as-conversation" happens. "As a work, the text produces its world of meaning in front of the text as a possible way of being in the world."[46] This "world of meaning in front of the text" includes the interpretive responses of the reader as well as the subject matter and questions of the text itself. Rejected in

---

45. Tracy, *Paradigm Change in Theology,* p. 43.
46. Ibid., p. 50.

this phrase is a settling too quickly for the historical critic's "world in back of the text," the fundamentalist's "world of the text," or the literary critic's "world in the text."

In his own formulation of this process, Tracy adds some features he believes are missing in Gadamer's analysis, ones that have to do with the critical and explanatory tools of interpretation. Needed at some juncture in the interpretive process is a hermeneutics of suspicion and a hermeneutics of retrieval. The former exposes the illusions that ancient texts and their conventional interpreters perpetrate on moderns (e.g., the pretensions to truth that cloak vested interests of class, race, sex, and condition). The latter takes seriously the form in which the ancient message comes to moderns by the use of historical-critical and literary-critical analysis. Both of these forms of exposure are required for a genuine conversation. Standing alone, however, critical methods never do bring one to definitive encounter with the text; rather, they are preparatory to that luminous exchange.

Tracy makes his proposal as an alternative to other current moves to which I have alluded, including historical reconstruction, intuiting authorial intent, abandoning the effort in playful self-edification, and control of the text for ideological ends. For my purposes, however, it is the classical hermeneutic that stands challenged. Here again both typology and correlation reenter the picture. Tracy denies the classicist belief that the reader can access Scripture to discern God's original and continuing textual intention. He requires a "new hermeneutical paradigm" to replace the retrieval theologies of Ratzinger and von Balthasar in the Roman Catholic Church, the neo-Barthianism of Lindbeck and Frei, and others striving to recover the identity of the tradition in the face of its perceived erosion. Evangelical retrieval would be included in this obsolescence.

Evangelical Response

The issues of revelation that underlie the correlational motif recur here under the rubric of conversation, with special reference to the text of Scripture. I have already mentioned the revelatory premises of incarnation, inspiration, and illumination.

Biblical hermeneutics is the art and science of interpreting Scripture. In my understanding, it entails these moves: the search for a common sense that reads the text in the company of believers past and present; a critical sense that employs responsible tools of historical and literary analysis; a canonical sense — called traditionally the "analogy of faith" — that situates the text within the whole of the canon and its pattern of teaching (the Story); and a contextual sense that draws out the implications and applications for one's personal and social setting.[47]

Exegesis undertaken on the foregoing basis questions an assumption Tracy borrowed from general hermeneutical theory that the cultural distance between Scripture and reader denies one substantive access to textual intention. Although Tracy has not gone all the way with postmodern commentators, what he leaves of the text is its capacity to provoke one's interest in, and provide access to, its "existential questions" and "subject matter." This encounter does not appear to have identifiable content that one can receive. Rather, the "world in front of the text" is the fusion of the text's provocations and the reader's interpretations. The moment of conversation that so emerges is the locus of authority. David Wells's description of some kinds of contextualization theory seems to apply here. He speaks of them as "rather like a police officer at a busy intersection,"[48] telling folk when they can stop and go, and where they can drive.

In the policing function of the conversational moment, two vital aspects of the text have been eliminated: the content and the normativity of the subject matter. If one cannot grasp the first, one cannot talk about the second. Tracy does indeed make a slight concession to access in the authority he accords to the

---

47. See my *Christian Story,* 2:157-340, and chapter 6 above.
48. Wells, "Nature and Function of Theology," p. 196.

retrieval capabilities of critical tools: not the retrieval of the authoritative content of Scripture, but the discovery of the circumstances and structures in which this elusive content took rise.

What accounts for the absence of classical content and normativity is the authority granted to the hermeneutical assumptions of modernity and postmodernity. One no longer has a conversation with the prophetic-apostolic substance but only with its questions and topics as they fuse with one's own questions and issues, a horizon found not in the text but at one remove from it. Thus the *voice* of the text itself is silenced. This "other" is told that it cannot speak, because the magisterium of today's hermeneutical scholarship has ruled it out of order.

I have already taken up some of the revelatory presuppositions of the classical and evangelical alternative to this closed conversation, and will not repeat them. I add here a few others related to the theme of conversation. The way to correct the limits and biases of readers — "sin" and "finitude" — in the Reformation tradition is through the epistemological access of the priesthood of all believers. Thus the *whole* people of God are invited into the conversation. The gift of illumination is given, as in Paul's Corinthian counsel, to the Body in its entirety, a community that ranges over both time and space. Trustworthy interpretation is catholic, universal, inclusive exegesis.

Even the culture's voices are not to be denied entrance to the conversation. The academy is welcomed to the table, with voice but no vote. On the grounds of a doctrine of general revelation, the best of the culture's insights enter the dialogue through the responsible use of critical and explanatory tools. Given the brokenness of the world's wisdom caused by the fall, the interpreter makes *eclectic,* not systematic, use of its insights, furnished thereby with the *bene esse,* not the *esse,* of textual meaning.[49]

---

49. See my *Christian Story,* 2:170-76, 259-69.

Ecclesial Conversation

The metaphor of conversation, applied initially to the dialogue of a reader with a text, moves also back into its interpersonal context. I denominate it here "ecclesial" conversation for two reasons: (1) Tracy's usage shows interesting continuities with characteristic Roman Catholic communal modes of authority and interpretation, and (2) a counterpart to the teaching office in that same tradition reappears, albeit relocated.

One can discern "the church," very broadly understood, in Tracy's descriptive and normative, textual and interpersonal, treatment of the theme of conversation. I noted previously that the text does not, as such, speak in a commanding voice, lodged as it is in its ancient communal setting, and meeting one in one's own communally shaped prejudgments. Communal tradition, there or here, exercises a decisive influence on textual questions.

Tracy argues that one needs to challenge narrow communal prejudgments brought to the text. Community conversation expands one's vision. Normatively now, in contrast to descriptively before, one requires a corrective forum. Who constitutes this community? It is certainly the church institutional, rich in the symbols that have already formed and informed the Christian theologian, and offering a range of diverse voices, exclusive of fundamentalism. But ecclesial reality extends beyond these borders. It includes those "others" long silenced by established white, Western, male, middle-class Christendom. Their critical consciousness exposes the ideological aspects of traditional theology, and one must honor the special access to truth given to the dispossessed.

Not among the oppressed, but crucial interlocutors nevertheless, are the members of the community of learning who have reflected deeply on human ways of knowing and interpreting. Their voices must be heard insofar as they bear upon analogous issues of method faced by theologians. Derrida, Habermas, Barthes, Lacan, Ricoeur, Saussure, Wittgenstein, Gadamer, Levi-Strauss — formidable figures in the philosophy of language and culture — speak to one about how to read and understand texts. They play a prominent role at the table of ecclesial conversation.

To pursue playfully an evangelical hermeneutics of suspicion on these matters of ecclesiality, one might inquire about the constituency, intentions, and auspices of the major conference on the "new paradigm" in theology from which the volume *Paradigm Change in Theology* grew. Convened by Tracy and Küng, supported by their respective institutions, the University of Chicago and the University of Tübingen, and funded by the Rockefeller Foundation, *Deutsche Forschungsgemeinschaft,* and the University of Tübingen, sixty-two theologians and philosophers gathered to explore the implications of the new paradigm for the future of theology. The intent of the organizers was to test the thesis that, even among the diversity of those represented (not so diverse as to include an evangelical presence), a revised correlational paradigm could and should set the terms for the next stage of theological inquiry. How is this conference not a hint of a new magisterium gathering in conclave to define the limits of acceptable doctrine? How is the sponsorship by the powers and principalities of modernity a sign of commitment to a "new" paradigm?

No one is so removed from either magisterial inclinations or the world's funding resources to be able to point a self-righteous finger and not acknowledge one's own complicity. Hence the role of the "other," whether it be the new exposing the pretensions of the old, or vice versa.

Evangelical Response

Some aspects of Tracy's theme of ecclesial conversation should draw positive responses from evangelicals. In principle, he has widened the range of participation in the Spirit's noetic work, pressing it beyond the official teaching office of the Roman Catholic Church to the whole people of God (and thus developing creatively the *sensus fidelium* tradition within that church).

222

This collegiality reflects the model of the Body of Christ found in Romans 12, Ephesians 4, and 1 Corinthians 12–14: the Holy Spirit gives gifts to the whole people of God, manifest in its many parts, each needing the others for the mutual upbuilding of the Body. The epistemological priesthood of all believers *is* the hermeneutical community.

Related to this point, a classical paradigm can also honor Tracy's concern to hear the communal voices of the marginalized other. Christ is present in the midst of the hungry, the naked, the prisoner, and those who feed, clothe, and visit them (Matt. 25:31-46). Christ preached good news to the poor and release to the captive, as well as mercy to the sinner (Luke 4:18).

One should listen as well to the words of wisdom from communities of wisdom outside the church, the children of Abraham raised up from stones here (Matt. 3:9). The sovereign God is the source of all truth, including that found in the broken lights of creation.

One should listen and learn, yes, but not allow this, or any expression of ecclesiality, to speak the definitive word. In evangelical perspective, "church" is a *resource,* not the source of authority. This assertion thrusts one back into the issues of textual conversation. Evangelicals must bear witness to the freedom of the Word to challenge the community. Although the church, descriptively, is present in one's theological prejudgments, and the church should be there, normatively, in the act of collegial conversation, its role is *ministerial,* not magisterial. As the Barmen Declaration put it, speaking for the Confessing Evangelical Churches in the midst of a struggle with questions of authority: "Jesus Christ, as he is attested to us in Holy Scripture, is the one Word of God which we have to hear, and which we have to trust and obey in life and in death."

One must also take issue with the makeup of the community that functions as resource. To the extent that the philosophical or literary communities of postmodernity take precedence in the conversation, or decisive authority over all claims to knowledge is given to advocacy groups, then the communities

223

of human experience speak with a louder voice than the church's own tradition and internal discourse. Scripture, the source, is "the church's book." The gift of illumination makes the whole people of God the resource hermeneutical community, drawing where it must on the common grace at work in the world of learning and action. When it is so positioned, and attentive to the Word, it exercises a fruitful ministerial stewardship.

CONCLUSION

Martin Marty was right. All theologians have business to do with David Tracy. The evangelical voice needs to be heard in the conversation. May the table talk be mutually consoling and critical.

SOURCES

"What Evangelicals Believe about the Bible: Commonality and Diversity." This derives from an overview essay for an issue of the journal *Interpretation* on "the evangelical approach to the Bible," published as "Evangelical Hermeneutics: Commonality and Diversity," *Interpretation* 43, no. 2 (April 1989): 117-29. Reprinted by permission.

"Political Fundamentalism: Distinctions and Directions." Most of this article I prepared for the conference on "Theology, Politics, and Peace," sponsored by the Candler School of Theology and the Carter Center of Emory University, April 1988, and published in *Theology, Politics, and Peace,* ed. Theodore Runyon (Maryknoll, N.Y.: Orbis, 1989), pp. 117-25. Reprinted by permission. I inserted a few paragraphs from "Evangelical Hermeneutics," the main source for chapter 1.

"The Use of Scripture in Theology." Published as "The Use of Scripture in My Work in Systematics," in *The Use of the Bible in Theology: Evangelical Options,* ed. Robert K. Johnston (Atlanta: John Knox, 1985), pp. 200-226.

"Evangelical Catholicity." Lecture given to the Mercersburg Society, June 1990, Mercersburg, Pennsylvania, and published in *New Mercersburg Review: Journal of the Mercersburg Society* no. 8 (Autumn 1990): 41-50. Reprinted by permission.

"A Narrative Theology of Revelation." Prepared for the conference on "Christian Theology in a Post-Christian World," March 1985, at Wheaton College (Illinois), and published as "God the Discloser," in *Christian Faith and Practice in the Modern World: Theology from an Evangelical Point of View,* ed. Mark A. Noll and David F. Wells (Grand Rapids: Eerdmans, 1988), pp. 93-118.

"Narrative Theology in Evangelical Perspective." Prepared for the "Conference on Narrative" sponsored by the Institute for Advanced Christian Studies and the Library of Congress, June 1992. Not previously published.

"The Place of Israel in Christian Faith." Based on materials prepared for the Theological Panel on Jewish-Christian issues, United Church of Christ, 1989–91, and published in *Gott Lieben und seine Gebote halten: In memoriam Klaus Bockmuehl,* ed. Markus Bockmuehl and Helmut Burkhardt (Basel: Brunnen Verlag Giessen, 1991), pp. 21-38. Reprinted by permission.

"Carl F. H. Henry, Ecumenically Considered." Published as "Carl Henry," in *A Handbook of Christian Theologians,* ed. Martin E. Marty and Dean G. Peerman. Copyright © 1965 assigned to Abingdon. Additional copyright © 1984 by Abingdon Press. Reprinted by permission.

"David Tracy, Evangelically Considered." Prepared as part of a lecture at Gordon-Conwell Theological Seminary, Spring 1991. Not previously published.

INDEX OF SUBJECTS